Open Moral Communities

Open Moral Communities

Seymour J. Mandelbaum

The MIT Press
Cambridge, Massachusetts
London, England

Set in Sabon by The MIT Press.
Printed and bound in the United States of America.
Printed on recycled paper.

Library of Congress Cataloging-in-Publication Data

Mandelbaum, Seymour J.
Open moral communities / Seymour J. Mandelbaum.
p. cm.
Some chapters previously published in various journals.
Includes bibliographical references (p.   ) and index.
ISBN 0-262-13365-2 (hc : alk. paper)
1. Community. 2. Community—Moral and ethical aspects.
3. Pluralism (Social sciences) 4. Communication—Social aspects.
I. Title.
HM756.M36 2000
307—dc21   99-43445
                                                                CIP

for our grandchildren

Contents

Preface

In the late 1960s, I dreamed of creating a two-way cable television system and public production center in North Central Philadelphia. I failed to realize that dream and settled for writing a book about it. Enthralled by the latest innovations in a long "communications revolution," I defined 'community' as meaning a group of people who communicated with one another. I poked and prodded at the ways of communicating in the hope of illuminating the tasks of enhancing intelligent governance by "democratizing access to knowledge" (Mandelbaum 1972).

By the mid 1970s I had largely abandoned my initial hopes for cable television and turned away from networks and telecommunication policies toward theories of planning. I never completely stopped poking and prodding, and I have lately begun to attend to the "new information technologies" and the "information infrastructure." (There are plentiful signs of that old and now refreshed interest scattered through this essay.) Thinking in an abstract way about planning has, however, changed the way I understand 'community'. There are no communities without communication, but there is a great deal more to a communion than the exchange of messages.

'Community' appears in this essay as a term in moral philosophy. The reframing of the term began with the realization that when we argue with ourselves or with others about the morality of collective choices our speech is embedded in communal images. For some, 'community' provides the elemental referent that allows us to distinguish "right" from "wrong." ("This is how we do it around here. This is our way.") Others insist that ethical judgments are appropriately grounded in abiding universals rather than in temporary communal claims: that God, Nature, or Reason dictates the major features of our moral codes and intuitions. Community operates only in the large but morally peripheral domain of local custom.

Both philosophic communitarians and universalists, however, share in an instrumental appreciation of 'community' as a description of the social arrangements that make it possible to cultivate a moral order. Alas, even the will of God or the obligations of a transcendent Reason require communities to socialize new recruits and to sustain the commitments and practices of members.

This essay is an exploration of three stylized images of these magical social forms. I've chosen to call these images myths because they are compounded of description and aspiration; of detailed narratives, parables, abstract theories, and archetypes. Each of the three myths—*contractual, deep,* and *open*—commands my respectful though not entirely equal treatment. I am principally concerned with the overtly simple idea that we *should* imagine ourselves as simultaneously belonging to a field of overlapping communities. In each community we encounter a moral order of rights, obligations, constraints, and opportunities. These orders sometimes unambiguously reinforce one another: acting appropriately in one communion bolsters the discipline of another. For the most part, however, the dense variety of claims—whether overtly conflicting or only intractably different—defies all efforts at radical simplification and unambiguous hierarchical organization. Even as we speak within one community, we subtly acknowledge other claims and multiple identities for ourselves and for those with whom we are (partially) associated.

This open myth shapes a robust sensibility that allows us to deal with ethical pluralism and essentially contested claims to truth without collapsing into skepticism, grasping for communal purification, or subordinating the field to a single way of talking. Robust but not heroic: the rhetoric of the open myth is often ironic and hesitant. At one point in the essay I describe it as "weak tea." (Alan Wolfe (1998), in a similar vein, writes of "morality writ small.") The myth, however, provides a compelling complement to its more confident and familiar competitors: the notions that communities are legitimate only when they are grounded in a voluntary contract or in a deep moral consensus.

I suspect that I understood the open myth in my bones long before I had words for it, knowing even as a child that Judaism both informed my conception of "enlightenment" and warred against it. Later, the myth provided a way of understanding how overlapping memberships threatened true believers and the communal boundaries they defended; how a tolerant "liberal imagination" could bolster complex fields against simplifying utopias and horrific malevolence.

Writing this essay, I've frequently opened the morning paper with a grim sense of vindication: it would surely be a better world if neighbors in the Balkans or the Middle East saw themselves in a field of overlapping communities rather than a cockpit of contending communions. Though good news is hard to find, it is not entirely absent. Whatever its ultimate fate, in its conception the Good Friday agreement in Northern Ireland articulated the sensibility I associate with the open myth: a willingness to legitimate overlapping and ambiguous authorities, to allow competing places to exist in the same space, and to treat passionate memories ironically.

This essay does not, however, point directly to the play of the three stylized myths in the bloody inter-communal conflicts of our day. Two chapters—one dealing with exclusionary zoning in New Jersey and the other with redemption after the 1985 attack on the MOVE compound in West Philadelphia—describe events and texts that in their moment aroused considerable passion. They are, however, of little global significance: New Jersey is not a Gulag, and West Philadelphia is not Pristina. Indeed, I want the two cases to be understood as only modestly "out of the ordinary"— just different enough to illuminate ubiquitous representations of community and daily communal practices. If the essay is persuasive, its power will rest in the reader's sense of recognition rather than in my compelling description of unfamiliar relations. I have largely taken that recognition for granted, exploring its implications rather than its origins.

This account of the communal myths we shape and within which we act is framed in the terms of the conversations that swirl around city and regional planning in North America and, indeed, across much of the world. I've chosen those conversations opportunistically: those are the arguments and the affirmations of collective identity that occupy most of my working hours.

There is, however, a better or at least less personal reason to examine the talk of planning: there is probably no other group of collective practices that points to 'community' more insistently as a description of its settings, active subjects, and moral objects. The urban and regional stage is populated with a great cast of communities, each entangled with another in a way that frustrates our simple hopes of understanding (let alone changing) one unit at a time. On that stage, families and firms overlap (at least a little) in their membership and moral claims: churches and street corner gangs, unions and neighborhoods, cities and nations. In that overlapping field we must invent public orders that sustain the complex pattern and make common sense of ethical difference.

The chapters are arranged in three parts. Part I sets out the role of communities in the creation of moral orders and the implications of the three stylized communal forms. In part II, I turn to six terms—*theory, story, time, city, tool,* and *plan*—that figure largely in both the lay and the professional construction of public orders. (Only the treatment of tools in chapter 8 is cast in the specialized language of professionals: the rest of the lexicon shows few marks of the planning guild.) In each of the six cases, my argument appears in a similar guise. The consensual dream of a compelling integrative discourse is "impossible," but that is not a damning flaw. Indeed, it preserves the instrumental and normative resources of communal pluralism.

In part III, I look at two cases in which compelling moral claims for redemption and justice challenged the ambiguity and pluralism of the open myth. In both cases, those claims were limited. Redemption was transformed into History, and Justice was moderated by Prudence. My appreciation of that "weak tea" is complemented in the final chapter by a reflection on the appropriately "thin" virtues of citizens in a liberal republic that serves both as a distinctive community and as a guardian of the field of communities.

At the end of the day, I suspect that very few readers will be surprised by my account of these three myths and their implications. I hope, however, that the recognition of familiar but usually tacit understandings will bolster an appreciation of the links between moral orders and communal practices.

Acknowledgements

Chapters 4, 11, and 13 have not been previously published in any form. The published versions of the other ten chapters have been revised—in several cases substantially—to further the argument of the essay.

Chapter 1 was originally prepared for a conference on planning institutions and technology. It was subsequently published as "Communitarian sensibilities and the design of communities" (*Planning Theory* 10/11, 1993–94: 187–203) and as "Sensibilita communitaria e progettazione delle comunita" (*Prometheus* 16/17, 1992–93: 109–125).

Chapter 2 was originally prepared for delivery at Virginia Polytechnical Institute and State University. It was published by the university as "Deserving communities" in part I of the 25th Anniversary Celebration Special Lectures of the College of Architecture and Urban Studies (1992).

Portions of chapters 3 and 5 were published as "Open moral communities" in *Society* (26, 1988: 20–27) and in *Explorations in Planning Theory*, ed. S. Mandelbaum et al. (Center for Urban Policy Research Press, 1996). The "fable" in chapter 5 relies on "A complete general theory of planning is impossible" (*Policy Sciences* 11, 1979: 59–72).

Chapter 6 was originally published as "Telling stories" in the *Journal of Planning Education and Research* (10, 1991: 209–214).

Chapter 7 was originally published as "Temporal conventions in planning discourse" in *Environment and Planning B: Planning and Design* (11, 1984: 5–13). The journal is published in London by Pion, Ltd.

Chapter 8 was originally published as "Making and breaking planning tools" in *Computers, Environment and Urban Systems* (20, no. 2, 1996: 71–84).

Chapter 9 was originally published (as What Is Philadelphia?) by the University of Pennsylvania's Center for Philadelphia Studies (1982) and (in a revised version titled "What is Philadelphia? The city as polity") in *Cities* (1, 1984: 274–285).

Chapter 10 was originally published as "Reading Plans" in the *Journal of the American Planning Association* (56, 1990: 350–356).

Chapter 12 was first published, under its present title, in *Explorations in Planning Theory*.

I

A Communitarian Sensibility

1

Moral Orders and Communities

A Communitarian Sensibility

From time to time, a voice—our own or that of an external challenger—questions the ethical bases of our actions and leads us to pause in the midst of making decisions. In the hiatus between one step and another, our ordinary uncertainty about the instrumental links between choices and outcomes is suddenly extended. We wonder not merely whether our deeds will be effective but whether they are morally right; whether the outcomes we seek will be normatively justifiable; whether our talk of morals and values will survive close scrutiny. Once we represent ourselves as speaking within an ethical domain—once we allow that some questions are distinctively "moral"—we must bolster our disposition to do this or that with something more than an appeal to ordinary practice, preference, intuition, or interest. With good reason, we may complain if those common forms of self-assertion are denied entirely, but something grander and less personal seems necessary if we are to respond in an appropriate form to the seriousness of our doubts.

The disposition to address those doubts with formal arguments is most intense whenå the pall of uncertainties is cast over collective rather than merely personal choices. In the collective forum, we confront other minds and voices reminding us of our own inner turmoil and asking for reasons. "Feeling right" isn't reason enough.

Whether we regularly or only occasionally don a philosopher's hat, when we pause in this way to examine, refine, and justify our moral choices it is difficult to avoid framing our search within the terms of a conventional dichotomy that characterizes ethical systems as either universal or communal.

Within a universal frame, we attempt to invent or (some would say) discover a small set of elemental ethical principles without which it would be impossible to imagine Man or Society. In the simplest cases, the principles we seek will speak so directly ("in their own voice") to a prospective deed that all doubts will be dissolved: it will be obvious what must and what must not be done. Most adults, I suspect, understand that, for the great mass of complex and murky decisions that fill their daily lives, the ethical mandates and decisions are not likely to be quite so apparent: our judgments will inevitably be infected by the difficulties of forecasting, of reconciling individual and collective moral claims, and of finding a way when principles that are harmonious in the abstract conflict with one another in particular cases. The search for an elemental ethical core is arduous and contested. The universalistic frame, however, shapes and sustains the search by defining the form and role of the core.

Within the communal frame, the core disappears and all that remains are groups of people struggling to define a moral order that they never fully achieve. Ethical principles may be immutable and universal in Heaven, but on Earth they require human interpretation and are embedded in the language, assumptions, and social relations of particular moments. Within the communal frame, the ethical search is shaped by our image of a community deserving of respect rather than by our (vain) aspiration for a transcendent set of ethical principles.

I have tried in this essay to locate a safe path through a ground strewn with the explosive mines of these philosophic arguments. Without embroiling myself directly in the arguments of philosophers, I've sought to cultivate a communitarian sensibility and a craft of community design.

I start to elaborate on those objectives with three quite simple observations that are, *mirabile dictu*, remarkably similar:

• Moses, preparing for Sinai and then coming down (twice) from the mountain, faced the problem of designing a community that could sustain the universalistic elements of the ethic inscribed on the tablets. All his successors—humble teachers, prophets, and professors alike—have faced the same problem. Even ubiquitous or innate human capacities for moral reasoning must be cultivated "in community."

• Communitarian critics of universalistic ethics must often (to their explicit consternation) evoke a community where none of sufficient moral heft appears to exist. They simultaneously lament the absence of community and rely upon the specter to provide a moral order.[1]

• Plans, policies, technologies, institutions, and the built forms of settlements literally and figuratively crumble in our hands if there is no community to attend to them.

Alas, these observations drive me deep into the dense semantic forest that surrounds the concept of community. Treating 'community' as a term of ethical discourse does, however, allow me to avoid some particularly overgrown thickets or, when trapped in conversations not of my choosing, to clear some of the underbrush. This introductory chapter consists of a series of forays into that forest.

We commonly speak of a community as a small group of people occupying a bounded space rich with affective meanings and shared memories. In these "places," the members of the community interact in many of life's domains, speaking to one another face to face. In contrast with the small circle in the delightful TV pub called Cheers, everyone may not "know your name," but they nevertheless ascribe to you an identity within a web of linked associations. When we talk in this way, we imagine that individuals may belong to one and only one community, as if membership were governed by the legal concept of a single political residence. We speak confidently in the singular, using the unambiguous definite article. We seek to improve "the community," designate some organizations as "community-based," and recognize some actors as "community people."

This common usage is not, however, strictly applied. From time to time we talk of great cities and nations, tribes scattered over space, professions, churches, business firms, and all sorts of voluntary associations as "communities." Lately we have begun to distinguish "real" and "virtual" communities (though not, I think, with a great deal of confidence in the distinction).

If somehow we could not speak without assuring ourselves and others that each of our words had only one meaning, this would be a very silent world. Accepting and even cherishing our polymorphic practices, we may nevertheless pause to reflect on our lexical flexibility. Is there a common set of attributes that mark the varied communities of our mind and our tongue?

Should we wisely attend to the word with greater care in order to speak in the moments of ethical uncertainty?

Places and Artifacts

There is no particular mystery to the ways in which inanimate objects such as national flags, historical monuments, and corporate logos symbolically represent communities. Most of us are not confused by such conventional devices. We know that communities are composed of human beings, and that signs and their referents may have quite different forms.

At times, however, our grasp of rhetorical conventions is overcome by the physical reification of communal relations. The land, the flag, or the city becomes one with the people and their faith. In a similar though less passionate way, local community development corporations and public agencies often pride themselves on the houses they have built, as if the physical structures were the community that they sought to design. We drive past a block of run-down houses and exclaim at the community in disrepair.

There is something vaguely idolatrous about such physical reification. The land or the flag may symbolize a community, but it can never be a moral subject. New houses may strengthen a community or attest to its vigor, but they cannot be cast as moral guardians. (New houses may also signal the conquest of one community by another.) We recognize the fragility of reification when we try in vain to imagine spaces and buildings acting collaboratively or conflicting—when (in the role of tourist, museum curator, or imperialist) we make a site or an artifact our own but realize that we do not possess the community that endowed it with meaning. (Symmetrically, we may be struck by the ability of the dispossessed to recreate their communities and places in unfamiliar spaces.) The spatial choices made in the process of rebuilding a devastated city may alter communal relations, but neither the buildings nor the place *are the community.*

Groups

We often perceive people as joined by an objective interest or as at risk from a common environmental threat from which they might possibly save themselves through cooperative action (residents of a flood plain endangered by the growth of an impervious cover on the land, neighbors of a toxic dump, inhabitants of Spaceship Earth peeking though a frightening hole in the ozone layer). At the other extreme but with a similar insight, we may see them as sitting on a golden opportunity (a sea of oil, a pool of untapped human resources) that they could exploit if only they would get their act together.

Community organizers moved by perceptions of interest, risk, or opportunity may be forgiven modest rhetorical excesses. For example, the "global community" threatened by warming or the "neighborhood" threatened by a renewal project is often represented as nascent or emergent. It must be "empowered," "developed," or "mobilized," but it is, at the outset, a moral fact. In the same way, we may ascribe a group identity to individuals—they are, for example, black, or rich, or hypertensive—and assume that they are, therefore, "members" of a community defined by that ascribed identity. In many such circumstances, however, honesty would compel an acknowledgment that there is no community there, only a set of persons to whom we have imputed a common fate, opportunity, identity, interest, or market niche.[2]

Even that formulation doesn't quite capture the political burdens of transforming groups into communities. New communities are characteristically designed and mobilized on a crowded communal canvas. Attempting to turn a politically or economically salient group into a community necessarily presses for adjustments across the canvas. As revolutionary parties have long understood, if the "wretched of the earth" are to act communally they must realign their established memberships in families, religious and neighborhood associations, networks of friends, and polities. In the United States, the American Association of Retired Persons enrolls "seniors" with the same message.

The geography of the community canvas is complex and contentious. It is difficult to distinguish the boundaries of communions and their interactions—to decide whether new identities and relationships can be built on established networks or whether the ground must first be cleared and the social web reconstructed. The difficulties are only multiplied if we put on blinders before we start by dismissing or ignoring existing communities or moral sentiments, by specifying the conditions for respect in a way that excludes virtually every established community. If the only true communities are noncoercive and fully responsive to all their members, then we are dealing with shadows; if they are united by a coherent and fully shared system of values, then the few examples of the species are so short-lived that they disappear under our gaze.

The transformation of groups into communities is risky for communities and groups alike. Communities often adopt a group as a moral object, insisting that "we" be concerned with the well-being of "them." (Service bureaucracies of all sorts make and justify their livings in just such ways.) The "other" who commands this obligation may consist of all living human beings, of unborn generations, of innocent children, of trees, or of adults who are vulnerable to our self-regarding choices. Those groups are not, however, thereby members of the community; they are not moral subjects (Feinberg 1980, pp. 159–184; Goodin 1985).

The relationship between objects and subjects is asymmetric: the initiative lies always with communities, not groups—with subjects, not objects. A community that obligates itself to external moral objects or that enjoins its members to care about "all the children" or "all those who seek freedom" must set limits to its role as a trustee if it is not to risk destroying its own internal moral commitments and structure. (This is the other side of the classic worry that the charitable impulse that begins at home may be exhausted before it reaches the distant needy.[3]) A community that has learned to deal charitably with moral objects must also be wary of stumbling on a community of subjects—for example, not all poor people, but those particular ones over there with voices, proper names, personal ambitions, and social commitments. A charitable community that refuses to acknowledge subjects and communities retains the familiar object relationship at the heavy cost of treating human beings as savages, wards, numbers, or children. The subjects, on their side, may risk losing their protected status and their entitlements as innocent victims.

Institutions

The line between institution and community is difficult to observe in the semantic forest. Even the most experienced guides may sometimes lapse from one word to the other. A family, for example, is undoubtedly a community; the Family, as a set of practices and normative relations, is undoubtedly an institution. Capitalism and Democracy are sets of institutions that shape communities and are shaped by them. Like communities, institutions often are articulated as systems of rights and obligations; like communities, they survive by maintaining a rough balance between predictability, discipline, and order on the one side and spontaneity and innovation on the other. Is it useful to distinguish between the crafts and technologies of institutional and community design when they are so tightly connected? Might I have as well started this chapter by suggesting that in the moment of ethical uncertainty we should ask "What sort of *institutions*—rather than what sort of *communities*—do we value?"[4]

In *The Good Society,* Bellah et al. (1991) struggle with that issue and implicitly suggest a reason to distinguish between communities and institutions and to appreciate and preserve their entanglement. They remark that Americans (and, one might easily suspect, most other people) are intimidated by the idea of institutions.[5] "Normative patterns embedded in and enforced by laws and mores" (Bellah et al. 1991, pp. 10–11) loom as faceless specters—roles, not people. Framed in this way, institutions belong to the world of stable "structures" that we cannot readily change and that we should perhaps (the Declaration of Independence warns us) be hesitant to overturn lightly. Communities, in contrast, appear as the domains of empowered "agents." The fatalists in our midst may see only institutions that severely constrain our options, but most of us want to believe that we can alter our individual families, neighborhoods, schools, or firms without undertaking the redesign of Family, Neighborhood, Education, or Corporation. It is that lower-case intimacy and plasticity that we should properly cherish even in huge communities. Russian planners engaged in a community may think and act strategically about the development of market institutions; the emergent market cannot in the same way engage to plan Russia.

The instrumental craft that serves a communitarian sensibility does, however, depend on a lively sense of the dynamics of institutions. Beyond some threshold, successfully changing communities—my family, this neighborhood, our profession—requires the reconstruction of institutions. Symmetrically, the maintenance and the adaptive change of institutions require communities to recruit and to discipline law-abiding citizens, reformers, rogues, conservators, soldiers, workers, and nurturing caretakers.

Institutional change without substantial coercion characteristically depends on the social capital of communities in which people trust one another and their own social competence enough to risk altering established norms and conventional practices.

Communities

The world is crowded with communities. Most of them—as communitarians often aver—cannot sustain a deeply reflective ethical discourse; cannot carry the burdens of universalism or justify their practices as part of a richly considered way of life or tradition. Even the humblest communities, however, create a moral order. That is their nature, and that is the stubborn fact that the communitarian sensibility brings to their design. Even the drivers in a group of closely spaced cars speeding along a highway develop a sense of solidarity and an appropriate practice. They resent and (weakly) discipline putative members who violate that practice by going too slowly or darting in and out dangerously, and they snarl at outsiders—such as the police—when they intrude on the custom of the road.[6]

The core of the communitarian sensibility and the beginning of the search for a craft of community design is the notion of membership. Members are bound to one another by a web of rights and obligations. The web is articulated in practices, sustained by recruitment and socialization of new members, and controlled by ongoing processes of reward and discipline. Nonmembers who interact with the community are also fairly entitled to forms of respect and are bound by a web of obligations: if they behave in valued ways, they are entitled to appropriately correct responses. Indeed, as I have already suggested, nonmembers may even be treated as moral objects whom a community is bound to regard solicitously without regard to their specific earned deserts.

The other side of membership is, of course, exclusion and difference. A community that does not distinguish between members and strangers cannot construct or sustain a moral order and loses its identity. Its borders are dissolved, its discipline ended. (What does friendship matter if everyone is my friend?)

Some communities survive even though they have very little control over the entry and exit of members and cannot distinguish sharply between those who belong and those who are simply passing through. Residential neighborhoods in the United States are characteristically in this situation. Some never become communities; they remain groups sharing a common territory. Others succeed in creating a modest discipline and order in the face of this openness, either because the larger community protects them from being overwhelmed by strangers[7] or because they are able—legally or illegally, formally or informally—to create a protected enclave. The devices are legion: guards, gates, parking privileges, gangs, political incorporation, zoning, restrictive covenants, homeowners' associations (Ellickson 1982; Suttles 1990; Rosenblum 1998). Mass political parties in a competitive democratic regime face the same issue in a quite different way. Confronted with the neighborhood problem—openness, vulnerability, lack of discipline and distinction—they sometimes choose to intensify their communion by increasing the commitment of dedicated members and building walls around the periphery. That is not, however, usually a winning strategy. The electoral incentive encourages opening the gates and reducing differences. Paradoxically, in order to sustain itself as a community, a party focused on the recruitment of strangers must develop small cadres whose commitments to one another are strong enough to sustain the largely undisciplined and weakly affiliated voters. If the "democratization" movement destroys the possibility of sustaining cadres, then the party becomes an occasional framework or theater for a coalition of communities.

Most of us belong to many communities simultaneously. Even tightly integrated communions built around a deeply shared religious faith are composed of communities superimposed on one another—sometimes by force of arms—and struggling always with the tension between competitive allegiances. In the pluralistic and fragmented circumstances of a liberal society, we live in fields of open and often temporary communities, reconciling our many faces and identities within our own minds and speech (Galston 1991, pp. 22–41).

The field of communities takes on qualities of its own. At virtually every scale, some communities assert their superordinate standing and their self-serving account of the open field's history and prospects. The field is shaped by the struggles over those hegemonic efforts. In a quite different way, some communities represent themselves as mediators across the field. Enrolling in these therapeutic communions, we seek to reduce and reconcile our competitive identities, learning (at least overtly) only to be ourselves (Bellah et al. 1985, pp. 113–141; Kadushin 1969).

The structure of the open field is simultaneously shaped and maintained by three distinctive modes of speech—each of which, I suspect, we may discern in our own conversational practices. Faced with a pluralistic field, we are sometimes tempted to be shrill and simple, our voice a bugle call to action or a bell clanging in the night, warning of danger. We are also tempted, however, to be tentative in our speech, accepting of interpretive differences, prudent, ambiguous, ironic, alive to dilemmas in our values, and proudly liberal in our rhetorical sensibilities. Finally, in many professional roles we struggle to create what Gouldner (1979) called a "culture of critical discourse"—a way of talking that will stand outside the field of communities and will be fully public and uniquely compelling. The frequent evocation of science (e.g., "planning science," "management science," "decision science," "complexity science") is an expression of this honorable but ultimately futile aspiration to overcome the merely partisan and the contingent in our (or, for most of us, "their") professional practices.

This brief tour has, I hope, suggested ways of designing communities in their respective fields:

• Change the conditions of membership, the relations between members and nonmembers, and the terms of exclusion.

• Shift commitments to moral objects and the relations of objects and subjects.

• Alter the processes of recruitment, socialization, and discipline.

• Weaken or strengthen a community's competence to command resources and to satisfy its members.

• Change the discursive practices of the communion and its field.

Even this brief and only cryptically specified list of tasks hints at a large but contested set of design instruments and a thick manual of both confident techniques and uncertain technologies. Thick manuals are not easily digested. Current expressions of a communitarian sensibility tend, understandably, to simplify the design craft into two broad accounts of the origins and character of communities and—within those accounts—styles of approaching the tasks in my short list.

The first account is that communities are essentially voluntary associations originating in a covenant among their members. The original compact may be far in the past, but it retains a commanding presence. New recruits—particularly those who join freely—are presumed to accept the community's obligations as if they had been parties to the initial bargain. Their acceptance is ratified and repeated in periodic rituals of affirmation and allegiance. If the community seems adrift, conservators of the moral order characteristically appeal for exceptional acts of renewal that reinvest in rituals that have been routinized, neglected, or stripped of their original meaning (Lincoln 1989).

This image, Janus-like, also faces in the other direction. A community that stems from a covenant may present itself (at some risk) as a set of autonomous souls and then undertake to form a new contract or to dissolve. The "members" of a firm that has lost its markets and its élan sit down together not to renew the original mission (whose time may have passed) but to re-create the enterprise in the present moment. Members of a family may act in the same way, setting new terms for their relationships or stepping away from them.

The image of "a new social contract" appears as a powerful design instrument even in a community whose scale precludes universal participation in the process of bargaining. The television images of vast parliamentary assemblies in Russia encourage a sense that we are watching "the people" at work, crafting a new community. (In comparison, the central room of Independence Hall in Philadelphia seems tiny.) On a much more modest contemporary scale, the elaborate forms of participation in what is ironically described in the United States as "comprehensive" urban planning suggest that the wisdom of the entire community is being mobilized to create a new vision and a new future.

We all understand, of course, that the new compacts are not written on a clean slate, that the processes of bargaining and the modes of participation are embedded in established organizational and discursive forms, and that there is a powerful theatrical element in the construction of the "political spectacle" (Edelman 1988). Indeed, a great deal of contemporary social and political theory has been driven by the image of simulating an idealized state that escapes from those biased forms. The simulation, we are encouraged to hope, might then allow us to specify the results of an interaction that we cannot possibly create on the ground. Just as we think of "shadow prices" as perfecting real markets for the purposes of weighing costs and benefits, so we have been variously encouraged to shape in our minds an "original position" in which we can define justice objectively or an "ideal speech condition" in which coercion is removed from our conversations. Such perfectionism does not sit easily within a communitarian sensibility.[8] If meanings and identities are shaped and reshaped by relations within and among communities, then how can the specters that survive the stripping away of bias or coercion be recognized and trusted?

The second broad account of the origins and dynamics of community does not depend on a covenant. In this account, the central concept is "practice" (or better, "practices") rather than "compact" (Oakeshott 1933, 1975; MacIntyre 1984; Turner 1994). Both our deep identities and the faces we present to the world are shaped in communities that, for the most part, precede our existence and are not of our making. If we want to design those communities, we must undertake to know "how we do things" within their social borders and then either to reinforce or to amend the practices that socialize and discipline members. We must ensure that members are protected in their entitlements and insist that they meet their obligations. (In a different voice: we must "help them meet their obligations.")

Even in communities that are of our making and that originate in a recent compact, the strategic style that is centered on practices directs us to attend to the countless ways in which original intentions are realized or thwarted in emergent traditions, in administrative procedures, in exemplary behaviors, in the web of daily life, and in the forms of speech. A constant evocation of what we said "before"—before the treaty was ratified, before we were married, before we agreed to be partners in the firm, before we undertook to stage the play—does not substitute for practices that sustain the flow of recruits, socialize them into the new arrangements, protect the boundaries, and encourage members to behave appropriately. (In contrast, of course, practices must and do take on a life of their own that largely displaces appeals to the original compact, to the vision of the founders, or—as many planners will attest—to an idealized future.[9]) Even shared values—the defining element of many images of community—seem secondary to practices: our communion is defined not by what we value but by what we do and what we allow to be done.

Ethical arguments within this account and within this strategic design style are particularly complex. Appeals to origins and compacts are largely misplaced. Abstraction of principle from practice and the construction of simple evaluative hierarchies risk the destruction of meaning and the distortion of exemplars and parables. Policy analysis as a sparse and analytic discursive technology (whose standard literary forms are the columns of a cost-benefit analysis and the graphic sweep of intersecting preference and production functions) gives way to the novelistic writing of scenarios that virtually defy consensual cardinal ordering of alternatives (Pincoffs 1986; Nussbaum 1990).

Paradoxically, when practices rather than compacts are the core of the communitarian sensibility even the design of new communities in a crowded field appears a classically conservative act: it appears to be engaged with daily life more than with commanding visions; with routines, social bonds, and the web of interactions (albeit new ones) more than with charisma. Calls to a new moral order are suspect unless they have the density of the mythic world of J. R. R. Tolkien.

2

Deserving Communities

Pruning the Tangle

Humans live in communities. They find comfort, support, and meaning in communion with others; a moral order in the discipline of membership. It is, of course, also worth remembering that they find oppression, denigration, and confusion in communion, and that they flee communities in great numbers. When unable to escape physically or emotionally, some lapse into a resignation that barely hides their distress; others openly curse the gods and guardians of community. Even in cities of strangers, however, the migrants rarely remain outside communities very long: they remarry, find new friends and places, and join in new social rituals and civil associations.

What I have described as the communitarian sensibility is deeply grounded in these robust processes of creating and recreating communions. Once we have accepted the notion that communities (whatever their deep philosophic status) are instrumentally vital in maintaining moral orders, we are bound to think about the resolution of the sort of ethical uncertainty that I evoked at the beginning of the first chapter by relating discrete behaviors to their communal settings. We reflect on the communities of our own minds: What are moral implications of our memberships? How will our decisions bear on the communal orders? (If members fail to attend to those questions, communities die.) In that moment of uncertainty we also reflectively ask the same questions of others: How are their decisions embedded in communities? What are their moral stakes in our engagement?

Looking out at the vast landscape of communities that enter into our inner dialogues, we are easily overwhelmed. Are all those communities (together with their practices and ethical standards) deserving of respect?

Aren't some of the communities patently undeserving—important practically, perhaps, but not morally? If the distinction will bear scrutiny, individuals in "undeserving" communities may be judged without regard for their communions. If the "family" is undeserving, the code of silence will not, for example, justify the behavior of a Mafioso. "Following orders" will not excuse the behavior of soldiers in the service of an army that violates the Geneva Convention. Neighbors who band together to recapture "their" streets from an undeserving community of drug dealers and addicts need not represent themselves as engaged in an inter-communal conflict in which rival moral orders claim legitimate access to public spaces; they may be forgiven a certain intemperate or uncivil quality in their speech, insofar as they deny the undeserving community any right to a "deliberative reciprocity" that appeals to shared values (Gutmann and Thompson 1996, pp. 52–94; Kingwell 1995, pp. 193–249).

What of the neighbors themselves? Do they deserve respect only if they abide by the norms of a superordinate communion? If they act as vigilantes, are they no better than the criminals they seek to punish, and are they without any standing in our moral accounts? If, however, the neighbors meet the superordinate test, then is it foolish to treat them as anything other than the mobilized, local members of the larger entity? If we can sensibly use "desert" to pare the tangle of communal claims, we might be able to replace my description of a complex field of overlapping communities with a simpler image of a few large communions that socialize and discipline members by generating and engaging "branches." Should we, for example, treat individual families—the most ubiquitous communal form—as if they were Boy Scout troops or Presbyterian congregations whose ability to manage their own affairs is subject to the oversight of a higher authority? How opaque is the shield of privacy that limits the public gaze into the dynamics of individual families? Who will hold families to account for the public implications of their (no longer private) ethical failings (Okin 1989)?

Undeserving communities are, of course, social facts. The neighbors would be well advised to understand the communal bonds of the drug dealers, and Italian judges would be well advised to understand the code of the Mafia. It would also be imprudent to stigmatize communities so freely that moral deliberation was limited to minor disagreements within an overwhelming ethical consensus. Nonetheless, in our moments of ethical uncertainty we would all be remarkably vulnerable to strategic manipulation if we could not distinguish between deserving and undeserving communities—if "community," like "culture," were endowed with a magical power to immunize groups against all threats.

I start with the question "How and why may we credibly distinguish between deserving and undeserving communities?" That question provokes a series of difficult queries: Who asks such a question? Who responds and who would attend to the response? Who is capable of distinguishing good reasons from bad so as to confer respect and trust on a community and its members? How do those sensitive critics manage that awesome responsibility? We answer these difficult questions in a practical way every day as we go about the business of evaluating moral claims, assigning blame, and rewarding ethical performances. (The moment of ethical uncertainty is, after all, not permanently disabling.) As we work our way through those daily tasks, I suspect, most of us rely, at least in part, on a stylized image of an objective judge who lives outside the fractious field of diverse communities and assigns merit without personal bias or interest. The judge of our dreams draws on standards that would command universal assent if only everyone were objective. Everyone is, of course, not objective; thus, it is the judge who must specify the content of that assent under the conditions of that hypothetical detachment.

We hold onto that stylized image because it preserves the precious notion of transcendence, allowing us to imagine that we can, however briefly, step outside ourselves. We all know, of course, that the image is a fantasy. Here and (as will soon be apparent) in many other circumstances, our speech is ironic, sharing a secret understanding that our words are not quite what they seem (Mandelbaum 1998). There are no such judges, legislators, or philosopher kings, and there is no way of talking about deserving communities without employing a language that is shaped by layers of (often conflicting) notions.

The conditions under which we undertake to judge communities requires that we act within them. We don't, of course, usually sit in the middle of a circle with all our fellow members watching and disciplining us at every instant. We represent communities symbolically in our minds and then respond to them. Our mental creations are subject to all the failings of images and forecasts: we don't anticipate responses correctly, and we mistake the normative interpretations of our behavior. We are "sure" that our friends will shun us but are delighted to find them accepting; we are confident that our colleagues will "understand" only to see them confused and angry.

As we experience life in a community over extended periods, we usually get better at distinguishing between appropriate and inappropriate behavior and at anticipating the forms and incidence of communal discipline. No matter how canny our judgments, it is nevertheless a mistake to think that we see things as they *really* are without the mediating structures of the mythic communities of our mind.

Within those mythic communities, we assign deserts from two quite different critical perspectives. In the first, a community is judged by either members or outsiders against its own standards; in the second, the standards of one community are brought to bear against another.

Judging from the Inside

The practice of the first (internal) critical standard is overtly simpler than that of the second because it raises no issue of moral relativity or of the invocation of extra-communal authority. Imagine that a community displays a set of traits and practices. It might, for example, teach its children to act aggressively or to honor artistic creativity. Judging from the inside, we point to a trait and ask "Does that merit respect by the community's own lights?" When we think about the future and new institutional arrangements, we adapt the same intellectual device. Reading a plan, we wonder: Would a prospective trait or practice be justified within the life of an established community? Would the community of our dreams, if realized, deserve the respect of its own members?

There are two common ways of answering those questions. The first designates a hierarchy of communal values. Traits or practices deserve respect if they conform to the values at the top of the hierarchy. A community is deserving if it attempts to perfect itself so that its ordinary behavior comes progressively closer to its "ideals."

The best-known example of this use of ideals is Gunnar Myrdal's 1944 critique of racial discrimination in the United States. Common discriminatory practices—even those of long standing—were flawed, Myrdal insisted, because they violated deeply cherished values. The conflict between practice and character created a dilemma that ultimately would be resolved by repairing the nation so that it would approximate its own ethical standards (Myrdal 1944; see also Southern 1987).

This strategy is ubiquitous. Planners, managers, mediators, and public leaders employ it repeatedly when they encourage organizations or publics to overcome temporary preferences and "narrow" self-interest in order to express their "true" or "best" interest. The "higher calling" is invoked to free communities from ignorance, sloth, and petulance.

The second mode of internal critique does not overtly depend on a hierarchy of values or on a small canon of ideals. Rather than ask whether a trait or a practice conforms to an abstract value, we attempt to assess whether it fits the communal culture and history: Is it truly American, or truly Christian? Is that how the Mandelbaums behave? Is that the GM way?

Communities usually depend on the ability of members to judge what is "fitting" in a smooth performance that is not interrupted by behavioral uncertainties and intellectual doubts. Indeed, in some settings hesitation is perceived as a threatening sign of an incomplete commitment. Reflecting on those "natural" practices, it is difficult to avoid idealizing a Culture and a History so that Our Way becomes an abstract principle, eroding the difference between hierarchical and conservative historicist standards.[1]

I have, however, posed the question of deserts in a moment of uncertainty that presumes at least a modicum of skepticism and a willingness to argue. In such a moment, there are three constraints on internal criticism in both of its forms: the absence of a normative hierarchy within many communities, the interaction of "high" and "low" values, and the ambiguous and contested quality of many communal norms. Taken together, these difficulties not only increase the complexity of internal judgments but also suggest that external perspectives play an unavoidably important role in the designation of deserving communities.

Every community distinguishes "right" from "wrong"; to put it more carefully, no group that does not make that distinction acts as a community. The norms of a community as expressed in its stable practices and in the character of its members may, however, be flat rather than hierarchical. There is a right way and a wrong way to act, but none of the virtues is superior to any other, there is not much opportunity for exemplary performance, and there are no "small" breaches. The community of the highway convoy that I evoked in chapter 1 does not distinguish conventional and heroic moral behavior. It does not remember its glorious past, nor does it sustain an internal cadre of moral guardians who hold the group to its lofty ideals. The code of the small community that is continually being formed, dissolved, and reformed is simple and depends heavily on consensus: "Drive as fast as the traffic will allow. Do not push the traffic by driving so quickly or retard it by driving so slowly that competent members are endangered." The code and the community have a limited scope. When one driver shoots another after a close encounter, outsiders take control.

That simple code is not adequate to assess the deserts of the community. We discover hierarchical norms that allow us to allocate deserts on an internal standard only by expanding the boundaries of the communion to include the police, citizens, manufacturers, and regulators, without whom there would be neither cars nor roads. We may then judge that enlarged community by its own standards: Does it maintain the roads? Are the police honest? Are speeders apprehended? Are cars designed for safety? Are drivers careful?

Expanding the community inevitably devalues the most immediate or intimate rules of interaction in the convoy. They are replaced by formal prescriptions—55 MPH! Pass on the left! Buckle up!—that evoke higher moral standards and guardians with coercive authority.

Neighborhoods—often represented as the prototype of community—are not, of course, auto convoys. As informal associations acting through a combination of friendly persuasion and coercion, they sometimes manage to sustain social relations over long periods. Homeowners come and go, but not at 60 miles per hour. The character, the ownership, and the edges of neighborhood places—schools, parks, shopping districts, houses of worship—change repeatedly, but at an irregular pace that provides extended periods of stability. The exemplary behavior of "good neighbors" is praised. If nothing else, propinquity encourages a set of simple virtues: curb your dog, watch the children, clean the stoop, don't make a fuss.

Despite their salience in the iconography of community, neighborhoods are, however, what Walzer (1983) describes as "indifferent associations" whose character is shaped by "personal preference and market capacity." They are highly vulnerable to their own inability to control the creation and destruction of land values, to constrain the exit of members, and to protect themselves from the views of strangers. Neighborhoods don't characteristically create deeply shared memories among the passing residents, nor do they require complex moral hierarchies. They elicit ethical depth only when they are conceptually enlarged by being transformed into cities with broad police powers and influence over schools, land use, and public services or when they are seen in the context of a larger institutional pattern of social differentiation and stratification.

In contrast, hierarchical ethical discourse and the apparatus of formal history seem to have been invented to fit the social structures and the conversational practices of nations, cities armies, universities, hospitals, corporations, unions, professions, and the great religious communions. The members of these communities repeatedly signal distinctions between ordinary and heroic behavior, between usual practice and the highest standards of the members, and between the style and sensibility of ordinary folks and those of exemplary guardians of the faith.

We are, however, easily deceived by such talk. The rhetorical distinction between "high" and "low" values obscures the countervailing and complementary relationship between the two. In virtually every complex community that comes to my mind, the "wisdom" of the "folk" or of "everyday" life is imagined as a powerful and valued discipline, limiting the pretensions of the guardians. Efficiency experts in firms and priests in the confessional booth are forced to understand the moral demands of life on the shop floor. Idealistic reformers and what Barber (1988) describes as "foundational" theorists are taught the realities of politics in the field; saints confront the robust adaptive strategies of sinners and ritualists. Simplifiers who articulate the essential "mission" of their institution find themselves repeating a set of hollow words when they confront dense networks of commitments that resist reduction (Lincoln 1989).

When we fail to grasp the dialectical relationship between high and low values we distort our judgments of desert. When we try to judge (or to control and plan) a community in the name of its "highest" standards, we inevitably cast ourselves as larger (or simpler) than life, bound to a noble journey that inevitably falls short, doomed by the resistance of an implicit moral order that we can barely acknowledge and that is never as just, as democratic, as efficient, or as community-regarding as its ideals demand.

A comedic or ironic perspective on the moral order of complex communities provides a salutary corrective to hierarchical and tragic simplifications.

Accepting our limitations, we understand that life in most complex communities is riddled with misadventures and confusion; only occasionally do
we succeed, for brief moments of laughter and tears, in reconciling with
one another.

That is, unfortunately, not a very exciting perspective. Nor does it provide a very secure base for assessing on internal grounds the fitness of policies or the deserts of a community. In any complex setting, we are likely to
discover that major values are contested rather than fully shared—i.e., that
the boundary of the community is at issue so that it is uncertain as to who
is a "stranger" and who is a "neighbor" and how their claims are to be
weighed (Rosenblum 1987, pp. 125–151). Even shared understandings
appear in sets that operate as dilemmas within the body of common sense
rather than as clear directives (Billig et al. 1988, p. 17):

The contrary themes of common sense provide more than the seeds for arguments:
they also provide the seeds for thought itself. . . . These are not necessarily the sort
of acrimonious arguments which take place between different communities and
whose acrimony derives from the lack of comprehension of each other's strangely
nonsensical common sense. These are the arguments which arise within a particular common sense, as people debate about the common sense which they share. . . .
These are the sorts of arguments which people must have with themselves if they
are to deliberate about matters.

When we observe the practices of any complex community we inevitably
encounter a flow of arguments punctuated by episodic agreements. We may,
of course, scratch deeper to reveal a common sense, a stable set of commitments, or a way of talking—a discourse—beneath the surface of events.
We should, however, be as wary of the metaphor of "surface" and "deep"
as we are of the simplification entailed in the designation of the "highest"
values of a community. The historicist sensibility that allocates desert by
marking some behaviors as "fitting" (or, judgmentally, as "befitting") the
"nature" or "culture" of the community succeeds only at the cost of minimizing differences, conflicts, and explicit choices. Virtues (like rights) often
conflict, and some that are highly valued may be disruptive of social peace.

Judging from the Outside

As outsiders judging a community from across a border, we rarely choose
to enter fully into this internal morass. We assess whether a community is

deserving of our respect only because we seek to create, maintain, reform, or destroy a relationship to a moral association in which we are members. The character of that relationship serves as a frame, shaping and simplifying the judgmental act.

Imagine a case in which the officers of a firm approach the managers of a union pension fund soliciting a loan. The borrowing relationship characteristically limits the scope of the conversation in their encounters and shapes the terms of the assessment. The managers of the fund may be interested only in judging whether the firm will be able to repay the loan. The borrowing history, balance sheets, and economic forecasts that bolster the application may seem far from the usual rhetoric of moral accounting. We should, however, suspend that visceral bias against the moral salience of money. Communities making promises to outsiders are "undeserving" of respect—or of loans—if they have not usually met their "obligations" and if they are unlikely to be able to meet them in the future.

The simple frame of promising and performance enables the fund's managers to meet their fiduciary obligations, though it does not, of course, capture the full moral life of the borrower. Nor does it provide a universal assessment standard. A municipal redevelopment authority considering a loan that will lead a manufacturer to relocate a factory, for example, may want to discuss the "fit" between plant and community when they meet to discuss the loan. Pollution and labor practices would enter into the accounting of desert. A high Dunn & Bradstreet rating would not suffice.

When we judge a community from the outside, the relationship also shapes our own communal identity. The union, as I have described it, is an association of investors like any other. The history of such funds is, however, marked by controversy over that casting. Proposals that the funds invest to favor a region, a type of firm, or an environmental policy are variously justified as maintaining the character of unions as moral associations or rebutted as ideological and inappropriate to the investment relationship. When fund managers respond to this debate by differentiating their portfolios so that individuals may choose among several investment programs, they (re)form the identity of the union.

Borrowing money is certainly one of the most familiar forms of a relationship leading to the external evaluation of a community's moral deserts. There are, however, other close competitors. We are often drawn into an external evaluation when we face the prospect of either emulating a community or imposing upon it.

Emulation and imposition may start modestly with a discrete trait. U.S. manufacturers may, for example, be attracted to Japanese methods of managing inventories. They may wonder whether they can use the "hurry-up" inventory method (the best-known of those methods in the United States), and they may begin to explore the possibilities. As the Japanese discovered in their long and continuing experience of emulation, exploration may not begin with a moral assessment but it characteristically concludes with it. Important traits are rarely "distinct." They cannot be carried from place to place without implicating a larger communal order. In asking about the contextual requirements of "hurry-up," the U.S. manufacturers inevitably are drawn into a moral assessment of larger features of a Japanese community that sustains the practices. In a complementary way, they are led to reexamine social relations "back home" to assess the fit of the new practice.

The dynamics of imposition have very much the same form though they characteristically present a much harsher evaluative face. One community imposing itself on another discovers that it is drawn into an external moral evaluation in order to implant the new practice in foreign soil; into an introspective evaluation of its own character to test whether the effort of imposition is fitting. Christian missionaries in the Spanish realms of the New World struggled—some more than others—with difficult issues. Their efforts and their faith implied a disrespect for the communions they discovered. How broad was that disrespect? Did it entitle them to coerce conversion and to extirpate every sign of the old practices? What sort of relationship was fitting for a Christian?

In this and countless comparable but less severe cases, the character of the relations between communities structures and simplifies tasks that are remarkably difficult when engaged within the terms of each communion independently. Our heavy reliance on market exchanges is grounded in the enabling simplicity of the external relationship. The arms-length exchange provides a discipline that an organization may not be able to sustain internally. Whatever the full range of our identities, we must see ourselves as bound to gain resources by exchanging our production with others. Whatever the character of the others, we are bound to see them as trading partners.

Indeed, we have learned how to sustain very large communities by allowing them to create smaller internal associations bound in a web of relationships that make the assignment of moral deserts possible.[2] Units are accountable for their performance, but their internal processes are not closely specified by the leaders of the community. Except under conditions of severe stress, communal conversations avoid exposing these internal dynamics in order to preserve the desired and desirable autonomy and accountability.

A great many large communities practice delegation and monitor performance. Often the performance units—whether they are machine shops or administrative bureaus—become the primary foci of communal affiliation. Units seek (often successfully) to devalue the externally imposed performance measures and to replace them with standards of their own choosing. The elite of the large community—representing itself as the voice of the communion rather than as simply one group among many—then is tempted to break the conversational constraints in order to regain control. For a moment, when the elite succeeds, the community appears as one before it begins again to rebuild the walls that channel internal relationships through carefully designed gates.

Large communities must be wary of attacking those walls so frequently that the many small communions are overwhelmed. The insistence on transparency ("Let us all know one another completely so that there are no secrets") makes it impossible to sustain large size, complex external relations, or stable institutions.[3]

Two communities may, of course, relate to one another in several different ways. I may, for example, expect a school to teach my children, control the children of others, prepare workers for my firm and citizens for my nation, husband my tax dollars, and sustain real estate values. In each relationship, both I and the school take on a different identity and may be morally judged on a different scale. I express my expectations in distinctive communal settings. I may, indeed, lose track of the plurality of claims, so that my mind—as a creation of these multiple communities—become increasingly incoherent. The school responds by elaborating its structure so that it can engage each setting appropriately. In some the school appears as a loosely connected collection of teachers; in others it appears as a set of managers supervising production workers. (It too, of course, risks incoherence.)

This plurality and this incipient incoherence cannot be suppressed. There is no purpose that justifies and no method that enables a holistic moral accounting outside the web of relationships. The external perspective provides a relatively simple mode of assigning deserts but the field of communities is fruitful and multiplies in its grip. In order to provide a moral purchase on the world, we repeatedly divide communities, making many out of one.

There are, of course, costs and risks associated with simplification. Markets, we have learned, always fail the most demanding performance tests; signals between communities are distorted and exacerbate the environmental problems they face. A great many people have repeatedly tried to reduce or control the dangers of pluralism by bringing trading partners into a single organization, tearing down internal walls so that strangers may act as neighbors, subordinating fractious units to a new moral covenant, or replacing discrete cooperative exchanges with coercive coordination. Making one out of many, they enter the complex tasks of internal assessment.

Internalization temporarily (or, better, episodically) reduces the number of overlapping communities. It succeeds, however, only by creating new walls and externalizing the assignment of moral deserts—by reshaping the cast—not by reducing the number of communities. Indeed, small units with narrow domains—specialized manufacturing firms, water districts, garden clubs—often face intense external competition or scrutiny and offer very little latitude for internal proliferation. In contrast, large units—diversified and vertically integrated manufacturing firms, the United States, the Roman Catholic Church, New York City—both require more internal proliferation and provide more latitude for it because they cannot specify so precisely the requirements for their communal survival.

The desire to create one out of many is entwined in both the ideology and the practices that Taylor (1989) associates with modernity. Our ambition to control negative externalities grows more imperialistic as we become increasingly skilled at tracking the paths of even minute pollutants across natural and social systems. We are able to understand the ways in which the patterns of energy consumption in the Northern Hemisphere influence development opportunities in the Southern; to measure the movement of minute traces of toxins across vast distances. We fantasize about eliminating all environmental risks (Wildavsky 1988). The claim of the ultimate community—all humankind sharing a common fate in the biosphere—compels us to fit every local attachment within the largest possible frame. We are positively obligated to undertake a moral inventory and assessment of the "community of nations" because failings in any unit implicate us all and threaten the moral principles implicit in the human community.

Humankind is, however, a group, not a community. We are not—nor could we be—a global "village" or "family." This is strikingly apparent in presentations of a universalistic ethic by Norman Care and Robert Goodin. Care (1987, pp. 164–167) insists that acting justly toward those with whom we share a common fate no matter where they live requires the members of rich, liberal societies to sacrifice—"at least for a time (perhaps as little as a generation or as much as a century)"—their liberty and their commitment to self-realization. Goodin (1985) provides a cogent analysis of the ways in which the authority we grant to "special" obligations owed to our families, our colleagues, our clients, our cities, and our nations exhaust us, leaving little for those who are far away or out of sight. A universal commitment to sustain those who are vulnerable, he insists, will justify many of the old forms of obligation but will realign them so that they are appropriately subordinated to general commitments to the welfare of the poor and the weak. Justice cannot be satisfied, Goodin warns, if we treat it as a residual claim to be met only after we have finished with the business of daily life.

The persons whose claims mandate this global reconstruction of obligations are objects, not subjects; a group, not a community. When, however, the casting is changed so that the poor or the vulnerable become a community—when they become "citizens" of India, Somalia, or the United States—their identity demands that they be treated as if their deserts are principally grounded in their behavior rather than in their needs. In a surprising and often troubling way, justice claims grounded in the needs of groups of individuals give way to the moral assessments of communities. Even external development workers who want to reach the poor without engaging national institutions discover that they labor in a field of settlements and associations—that they must speak to persons *in community* rather than to persons as detached objects. Whether they use internal or external criteria, they find that some communities deserve respect and some do not. If they fail to make, announce, and act on the distinction, they destroy the credibility of their own values. If villagers who blithely eat all their seed and ignore weeds are treated as the moral equals of their "responsible" neighbors, then what is the value of virtue?

Intractable Pluralism

The world we see in front of us is crowded with communities. Is it possible that today (or perhaps the day after tomorrow) the crowd will be thinned, the tangle pruned? Is the compelling practical distinction between deserving and undeserving communities the instrument that will reorganize the communal landscape?

My answers to those questions are, I hope, clear enough. We do, indeed, sensibly make the distinction between deserving and undeserving communities. The ways in which we make that distinction leave us, however, with an intractably pluralistic landscape rather than a simplified one. The processes of assigning moral deserts and arguing about them complicate rather than simplify the communal field. Although we sometimes make one out of many, the integrative strategy is characteristically paradoxical, generating communal diversity rather than suppressing it.

3

Three Communal Myths

Arguments, Images, and Stylized Myths

When we try to persuade one another about the "right" course of action, we usually set our arguments within images of a communion whose members are capable of listening to our words and responding to them, of understanding our experiences, and of correcting our misperceptions. Only within a community that sustains, legitimizes, and disciplines practices and that cultivates a moral order does it make sense to talk a certain way or to believe that anything is worth knowing. Only in a community will individuals speak with a shared understanding of the pragmatic implications of their words and act with a shared understanding of the meaning of their deeds. Consenting (albeit often tacitly) to argue within an image, we create a world that shapes our speech. Pleading at the Bar in the appropriate forms, we maintain communities that sustain the institution we call the Law. Presenting the annual State of the Union address to Congress, the president of the United States affirms the terms of the political spectacle in which opponents join in a shared communion.

The communities that infuse our arguments with meaning are always creations of our imagination. Indeed, it is precisely because communal assertions are so important in justifying speech that they are used with great rhetorical abandon. Skeptical observers may often wonder whether signs of communication have been given inflated moral significance. Are there members with rights and obligations, or are they wholly creatures of the speaker's imagination? Are new recruits socialized and members disciplined? Is the putative moral order realized in practices, or is there no community there?

As I have already argued, imagination shapes our communal lives even when there are plentiful signs that we are engaged in vital social relations. We rarely sit in the middle of a circle in which we are instantly and unequivocally rewarded for behaving appropriately and censured for our mistakes. Instead, we represent a community in our minds, we act, and then we monitor and interpret the external response. Sometimes we discover that we have mistaken our community, that no one seems to have been listening, or that our words and deeds have lost their meanings. The overbearing communal circle—where it appears—is usually cast as a horrific attempt to take us out of our minds and our ordinary social relations by controlling our attention absolutely, giving us no place to hide, no view beyond the perimeter, and no possibility of publicly affirming variations in interpretation.[1]

Sometimes we know all the members of a community personally and represent them symbolically with names, personalities, and distinctive accents. Other communities, however, are composed of the dead (who can speak to us only with the voices with which we endow them) or of legions of strangers bound to us by a common membership—our "fellow citizens," "worthy adversaries," "co-religionists," and "comrades in arms." Even in their most obscure and anonymous modes, however, our images of community are stamped with the marks of shared events, persons, and practices—familiar dramas in which we have cast ourselves or been cast: "my neighborhood," "my gang," "our nation," "the company," "the profession," "our fathers."

These grainy images are subtly and, it often seems, secretly shaped by stylized myths capable of sustaining abstract and formal arguments. My neighborhood, profession, or nation must appear to be a community of a particular sort before I can generalize my communal claims in a way that may persuade skeptics or strangers. The stylized myths that serve this shaping role are few in number, enormously influential, and remarkably stable over time. When our eyes and ears are attuned to these stylized myths, even the casual evocations of a beatific calculus—"Overall we'll be better off with that plan than any other"—are interpreted as an allusion to a community in which members are appropriately and consensually governed by one or another utilitarian decision rule. Overtly simple rituals—e.g., that a "gentleman" opens a door for a "lady"—evoke images of ancient meanings and deep commitments.

Without claiming to be exhaustive, I distinguish three such stylized myths that appear in social settings around the world. (The particular way I have represented the myths and my illustrations may be "Western" and predominantly "American," but the stylized forms are ubiquitous.) Each form sustains arguments in a particular mode and generates rhetorical difficulties that are the vulnerable side of its intellectual and emotional strength. Each also implicates the other two, so that even when they explicitly conflict the three seem to require one another. In large social settings—nations, corporations, cities, major religious groups—one stylized myth rarely appears without the others. I have labeled these three myths as distinguishing moral communities as "contractual," "deep," or "open." I am principally concerned with the final form (the myth of "open moral communities"), but I cannot describe it effectively without setting it within the triad.

Contractual Moral Communities

The contractual myth is grounded in two complementary ideas. The first holds that a community is legitimate only if it is initiated by a voluntary contract among its members. The contract may be quite explicit, as in the case of a signed text to which everyone can refer. In the absence of such a contract, however, a community is legitimate if the members would voluntarily agree to its practices and relations if they were to engage in a process of uncoerced negotiations. Participants in the affairs of a community joined in an argument about collective choices are bound to interpret explicit contracts and to represent (and justify) tacit bargains. When explicit and tacit contracts conflict, participants are encouraged to seek a "new covenant" consistent with respect for the authority of mutual promises.

The second idea at the core of the contractual myth responds to the problems attached to the notions of voluntary consent and the authority of promises. Every process of bargaining proceeds in a structure that constrains the choices of all the participants. We bring to those processes experiences and dispositions that we cannot freely jettison in order to "voluntarily" engage with others. The very acts of promising and depending on promises require background institutions that allow us to respond to unimagined contingencies, to protect ourselves from destructive interpretations, and to balance the claims of tacit and explicit contracts. Those institutions cannot, however, survive and function if they are at risk in every promise we make and in every contract we write (Attiyah 1981).

Interpreted strictly, the first idea in the contractual myth would set such a stringent standard that we would be forced to deny legitimacy to most communities. If, however, we back off from that counsel of perfection, the first idea does not help us judge how much "structure" (or "coercion") is acceptable before contractual arguments about collective choices lose their meaning. The second idea, which is central to much of what we think of as "modern" and "liberal" thought, relaxes that standard. Imagine, we are told, that the biological organisms we identify as "human beings" are also moral entities endowed with elemental rights that precede any social arrangement or bargain. These pre-social Selves engage with one another in order to protect their lives and well-being or to achieve a goal that cannot be obtained without the discipline of community and the order of settled institutions. This primal contract provides a frame within which it is possible to articulate standards for particular and necessarily flawed bargains. Of course, those labor negotiations or that pre-nuptial agreement were imperfect. They should be accepted, however, if they sustain the general social contract; they should be rejected if the taint endangers it.

In almost all settings, this account of a general social contract is elaborated (variously) in accounts of the "state of nature," of an obscure generative period in which heroic primitives strode the earth, or an historical "founding" in which we our ancestors endowed us with a transformative gift. The myth need not, however, be cast in these terms. The great social bargain may be tacit. In the form that John Rawls has employed so effectively, we are asked to imagine that we contract with one another behind a "veil of ignorance" that prevents us from knowing our social position or our place in the sequence of generations. That "objective" bargain is not trapped in the past, never to be repeated. It is immanent in the present and constantly accessible (Rawls 1971).

MacIntyre (1984) wrote an obituary for the attempt—he called it the "Enlightenment Project"—to construct a social order and to define a moral code within the contractual myth. The death notice was premature. The myth has passionate advocates and is so deeply embedded in the language of collective choice and individual rights that we can barely speak without employing its terms. Of course we know, as Kymlicka (1989) reminds us, that there has never been a pre-social Self. The notion that we are free to choose outside of a shaping social environment is a product of the salience of choice and the experience of pluralism and not of a heroic primitivism. It is that Self crafted into myth that is at the core of much of what we mean by modernity (Taylor 1989).

The power of the myth lies in the interplay of its two elements. Looked at from one direction, the ubiquitous use of the contract as a model of association is sustained and disciplined by a general social bargain. That bargain commands our attention to a superordinate community that must be maintained if the entire web of associational life is not to come unraveled. (If that community is threatened, "anarchy" takes hold and no particular contract—explicit or tacit—is safe.) Looked at from the other direction, the image of the uncoerced contract as a ubiquitous social form disciplines our representations of the general arrangement. The conditions in which the general contract was (or might be) struck cannot violate our ordinary conceptions of voluntary bargains: signatures elicited with a machine gun or with fraudulent representations are not binding (Gauthier 1990).

This interplay of the general social contract and ubiquitous contracting shapes the rhetoric of public argument. The language of economics infuses the talk of policy circles with images of spot and general contracts and of the reconciliation of collective choices with the rational calculations of individuals. We are simultaneously drawn to markets as the settings that promote voluntary contracting as the basis for social life and warned that markets are always imperfect; drawn to organizations to redress those failures and then warned again that they too are flawed. We are asked to respect a contract or are told that the old bargain is no longer binding and should be replaced. Our attention is called to the boundaries of the superordinate contractual unit and to its moral claims as the bastion of voluntary assent; we arewarned that parochial judgments should not interfere with the general welfare, which (in one or another of its faces) is the object of the social contract. Dialectically, we are warned that the boundaries have been misdrawn, the parties misspecified, or the claims of the Leviathan pathologically distorted. We are led to wonder in public about the interaction of general and particular contracts. If the general contract requires "justice"—

wearing one or another of its several faces—must every family, every city, and every firm be held to that standard?[2]

The discursive forms of the contractual myth are so dense, so pervasive and so attached to experience (even children enter into contracts with their teachers) that we often forget that we are dealing with stylized images rather than ethnographic descriptions. We cannot observe either the pre-social Self or most of the contractual processes that legitimize communities and institutions. Though it has the feel of everyday experience, the mythic image of contractual relations is a highly stylized expression of complex social behaviors. Within the myth, the structures of both overt and tacit bargaining processes—unequal power, the language we employ, the background institutions—taint voluntarism. There is a great deal to be explained (or explained away) if contracts are to legitimize collective choices. Outside that mythic form, the taints are often represented as vital elements of the social order. In the common but not fully adequate spatial metaphor: our mutual promises are grounded in community rather than vice versa.

Deep Moral Communities

The myth of deep community—the second of the three myths—treats all human beings as social. In this myth, the counterpart to the image of the contract is an insistence that arguments about both personal and collective choices fit within the discursive forms of a community that engages its members in an integrated view of their place in the cosmos, their history, their culture, and the meaning of personal experiences. Practices in overtly distinctive domains—factory, family, mosque, club—are represented as parts of a single fabric so that a violation in one area endangers the entire skein. With or without a theistic claim, the ordinary events of daily life, the protocols of social relations, and the cycles of the natural order are invested with sacred meaning. The most passionate arguments often deal with the conditions of entry, the punishment and even exclusion of violators, and the interpretation of apostasy.

The myth of deep community may seem the stuff of anthropology: tales told of little communities, primitive peoples, and insular groups who resist the blandishments of modernity. Members of complex civilizations that confront cultural conflicts both inside and outside their borders also speak, however, of deep and extensive mutual obligations, a shared history, and a sacred ethical code. The intellectual advocates of nations and empires as moral entities have often represented them as communities whose claims to superordinate authority—above family, religion, locality, or clan—rest on the shared identity of a "people." Neighborhood associations, large corporations, and suburban churches in American cities may similarly present themselves as extensive (if not all-embracing) moral entities.

Rationality within the contractual myth means, in one of its many aspects, that collective choices accurately express personal preferences (Hardin 1988). The myth of deep moral communities, in contrast, is centered in the range and coherence of the moral order: to be "rational" means to fit within that order and to respect it.[3] Contracts are common, but, as I have already suggested, they express rather than create communal orders.

Both in practice and in their mythic representations, deep communities are marked by individual deviance, by group differences, by social conflict, and by the stress of collective decision making. (They are in and of the world of human beings, not angels.) In the contractual myth, the processes of control, management, and planning that prevent variety and conflict from getting out of hand are often treated with suspicion. The demonstration that a "way of life" has been designed by one group to control another strips the supposed contract of its mantle of legitimacy.

In contrast, arguments set within a deep myth characteristically assume that true belief and correct practice must be designed and maintained; that both voluntary adult recruits and children must be socialized so that they come to believe that "Japan," "America," or "General Motors" is a deep community that defines and nourishes them. The danger is not authority but primitivism (which devalues current practices and historical experience) or antinomianism (which denies authority its domain).

Speaking and acting within the deep myth provides welcome opportunities to exercise authority so as to sustain integrative capacities. In a study of a Baptist church in an Atlanta suburb, Greenhouse (1986) uses a telling phrase: faced with a dispute, the members come together to "pray for justice." The process of quoting from sacred texts (the Koran, the Constitution, tales of the founders), even to support diametrically opposed positions, allows the community to discipline change and to cope with conflict. (Symmetrically, failure to employ the appropriate quotations is an

assault on the shared order.) In the midst of a debate, speakers evoke parables or archetypal accounts of moral choices without explicating their current meanings or justifying their relevance. Listeners must invest themselves
in the incomplete account, enacting the myth in their own speech. If they
cannot do this—if the story makes no sense to them—they must give themselves over to the pedagogy of the initiates in order to join the community
(Burt 1984).

The myths of deep and of contractual communities are related in complex and unexpected ways. At one level, they appear simply to compete.
From the perspective of deep communities, the contractual myth seems
idolatrous and shrill (in that it is readily enlisted in the service of ethically
distorted and outrageous judgments); at the other extreme, it seems banal
and self-serving. If we specify the environmental constraints appropriately, even the most complex social arrangements may be represented as products of a sequence of contractual exchanges among (superficially) rational
actors. Seen from the other bank, talk of deep and sacred obligations is
often both obscure and deliberately obscurantist.

At a more profound level, the two myths depend on and merge into one
another. The initial links are historical. The voluntarism and the suspicion
of coercion that mark the contractual myth have been forged in the long
search for respite from the violent clash of deep claims: only a social compact grounded in tolerance could sustain social peace and, paradoxically,
create a virtuous commonwealth that would (in various times and places)
serve Muslim and Hindu, Catholic and Protestant, Jew and Greek, Puritan
and Friend. Inevitably, the uses and limits of tolerance that characterized
each commonwealth were shaped by the practices of the deep communities from which it arose, the character of the persistent deep communities
by the ways in which contractual alternatives were represented.

That historic pattern is continually repeated. There is also, however, a
less anguished or at least more usual connection between the two myths
where they are simultaneously (even promiscuously) employed. The deep
myth teaches us that we are not alone; we are not the first to feel the burden of coercion and pain. We need not, therefore, turn in our ticket. We
may cherish parables and collective memories that defy critical historical
standards to maintain our moral intuitions against the cold logic of voluntarism. On the other side, the idea of a Self with "human rights" that

precede the social order provides a shield against the buzz of claimants who would consume us entirely. The special role of Contract, in the myth, allows us to be held responsible for our individual deeds but limits our collective guilt for the sins of others—even our own parents—to which we did not (even tacitly) assent.

Open Moral Communities

I am tempted to describe the myth of open moral communities—the principal subject of this essay—as lying between the other two myths. I have not, however, established much room in the middle ground. When the first two myths compete, they often appear to drive out any tepid alternatives. If you reject what George Parkin Grant (in a critique of Rawls—see Grant 1985) calls "English speaking justice," then the coherent options appear to be the deep agreements expressed by the great religious faiths. Any other version of communitarianism seems pale by comparison. When myths are not competitive but complementary—when we embed one myth in the other or shift back and forth between them—the middle ground is similarly eroded.

The appropriate spatial metaphor locates the myth of open moral communities as suffused through the more familiar forms of deeply consensual or contractual justifications of the social order. Consider the simple question "Where are you from?" Those of us who have moved from one city to another know that the answer expresses a morally significant choice. We can respond with the name of the place in which we were born, in which we were raised, or in which we currently reside. In some settings, one of these responses is all that is called for or all that we are willing to offer. In its most compelling version, however, the question asks for marks of identity and affiliation: "I was born in Chicago but I am from New York," or "I'm from Calcutta, though I have lived in Delhi for a long time."

What are the implications of a voluntary act of affiliation with a place? What rights are implied? What obligations? Even the most ardent civic booster (eager to provide maximal answers) will understand that the communities implied by the terms of these questions engage us only partially. We are simultaneously members of many communities, and we assess the implications of affiliation with one or another by locating it within the dense pattern of the entire set.

The myth of deep moral communities represents this pattern as a jigsaw puzzle in which each association has its place within a relatively closed society. Temporary confusions or uncertainties about the placement of a particular piece will be resolved as the pieces are meshed in a uniquely appropriate order. In a jigsaw puzzle, each community—nation, city, neighborhood, family, firm, church—would create a distinctive ethical domain. When undecided as to whether one set of obligations or another applied to a particular issue, we would evoke a rank order: nation over family, family over firm, firm over city, and so on. Deep communities may be pluralistic in practice, but in the normative world of myths their major institutions "fit together into one unified system of social cooperation from one generation to the next" (Rawls 1993, p. 11).

The myth of open moral communities denies the jigsaw image and the rhetorical insistence on "fit" and "fabric." In the open myth, the boundaries of the total "society" are contested and emergent, so we cannot securely set the external straight pieces in place before beginning to fill in the pattern. We are forced to link the pieces in order to represent the boundaries. That would be difficult enough with an ordinary puzzle, but in the open myth some of the elements are overlapping, many of them are conflicting, and others are only loosely coupled. The principle of "fit" and the geometry of the pattern are also obscure. The puzzle, in its mysterious ways, must even accommodate the strange communion of long-term adversaries whose identities (shaped by their battles) come to depend on one another. Some of the members of community A also belong to B, but not all do. No members of C belong to A, but A and C are connected by members whom they share in D, and so forth and so on through the chain. We move within this complex pattern—now emphasizing one group of claims and then another, leaving one identity and adopting a new one—without usually encountering a charge of apostasy. The possibility that members will exit is implicit in every community. Images of routes of movement between communities and free spaces in which we can be anonymous or unidentified without being stigmatized sustain the openness of the entire structure.

Criticism and conflict are so common in the field of open communities that they are sensibly understood as part of the symbolic structure of the myth. The CEO of a large corporation may, for example, want to encourage employees to identify with small units while retaining a sense that every part of the firm is a cog in a single machine. The employees, for their part, may resent the "folks upstairs" who intrude periodically into the vital community of co-workers. Their firm is a field: out of one, an intractably messy many. In the same way, nation builders may denigrate "tribalism" only to find that their attack generates a defensive though ambivalent reaction. "Thus egalitarian, nationalistic ideologies," Marris (1986, p. 71) observes, "generate tensions which they cannot handle, unless they also embody their apparent contradiction."

The stylized myth of communal openness allows us to navigate within a field of communities without either minimizing their claims on us or diminishing them as inferior to those of a "real" community. They don't, however, provide a simple standard, comparable to a contract or an integrated moral order, that would cogently shape and discipline our speech within this myth.

How should we argue when we represent ourselves as belonging simultaneously to an array of moral communities? That is a difficult question, and I will wrestle with it on every page in the rest of the essay. Let me start the struggle with a simpler query: Is there really any reason to employ a third stylized myth, or can the first two—each with a distinguished philosophical pedigree—make sense of the array of grainy communal images that shape our public discourse? Even when the notions of implicit social contracts and integrated moral orders are suspect—when we would prefer not to talk "that way" anymore—they often seem to control our imaginations and our speech. If we follow their forms and accept the inevitable intellectual legerdemain (and limits) of mythic discourse, is there anything that is morally relevant that has been neglected? In an imperfect world, is there, for example, a compelling substitute for the image of an autonomous individual endowed with the marvelous capacity to stay or leave, choosing identities at will? May the shaping influence of communities be simply interpreted as the terms of a generalized contract whose content we can't fully forecast or understand in advance? That is, after all, not a particularly difficult idea. We all appreciate that even with extensive advance preparation, we join the Army, choose a college, get married, or take a job recognizing that we don't quite know what we have done, what will be done to us, or what we will become.

Similarly (but from the perspective of deep communities), suppose we see ourselves as engaged in many overlapping communities with at least partially conflicting values but with a willingness to compromise and trade, a readiness to cooperate (if the terms are right), and a commitment to the maintenance of a system of diverse options. If the communities bargained, we might, in the magical world of myths, represent their "overlapping consensus" (Rawls 1993, p. 11) as the will of a superordinate community integrating the pluralism of associational life. The deep myth and its rhetorical forms would then take hold.

The idea of an inevitably uncertain generalized contract emphasizes the voluntarism in open moral communities—particularly an idealized consensus and the dream that detached analysts can specify the public interest. Those two ideas do not, however, exhaust the uses of the third myth. Openness makes sense of a pervasive perception of mutual misunderstanding that neither the contractual nor the deep myths illuminate.

The myth of deep communities points to a shared lexicon that organizes arguments and the worlds they make—to a shared understanding even of speech differences. The prince and the pauper, and the theologian and the peasant, may attribute significantly different shades of meaning to the same terms. (They certainly pronounce them differently!) The linguistic variety integrated into social roles enables deep communities to act collectively by providing markers of authority and by allowing vulgar and elite perspectives to coexist. Both are protected by acknowledged differences.

The contractual myth doesn't elicit a comparable imagery of social differences and of language. The parties to the general social contract are impelled by powerful requirements (such as the incipient threat of warfare or the search for justice) that are not inflected by shades of competing meanings. The parties to ordinary contracts often mistake one another's words, but in the event of a dispute background institutions impose conventional meanings. If misunderstanding is endemic, the entire contractual structure as the foundation of a moral order collapses.

The myth of open moral communities sets the problem in a quite different light. If communities overlap and if they are located in a shifting and amorphous field, it follows that they cannot fully control their own discursive order. The myth transforms our perception of communicative failure into a measure of the intrinsic (and often deeply valued) structure of our worlds. Even intense communities cannot fully control their own conversational forms. Parents and children living in a complex communal field find that words are polymorphic: they mean different things to different people, and they assume varied forms as contexts shift. In large (and perhaps less intense) communities—cities, labor unions, neighborhoods, professional associations—ambiguity of speech and indeterminacy of interpretation are ubiquitous. Asking people (in the classic image of policy analysts) to choose a mix of "guns" and "butter," the myth of moral openness encourages them to ask after the meaning of the terms and the social context in which the balance would be struck. Absent a lexicon and a location, we should—within the myth—refuse to choose.

Lexical variety and polymorphism structure how we argue about means as well as how we argue about ends. Consensual instrumental knowledge depends on stable conceptions of the forms employed to describe our actions, the settings in which we are engaged, and the valued outcomes of our behavior. If our descriptive protocols are ambiguous and our interpretations are embedded in conflict, we are likely to argue over means as well as over ends. The overtly simple designation of one bundle of technologies as more "efficient" than another becomes a complex process of bargaining among the advocates of rival measures of both inputs and outputs. Again: absent a lexicon and a location, we should—within the myth—refuse to choose.

That rule of refusal and the premises on which it rests provide a point of departure for my search for rhetorical forms appropriate to the myth of moral openness. They also articulate a threat. Suppose the rule is crudely summarized as follows: "All social knowledge and all choices are political." If that is that case, must we abandon all faith in the dream of a consensual social knowledge as the working clay of collective choices? How do we agree on what we "know" within the myth of open moral communities? How do we sustain a bargaining process that results in a workable public discursive order? What are the institutional and rhetorical forms of this bargaining?

4
Community and Communication

The three stylized myths shape the stories we tell to address our ethical uncertainties and to frame our communal arguments. They also shape the media and channels we choose and the characteristic dilemmas of our communication practices. The myths as I have described them are literary responses to the limits of direct experiential persuasion. If we could fully share our complex experiences, we would not require such abstruse simplifications. But we cannot! Strangers, no matter how empathetic, cannot be transformed into instant members. Their gaze alters an experience that is not their own.

Each of the three communal myths responds to the difficulties of reconciling members and strangers in a different way; each articulates a distinctive set of approaches to the assessment of communication technologies, networks, and policies.

The Press of Strangers on Deep Communities

In a deep community integrated by an extensive moral order, policy arguments are resolved by testing them within that order. New patterns of communication, whether they emerge from within the community or from without, are ethically threatening when they promise individual or collective benefits but interfere with the processes of socialization and discipline. The communal guardians may respond by rejecting the innovations or may seek to assimilate and control them. Unless the benefits are very great, rejection is morally simple (though often very difficult in practice). Revolutionary texts, sexually explicit videocassettes and CDs, violent computer games, and programs pulled from the air by small satellite dishes and hand-held transistor radios evade the gaze of the most assiduous moral guardians. (Clever guardians may sometimes, of course, choose to look away rather than test the limits of their authority.) When deep communities are colonized by powerful outsiders—whether in the merger of firms, in the gentrification of blue collar neighborhoods, or in the march of imperial armies—failed rejection only accentuates the loss of competence by emphasizing that the communion cannot control its own moral order.

Assimilation is a much more morally demanding response. Its proponents must reconceive the forms and the limits of socialization and discipline (e.g., using radio and television to accomplish the Lord's work, creating universities that may be resistant to control, adopting the language of interlopers to combat their influence). They must also face internal complaints of abandonment or naiveté—a birthright sold for a mess of porridge—and struggle against simplified but emotionally compelling memories of a community that once was uncontaminated by foreign influences.

Whatever their difficulties, the responses of rejection and assimilation suggest a world that is amenable to communal control. Debates over the new networks or media provide an opportunity to cultivate the shared moral order. France, India, or Saudi Arabia, by censoring American films or limiting their distribution, asserts its own status as a moral community deserving respect. Similarly, boycotts and V-Chips assert that parents can and should control the flood of messages directed toward "their" children.

There are, however, aspects of the development of communication networks that virtually defy control because they frame dilemmas, simultaneously serving and threatening communal norms.

Every deep community describes a universe of nonmembers who are moral objects. Attending to their welfare expresses and strengthens the core values of the communion. In this way, members may be variously enjoined to protect vulnerable animals, feed hungry children and safeguard guests but to avoid sleeping with infidels or befriending colonial officials. Every deep community must establish and maintain a balance between the claims of strangers and those of members. For some this is an easy task because few strangers intrude on their worlds. For others it is particularly difficult: either the powerful strangers are morally imperialistic and impose their own order or, paradoxically, the community is transformed by its own desire to open its borders and to evangelize the immigrants. A universalistic theme in the ethos of a deep community—one God, one globe, one humanity, and one moral code—renders it particularly vulnerable to the temptation to stigmatize its own parochialism and to convert strangers by assimilating their practices into the universal creed. As Buddhist, Muslim, and Christian missionaries spread outward from their core territories they incorporated large elements of the worlds, they encountered as (often passionately defended) variations of the original communion.

Communication innovations since Gutenberg (or, in a more limited perspective, since the development of telegraphic networks) have increased the range and the salience of nonmembers in the worlds of deep communities. "Simple" military imperialism and economic exchange have been generalized into a profound cultural encounter: not only were French troops in Saigon and Algiers; Paris was there. In an equally compelling way, Saigon and Algiers were in Paris. The citizens of national polities are encouraged by international conferences and agreements to imagine that the preservation of species and ecosystems everywhere depends on their moral choices. In most places where radio and television reach, audiences cannot escape constant images of the pain of innocent children and the consumption modes of faraway peoples. Computer networks bind strangers to one another in the intimacy of a global labor market created by footloose industries and the inexpensive movement of information and capital. It is difficult to find communities anywhere in the world whose speech is not inflected with the rhythms and disciplines of the written word and the clock, or whose sense of what is immediate and what is remote has not been reformed by radio and television.

The mass of external moral objects is overwhelming and defies the integrative capacity of deep communities eager to incorporate them. Not, however, for lack of trying! The image of a new ethos infusing old ideas and social forms remains a vibrant dream articulated in transnational bureaucracies and parliaments; in religious, social, and political movements; in professional associations; and in development organizations. In significantly different styles, it appears in Tehran and Cairo as the fundamentalism of intellectual elites and in Brussels as the dream of European social "cohesion."

Thick and Thin in Contractual Communities

Involuntary ignorance is the enemy of legitimate contracts. If I have knowingly decided not to inform myself about the conditions of the world in which a contract is launched, my assent is binding. If, however, I have been deceived by deliberate lies or by structural obstacles to knowledge that I could not overcome, then the contract is tainted by coercion—albeit of a very subtle sort.

Obstacles are, alas, defining elements of every social system. A world in which all knowledge was universally shared would be horrific were it not unimaginable. All communities that employ contracts as part of the fabric of everyday life must sustain a public order that distinguishes between structural obstacles that do not vitiate contracts and those that are so severe that they stigmatize every relationship that depends on them.

When we envelop ourselves in the contractual myth, we shape that order so that coercive obstacles are suspect. In general, fewer constraints on "speech" are better than more, media pluralism is better than monopoly, and broad access to knowledge is preferable to restricted intellectual privilege.

Innovations in communication have often concentrated rather than dispersed control over the media; stratified rather than democratized access to knowledge. Faced with apprehensions about "mass society," about the manipulation of opinion, and about inequalities in the distribution of knowledge, the contractual myth sustains a buoyant insistence on the value of more and cheaper communication and more stringent criteria for informed consent and full disclosure. Secrets are not the appropriate remedies for failed or illegitimate compacts, and limiting innovation is not the remedy for monopoly.

The core of this political orientation is the assumption that communication processes can be analytically distinguished from other social relations, the thin meanings of distinctive texts from thick contextual messages, and the communication infrastructure from the communities it sustains. These are familiar distinctions, and it would be difficult to talk within the contractual myth about the information required to legitimize social bargains without employing them. They are, however, symbolic constructions, not elemental social facts. Engaged in the workings of a complex community, individuals do not distinguish sharply between the information content of texts and the social relations in which they are grounded. The meaning of even pedestrian messages shared by lovers is implicated in the character of their affection. When co-religionists join in song, the message is in the communion more than in the words or the melody. Even detailed work protocols—"Put tab A in slot B and then turn screw C 180 degrees"—conjure a world of authority and competence in which giving and taking instructions makes sense. (Deferring to that authority, I will try to follow "do-it-yourself" directions long after I am sure that they must be wrong.) Texts entering a communion from outside are tamed and thickened by talking about them in conversational circles and reshaping them into integrative rituals and marks of distinction (e.g., chatting around the office coffeepot about last night's television program watched at home, or embracing an elaborately staged rock concert within everyday collective fantasies).

The process of developing innovations that substitute one mode of communication for another begins by treating established relations as problematic and devaluing interactions that cannot be conveyed in the new mode. When it succeeds, the analytic distinction between a message and the relationship in which it is embedded—between thick and thin communication—creates a space in which individuals and communities tolerate the change and even embrace it. Acting inside that space, we accept that a telephone conversation substitutes for a face-to-face encounter, or that watching television replaces going to a movie house, a "real" theater, or a "real" baseball stadium. Over time, the substitute modes are themselves enfolded in social relations, only to be subjected again to devaluation and detachment.

The stylistic preference for more information feeds on and sustains this repeated process. The social rituals and forms in which communication is embedded are stigmatized as marks of privilege or restrictive access; as structural obstacles that should give way to the voluntary contract. Insistence that understanding requires a complex engagement implies that knowledge cannot be widely shared in a medium that is not designed to replicate thick meanings: that the computer network cannot replace the classroom teacher, the classroom the apprenticeship, or the library the college.[1]

The contractual myth is a restless master. Thickened meanings must repeatedly be decomposed into their elements if the taint of coercion is to be removed. The myth, however, provides very little guidance as to how contracts are struck and how meanings are sustained. Complex engagements in families, firms, professions, and polities and across the great array of communities require all the thick (and suspect) devices of authority, trust, tradition, affection, and discipline. More information may strengthen or weaken these devices but does not replace them.

The poverty of guidance is particularly significant in the design of representative institutions in liberal polities. Whether or not the founding of these polities is ascribed to a discrete compact, they are legitimized by the bargains struck every day by representatives who are subjected to periodic elections.

Representatives are subject to periodic elections. Within the myth, we fairly ask: How do the representatives come to know about the world they attempt to shape? How do they arrange their own affairs to allow them to engage in intelligent decision making? How do they avoid having their intelligence frustrated by the ignorance or imprudent passions of the voters? I will turn to these questions explicitly in chapter 13. Anticipating my argument there, I offer only a modest proposal: None of these tasks and none of the dilemmas they spawn is adequately addressed by the substitution of thin for thick information or by the simple expansive insistence on more communication. In ways that are often conflicting, enhancing the knowledge of representatives requires more access to privileged expertise and to the advocacy of discrete interest groups, more accountability, and more insulated statecraft. The capacity for intelligent decision making depends on the often unreconciled disciplines of frankness, civility, hierarchy, consensual public orders, and frame-breaking negotiations.

"More" is not enough even for the creation of informed publics that will sustain rather than inhibit intelligence. Knowledgeable voters will be organized in a way that allows them to construct a reliable sense of their own "special" interests and also to imagine (as if they were representatives bargaining with one another) how those interests interact in a shared field rich with possibilities of conflict and cooperation.

Thin communication technologies are implicated in each of these design problems, but they principally require communal and institutional responses. The transformation of a parliament of strangers into an effective legislative community may be facilitated by computerized tracking of bills and access to data and expert knowledge. In parliaments as in neighborhoods, however, community development depends principally on the creation of trusted "old hands," on the articulation of interpersonal networks, and on the maintenance of a permeable but distinctive boundary within which members attend solicitously to their relations with one another.

In the same way, the articulation and the mobilization of publics may be enhanced by the design of mass and personalized media of communication. Television channels, computerized mailing lists, fax and e-mail networks, and inexpensive newspapers may make it possible to engage large groups in a common cause quickly and at low per-person cost. The construction and the interpretation of interests that will sustain collective intelligence, however, depend on the norms rather than on the forms of communication: How do advocacy organizations relate to their members and position themselves within the often-conflicting claims of mobilization and the formation of coalitions? How do they value the craft of legislators who shape public policies from the confusing mass of well-articulated special and diffuse public interests?

These communal and institutional choices are only dimly illuminated by the contractual myth. Boundary maintenance in a legislature or in a community of intense partisans is suspect, and the articulation of special interests is stigmatized in favor of a fascination with dispositions that cannot be ascribed to any set of well-marked persons but are ascribed to "everyone," to generations as yet unborn, to Nature, or to all sincere and rational citizens. The meaning of messages may lie in the minds and in the social relations of actual readers. We cannot, however, self-consciously design readers without subverting the equivalence of thin and thick communication modes and the moral authority of overtly voluntary contracts.

Division of Labor in Open Moral Communities

The stylized myth of a field of overlapping moral communities engages both the overwhelming burden of strangers and the attractive advantages of more though thinner information. In that engagement, the burden and advantages are shaped in distinctive ways that protect the complex fabric of the myth.

The open myth does not require that starving strangers and dying whales be assimilated into an integrated communal order. Instead, in a rough moral division of labor, they are implicitly assigned to established or emergent communities that embrace their cause. Only in these communities must members struggle with the conversion of moral objects into subjects or with the transformation of "relief" organizations into cooperative partners in development. For others, as observers, the obligations of hospitality or beneficence are limited.

When powerful communities extend themselves to strangers in new ways, they pull the field in which they are embedded with them. The British raj pulled English churches, families, firms, and localities into India even though they had not specifically chosen the path of empire. The conception of a transnational identity similarly touches communities that are not explicitly parties to the European Union. As long, however, as powerful communities are represented as elements in an open field, their moral authority does not depend on a capacious or integrated domain. My citizenship legitimately binds me to pay taxes to the U.S. government (or to accept punishment for my disobedience no matter what its motive), but I am not morally implicated in each of its wars or in each of its grants to artists. Within the ethical framework of representative institutions, neither individuals nor communities are obligated to protest every deed that repels them or to affirm each deed in which they delight.

The ethical division of labor that is implicit in the myth of overlapping communities balances (often unsteadily) between hyperattention and moral sloth. At one extreme, it is vulnerable to the overwhelming sense that the pictures cannot be ignored; that a universalistic justice or the very survival of the human race demands the creation of a deep global community that mobilizes its citizens to repair the world. At the other and more significant extreme, the division of labor readily deteriorates into the facile assumption that merely observing the world is sufficient; that by following the news we sustain the game and assure its continuity just as if we were spectators who had paid to watch a soccer match.

The open myth engages, sustains, and even requires the ubiquitous processes that replace thick with thin communication. At a very simple level, many of the communities in a dense, overlapping field are justified as contractual, resting on explicit terms and voluntary assent. At a deeper level, the pluralism and the openness of the field are cultivated by fictions and simulations that allow individuals to detach from their immediate selves and to navigate from one community to another. Like crafty novelists, we create ourselves in (often unreconciled) stories, both fitting and shaping communal dramas as we talk. Knowing about strangers—however meager and unengaged our exposure—lowers the barriers to telling new stories, assuming new relations, and migrating across physical and social space.

The open myth as a stylized way of thinking about communities is not, however, critically focused on thin communication or on the perfection of contracts. It offers no compelling ideological justification of equalizing access to information. Instead, it directs those who speak within its terms to the conditions that create, sustain, and recreate limited communions: to the work of attracting and transforming resources, socializing new recruits, disciplining members, and relating to outsiders. Commanding attention to these conditions does not, of course, prevent communities from making foolish or inept decisions—e.g., from resisting innovations that would enhance their operations or buying devices that do not fit. Unused or under-used computers in business firms and darkened television sets in schools testify to the capacity of communities to be lured into fashionable but unwise investments and, simultaneously, to their sometimes sensible and sometimes bullheaded ability to resist changes that do not mesh into their thick communication patterns.

The open myth articulated in simple and quite ordinary assertions of multiple affiliations and disciplines sustains two complementary sensibilities.

First, if we seek to live in a field of overlapping communities, we must preserve modes of passage from one community to another and expect to struggle with the sometimes conflicting claims of communion and openness. Rather than define ourselves in that conflict, we may attempt to simplify the field so that every person belongs to one and only one moral community. The retreat from pluralism, however, characteristically fails, or else it succeeds at a cost so high that it blackens the name of victory.

The second sensibility is an appreciation of what I have come to call "reading in public." Many communities organize themselves around written texts: lawyers and judges, religious communions, scholars, legislative committees. Why don't the members of those communities require translations? Why don't they find extended written arguments virtually impenetrable?

As I reflected on those questions one Sabbath morning, it occurred to me that in all those communities readers engaged written texts "in public." That image expressed several complementary qualities. In those communities, members assumed that written texts had to be interpreted by readers; they did not speak for themselves! Interpretation was, however, a public act, not a uniquely private one. Its content and its form were shaped by the community into which it was launched. Readers give meaning to texts; however, they must defend themselves in a community of interpreters, creating themselves in that community as they speak.

Sustaining public interpretation requires a complex set of institutional arrangements. The public reading must be done over and over again, texts must be stored in a way that allows them to be readily retrieved, and the interrogation of readers and authors must shift back and forth between the written and the spoken word—one complementing rather than replacing the other.

These arrangements differ across settings, but something like public reading appears in every community that integrates new modes of communication into its thick patterns of shared understanding. Information in the new mode is interpreted, contested, translated, and repeated as it enters into the lives of individuals and reshapes their communal roles. It barely matters whether the text in hand is an old biblical passage or a new digitized map that can be flexibly reconfigured to serve different purposes: reading in public engages members in a community of interpreters.

Today the agenda of communication policy is dominated by talk of "superhighways," "infrastructure," and "digital divides." There are indeed great decisions to be made (in the United States and around the world) about the forms and the financing of telecommunication networks. The hard work of shaping the new capacities, however, will be done in the varied settings in which information providers transform thick into thin communication and communities struggle to make thin communication into thick. IBM, Microsoft, AT&T, and their competitors, in repeated waves of innovation, will market information systems and advice in using them. Only customers, however, are capable of adapting system and advice to create and maintain their communal orders. Over time, the great differences in the ways in which individuals and groups command information resources will not stem from the tolls on the superhighway or from the design of the communications infrastructure. Individuals and communities that elaborate public reading will command the new capacities; those that do not will be bombarded by information that remains strangely mysterious and impenetrable.

II
Public Orders

5
Theory

Knowledge and Planning

I think of myself as a member of a small community of urbanists concerned with the "theory of planning." Most of my colleagues in this community make their living in academia, attempting to understand and shape the enterprise of city and regional planning and to prepare students for careers within it. Comparable circles concerned with planning are linked to virtually every profession and organizational practice, and I think of the members of these other theorizing clubs as close relatives, joined to my home circle by their shared experience of life in universities and in extended invisible colleges. They are also linked by bridge figures whose work spans specialized intellectual domains, a small canon of common texts, and a process that rewards inquiry at the margins of disciplines. I also feel close to these other circles because we struggle with two troubling relational issues. We all must reconcile our interest in abstraction and in "things in general" with the "practical" concerns of professionals in the fields to which we are linked—with our interest in intervention, control, and change and with the methods and explanatory goals of the social sciences.

Much of the talk and writing of these circles bears the mark of the institutional arrangements and intellectual arguments of the twentieth century. The theorists are, however, heirs to a tradition of dreaming about the possibilities of knowledge that is very old and that has appeared from time to time and in different accents and modes in virtually every corner of the globe. Two aspirations are coupled in that dream. The first asserts that it is possible to develop a shared understanding of the social world, the second that the understanding will support a consensual repair of that world. That cryptic summary does not, of course, capture the complexity, the conflicts, or the subtleties of the communities that have pursued the dream. Some of the dreamers have radically distinguished between the first aspiration and the second: We may be able to know the past, but we cannot pretend to know a future that as yet lies outside the world of fact. Others have turned that proposition on its head: We cannot pretend to know the past until we can forecast the future with confidence and shape it with the tools of a robust science. (A small voice replies with incredulity: How can we forecast a future that we are capable of changing?)

For many theorists, the dream has been confined to the intellectual technologies of instrumental planning and does not extend to objectives and values that are likely to remain intractably and appropriately varied. We may expect to agree on the ways of minimizing travel costs in a complex network, controlling inflation, reducing pollution, or teaching reading. There is no prospect, however, of consensually establishing an ethically compelling level or distribution of travel costs, inflation, pollution, or reading competence.

Others have been more ambitious. They have seen fact, value, and method as intertwined. If we believe that we can develop a science of planning (or "repair"), then, at the very least, it follows that some social forms are ethically impossible or (more classically phrased) "irrational." "Racism," for example, may violate what we securely "know" about human differences, and coercive persuasion may violate our commitment to the methods of scientific inquiry. The dreamers—as is to be expected—have argued among themselves: How large is the set of excluded forms? What is left when the excluded forms are deleted? Are there ethically compelling positive mandates that are attached to the dream of knowledge?

Myths and Dreams

The enterprise of dreaming about knowledge sustains the mythic forms of both deep and contractual communities. Within both myths, it is essential that in principle a community be capable of developing a common understanding of its internally defining elements and of its relations with the external environment. Even when the common understanding is contested and the dreamers are controversial, there is no essential conflict between the aspirations articulated in those myths and those articulated in that dream.

In contrast, the myth of open moral communities poses an essential threat to the dream. In principle and in practice, a field of communities without a settled boundary and with overlapping memberships may not be able to create a consensual body of knowledge about itself and about its multiple environments. The same idea reversed: The notion that social knowledge can be formulated in a coherent synthetic theory threatens the credibility of the myth.

If we are capable of understanding one another consensually, why can't we eliminate the conflicts and the disconcerting babble that characterize the field? The answer to that question running through this account of "theory" and other terms associated with the dream is simply that we are not capable. Rather than rue that failure, I embrace it. Only when we abandon the notion of a consensual social knowledge can we fully accept that we live in worlds in which conflicting communal myths sustain and re-create one another, in which our instrumental judgments are intractably ambiguous and dilemmatic, and in which our plainest words are subject to diverse interpretations. Before I explore that incapacity, let me turn to the two myths that sustain the dream in its most ambitious forms.

Every association that imagines itself as a deep community must develop a shared conception of its history and an instrumental technology for controlling its future. It must know enough of the world outside its borders to respond effectively to threats, to elicit the external resources it may require, and to assess its obligations to strangers. Its ethical discourse must allow it to address and tame the various normative claims it characteristically encounters among its members and in the outer world.

Some communities address these tasks by insulating their members from external contacts and socializing them intensely. The community knows itself confidently because, for the most part, it is what it wants to be. The methods associated with specialized communities dedicated to the pursuit of knowledge are either unnecessary or positively threatening in such insular settings. That pursuit of knowledge challenges everyone's putatively shared understanding of both the cosmic and social orders and the authority of moral guardians.

In contrast, larger and less insular communities that wrap themselves in the mantle of a deep moral order—whether a "way of life," a collective mission, or a religious tradition—have characteristically endorsed and promoted the dream of knowledge. Around the world and across vast stretches of time, they have repeatedly cultivated the professionalization of history and philosophy, the invention of "culture" and "moral integration," the foundations of what we now call "sociology" and "anthropology," and the statistical accounting that provides a common metric disciplining collective choices.

The promoters have, of course, sometimes been disappointed by their creations. As epistemic communities develop their own internal norms and disciplines, they characteristically became more difficult to control externally. In a play that has been repeated many times in different costumes and accents, both secular and religious regimes have been gored by scholars whom they have appointed and trusted and have come to wonder about these new guardians. Communities dedicated to writing produce a corpus of texts that outsiders often find overwhelming and impenetrable. "Inside" critics, in a complementary way, lament that their colleagues have become so self-absorbed that the links between knowledge and the social order are invisible or distorted.

The arguments over these issues highlight the connection between the dream of consensual social knowledge and the myth of deep communities. If the dream were an indulgence, there would be no passion in the indictment of failure. Knowledge plays a particularly important role within the myth in the attempt to anticipate the impact of change in one social domain on another domain. How, we ask, are our economic practices connected to the ways we raise our children? How might we design our television systems to encourage citizenship? Since both secular liberal regimes and fundamentalist religious regimes may justify themselves as deeply integrated by a shared moral order, in one setting we may ask whether even overtly minor violations of rights will endanger the entire fabric of entitlements; in another setting we may ask whether the failure to ferret out minor errors will inevitably corrupt everything we value.

There is an equally intense connection between the contractual myth and the dream of knowledge but it characteristically takes a quite different form. Although a concern with contracts as the basis of social order commands attention to the historical record of contractual engagements, the historicist regard for the fabric of a culture is missing. The contractual myth replaces it with an intellectual strategy that often treats the historical record as imperfect and distracting. In order to free the world from the taint of coercion, we must perfect it in our minds, peeking around the obscuring wall of current conditions to explore what only might have been.

There is no conventional name for this perfectionist strategy, but it is ubiquitous. The contractual myth requires that we repeatedly assess the legitimacy of tacit agreements. How, we must ask, would we arrange our collective affairs if we were not constrained by our ignorance and fear and if we were not intimidated by power and the difficulties of replacing one set of social forms with another? Will this or that arrangement meet the standards set by those idealizations?

When these questions are addressed strictly within the terms of the stylized contractual myth, they demand a high level of artistic craft, carefully adjusting assumptions about the nature of the Self and the terms of engagement. Legitimate bargains are constructed on the strongly determinative foundations of a normatively compelling but unobservable Self.[1] The forms and language of knowledge become, in effect, ways of elaborating on the primal notion of Contract.

Suppose, for example, that members of a community are trying to agree on a choice of competing public projects. When they attribute prices to the costs or benefits of each, should they accept the terms of a real marketplace, with all its imperfections, or should they insist on what economists describe as "shadow prices" set in a perfect market? The contractual myth as it appears at the core of utilitarianism answers simply: If they do anything but the latter, they are, in effect, contaminating their choices with conditions (such as monopoly or the imposition of costs on innocent victims) to which they should not reasonably agree. Indeed, they should go further, removing all taints of injustice in the distribution of income or of manipulation in the representation of preferences. In effect, they must perfect the society and polity in their minds before they can justify any particular bargain. In one or another formulation of this perfectionist sensibility, we imagine ourselves speaking sincerely, acting objectively, or controlled by the dictates of reason.

The same sensibility appears repeatedly in a more empirical and less formal vein that accepts some but not all of the imperfections of the world. Suppose, instead of perfection, that we assume that in every setting some background arrangements are not amenable to change. All we can do is attempt to tease from the historical record an assessment of the differences between arrangements. Which arrangements enhance freely chosen bargains and which discourage them? What is the best we can do within a particular set of constraints?

These questions and the answers that they elicit are vulnerable to a critique of their assumptions: the acceptance of background institutions, the specification of constraints, and the notion that freedom can be calibrated in little increments. Within the world of those questions and answers, however, the contractual myth is sustained by its elaboration in the language of science and by the dream of social knowledge. When our investigations of unions, families, firms, cultures, and polities all lead us to ask about the conditions of voluntary cooperation and exchange, the stylized myth of Contract is never very far from our minds.

The connection between myth and dream is particularly intense when the attempt to reduce or eliminate the taint of coercion is morally centered in the dream. We may employ the most imaginative thought experiments to remove the taint of coercion from imperfect social relations by an act of surgical analysis. It is unlikely, however, that we will have similar success in a world in which the players are real men and women interacting with one another rather than ethereal parties to an abstract game. Suppose, however, that a consensual knowledge of the world as seen from the myth requires a method and a community of votaries that is uniquely open to experiment and inquiry. The practices of that community of inquirers would then approximate the ideal of the uncoerced agreement. Social practices would be tested against the standards of this community: Do they sustain experimentation and error-correcting inquiry? Do they engender and maintain imperfections in information that generate inefficient instrumental choices and unstable bargains? Do the rules that govern the relations between organizations encourage truth telling or strategic bluffing? Subjected to these tests, over time only liberal contractual societies could sustain the experimental temper. Given free rein, the experimental temper would sustain only liberal contractual societies.[2]

A Fable

It is both easy and reasonable to treat the myths of deep and contractual communities as if they were persons accepting or rejecting certain ideas as fitting complements or as uncongenial threats to their personalities. The myths have a history and a literature in which so many men and women have invested that their efforts and the myths are indistinguishable.

The notion that we argue within a field of overlapping and open communities speaks to a ubiquitous fact and to a common practice. The myth itself lacks a grand tradition, however. I am reluctant, therefore, to impute to the myth a particular attitude toward the dream of knowledge. Instead, I have constructed a fable that allows me to describe how the dream fares when it confronts the plurality of overlapping communities without a fixed collective boundary, a uniquely specified environment, or the mooring provided by the notions of either moral integration or contract.

Suppose (fictionalizing the activities of my colleagues) that a band of planning theoreticians, working within a field of overlapping communities and captivated by the dream of knowledge, seeks to develop a theory of social guidance that would be both complete and general. (I could tell an identical story as a quest for a social theory intended to explain the past rather than to shape the future. By any other name or focus, the lesson of the tale would be the same.)

In principle, the core of such a theory is not particularly difficult to construct. (At least it is no harder than that in any other social field.) The core should include relatively few elements and should not present massive problems of organization, data quality, or information storage and retrieval.

The difficulties appear when the theorists in my fable step outside the core in order to subject it to empirical testing and revision. (My fable is only a pleasant fiction, but theories, after all, are not to be simply judged on their aesthetic appeal or on their internal logic. They must work.) As they step outside the core, the theorists face an enormous array of partially formed generalizations and ideographic accounts of planning practice. Will they be able to the bring their core to bear on this array, first organizing it in a compelling way into statements of the potential relationships between the attributes of each planning process (or combinations of processes), the settings in which they operate, and valued outcomes, and then testing those statements empirically? If we seek justice (defined in one way or another), how should we plan in this or that circumstance? If we plan in a particular way, what sort of justice (or injustice) will result? What about the relationship between process and setting when effectiveness, stability, coherence, efficiency, or beauty is the valued outcome?

Will the theorists succeed in this enterprise? Will they be able to develop and refine a theory that will allow them to inspect any list of assertions about the relationships among processes, settings, and outcomes and then to predict accurately those that will survive both historical and practice tests—that will make sense of the past and guide the future?

Within the terms of the characters and the plot of the myth of an open field, there are, I think, only two credible answers to those queries. If I assign vast resources and heroic discipline to my theorists, they will succeed in their labors, although the intellectual tools they create are likely to be unusable. If I am more limited and more realistic in my assignment of resources or if I am more insistent on practicality, they will fail.

A general theory of planning must generate a set of propositions that relate all the necessary categories of processes, settings, and outcomes. Imagine these propositions arrayed in a table in which the columns are designated as types of planning processes and the rows as settings. Outcome measures appear in the cells. There may be many such tables arrayed in an hierarchical order. The first ("prime") table summarizes the most general empirical propositions that flow from the core of the theory. It includes only those descriptors that cannot be derived from some other attribute.

The canon of descriptors for the prime table cannot be settled through formal literary or linguistic analysis. We can't closely read a set of texts, compare usage and interpretations, and know confidently that terms derive from other terms. Setting the canon and adjusting it requires that we leap into the act of inquiry directly, assess the performance of symbolic indicators, and then circle back to adjust the way we describe processes, settings, and outcomes.

With enormous resources and with discipline far exceeding that found in any real-world epistemic community, my fabled theoreticians could maintain an archive of tables and propositions—a record of research and of debates over contested measures. Noting an anomalous finding, a gap in the information system, or a failure to anticipate the ways in which individuals or communities played against the characters imputed to them by the theorists (Bohman 1992), they could commission studies, lexical revisions, and (most serious) the elaboration of alternative theoretical cores. The catalogue of the archive—far more elaborate than any conventional information system—would update the tables and the core options, signal problematic findings, and lead users to alternative ways of framing issues or interpreting evidence.

This mythical archive is an information scientist's response to Jorge Luis Borges's (1964) nightmare of a library that includes all human knowledge but whose order passes human understanding. For ordinary users, however, the differences would be trivial. When the theoreticians returned to their communities for a short visit (the work of theory building would not allow a protracted absence), the home folk might well wonder what they had wrought. Would any but the builders move easily through the system? Would engagement in the archive sophisticate a reader's sense of the complexity of the world but reduce his or her capacity for decisive action? Finally (and perhaps most decisive), had the analysts forgotten the language, the experiential wisdom, and the purposes of the communities from which they had come?

Suppose—to continue the fable just a little while longer—that the communities rejected the archive and sent the analysts back to work with new and more stringent design criteria: in order to be useful, they insist, the prime table must be brief and neutral.

The criterion of brevity is simple enough to understand. If the core of a theory cannot generate a powerful but relatively short set of general propositions, the theory is likely to be too complex to use and very expensive to maintain. A long prime table would enter again into the world of the capacious but daunting archive.

The neutral criterion may seem less obvious, but it flows directly from the conception of the open field. Suppose a particularly creative scientist proposed an imaginative core theory and a prime table brief enough to be tested and refined within the resources of the group. The brevity would be aesthetically pleasing, but it would be inadequate if the table failed to address four matters that would be critical to the communities:

• It would have to include the various terms in which each of them described processes, settings, or outcomes, or it would have to justify the appropriate location of the terms in secondary tables. To ignore the words of a community would be to devalue its identity and the rules it used to make sense of its moral universe.

• Beyond attending to their lexicons, communities (as I have imagined them in this fable) would be concerned with the balance of the prime table. Suppose, for example, that the theoreticians, sketching with very broad strokes, assigned all planning processes to a single continuum from "market" to "hierarchy."[3] Such a canon for the description of processes would be general but would be vulnerable to fair complaints that it biased the potential products of research by structuring the dimensions of relevant settings and outcomes. Alternative descriptors focusing attention in quite different ways (with different biases) would be necessary to balance the normative implications of the elegant market/hierarchy continuum.

• The theorists would have to ensure that the table was neutral in regard to the contested boundaries of individual communities and those of the field itself. (The open myth, remember, does not describe a jigsaw puzzle.) Within that polymorphic geography, a neutral table would have to address the attributes of individual communities and the field in which they were embedded, since, presumably, the dynamics of planning are influenced by the pattern of overlap, by the costs of movement from one communion to another, and by the ways of resolving disputes between communities and within them.

• Adding to the complexity of that geography, the table would have to be neutral with regard to the contested world of moral objects. Imagine two communities with overlapping but not wholly identical membership. Some members of the first community will treat members of the second community as "strangers" potentially but not certainly meriting respect. Others in the first community, however, will treat members of the second community as fellow citizens—"moral subjects" engaged in a web of obligations, rights, and disciplines. The theorists must find a way of representing these differences if the prime table and the tables that flow from it are to be regarded as neutral.

A table would be complete and neutral when no additional adjustments were necessary to satisfy any community. That is, however, a demanding criterion. Presumably, every community in this fabled world would come to understand itself and the field in new ways through the process of evaluating the work of the theoreticians. Propositions that were satisfying at one stage of the process might seem irrelevant or biased as communities changed their own images of the geography of the field. Communities might even bargain with the theorists to get the best possible deal in the construction of a theory. (Many theorists will be amused by this possibility: would that communities cared so much for our labors! Perhaps, however, the fabled contingency is not so outrageous. In Eastern Europe and in the former Soviet Union, debates over markets engage theorists and politicians in a passionate conversation that is similar to the critique sketched in my account.)

The easiest way to meet the criterion of neutrality would, of course, be to add descriptors to the prime table until the fund of complaints was exhausted. Such a procedure would quickly violate the criterion of brevity, making it impossible for the theorists to avoid the complexity of the clumsy archive. The task would be more manageable if the theorists could throw out ignorant or inappropriate objections. They would be empowered to turn away a complainant who did not understand the canon, could not demonstrate bias, or failed to appreciate the necessity of a hierarchy of descriptors.

Even bolstered by such authority, brevity would not survive. Suppose, for example, that the theorists, acting as a panel of judges, faced a community in which differences in language or dialect were laden with social and cultural meaning—e.g., in which one group spoke the parole of subjects and the other spoke that of colonizers, or one the parole of wealth and the other that of poverty, or one the parole of tradition and the other that of faraway cosmopolitan centers. A complainant might insist that, although terms may appear to outsiders to carry identical meanings, native speakers understand that their connotations are distinct and the moral implications of the differences profound. Could the judges legitimately dismiss this complaint as unfounded? Could they meet the criteria of brevity and neutrality the moment they entered the world of linguistic variety and power? Wouldn't they be forced to turn again into the archival labyrinth, with or without the guiding discipline of a magnificent information system?

Public Orders

End of fable! If we represent the world as a field of overlapping, open communities, and if we seek a moral order within that framework, we cannot construct a consensual body of social theory, whether one directed to the past or one directed to the future. The classic literary form I imposed on the theorists of the fable—a simple core amplified in a complete hierarchical set of empirical propositions—is never realized and rarely attempted. Because the theorizing enterprise within the myth of open moral communities is inevitably so partial and so episodic, it cannot soar above the world it describes and expect to shape it decisively. That is not a terrible failing, and it need not be corrected. No community I know guides collective choices by relying in any direct or simple way on the theories of formal social science. Even overtly straightforward assertions of "fact" enter into policy arguments as value-laden expressions of competing images of the world and of the possibilities of action. Causal propositions, models, and theories—the high talk of serious scholarship and of my fable—form a glow of often ambiguous enlightenment, suffusing debate and practice without dominating them. The enlightenment establishes or (more modestly) confirms the salience of tentative explanations. It rarely, however, penetrates deeply enough into the foundations of belief to stigmatize ideas effectively as outside the domain of justifiable speech or action (Lindblom and Cohen 1979; Lindblom 1990).

I recognize in myself two conflicting responses to the limits of social science. When I am an outsider proffering advice to others, I rue the gap and look forward to the day when it will be eliminated. More wistfully than bitterly, I complain of the "political" influences that restrict the applications of "knowledge." In other moods, however, I embrace the gap and celebrate the wisdom of experience. When I am in those moods, it often seems to me that groups that cultivate abstraction and deal with things in general are insensitive to the requirements of (my) particular circumstances. I treat their advice warily.

These responses speak within alternative communal myths. The progressive dream that anticipates constantly narrowing the gap between theory and practice bolsters aspirations for moral integration within the deep myth; for the elimination of coercion in the contractual myth. The celebration of intractable limits on theory and theorizing, in contrast, embraces the persistent (even if partial) immunity of that variety to external control.

The high talk of scholarship appears within the myth of open moral communities as part of a public symbolic order that sustains the belief that we understand one another, our collective actions, and the world around us. Such orders are dominated by the thick structures of ordinary speech, a repertoire of common metaphors, and a fund of archetypal stories (such as biblical accounts and Greek myths) that both explain behavior and assert the comforting continuity of past and future. This dense mass of conventions is difficult to manipulate directly, but it is not impervious to change.

The thin language of formal social inquiry is in but not quite of this dense order. At one level, if you scratch the overtly severe and tightly specified talk of any of the epistemic communities that dream of knowledge, you discover a layer of metaphoric speech that elicits assent because it is attached to widely shared conceptions of the world whose stability depends at least in part on their ambiguity. We could barely speak if we were forced to explicate each metaphor and to address every variant of meaning in describing "mechanical" and "organic" institutions, the "diffusion" of ideas, the "development" of a labor "force," or the "structure" of an economy (McCloskey 1985). We can and often do manage to argue about collective decisions without ever defining terms or enumerating those who fit into the categories we have created. We explain phenomena, judge the parties, and articulate who we are in relation to them, but we do not specify our meanings and we do not count.

At another level, however, the thin symbolic order of the dreamers has a distinctive quality that separates it from the conventions of ordinary speech and cultural tradition: it is both peculiarly plastic and peculiarly subject to frequent and overt (though hardly uncoerced) negotiations creating public orders that operationalize meanings and measure the world. Under most circumstances, we inherit those orders and treat them casually as if they were as natural as daily speech. If we are arguing about employment in the United States, for example, we are bound by fragile chains into the terms set by the Bureau of Labor Statistics. We may choose to break from those terms (challenging, for example, the bureau's definition of the labor force and its treatment of discouraged workers), but we do so at the risk of falling into the free form of unspecified argumentation.

Public orders appear both within and between communities. In a city, a university, a labor union, or a business firm, for example, accounting procedures provide a way of describing costs and resources, allowing participants in these communities to debate policy options without simultaneously arguing over the framing protocols. The internal accounting order is disciplined by general norms that allow external supervision and support the flow of funds between communities. When the intentions and forms of the two orders conflict, communities often adopt two sets of "books." One serves external requirements; the other captures internal understandings of goals, costs, and resources. In open moral communities, participants must repeatedly struggle to define the relationship between conflicting modes of speech. Should a school be run like a business? Does "productivity" mean the same thing in every setting? If we have agreed in political discussions to designate members of a certain group as "victims" who are immune from blame, are we required to abide by that convention everywhere? Can people be trusted if they fail to observe the public orders of particular settings even at the costs of honesty? What are the limits of mature hypocrisy?

The character of these public orders is set both in explicit negotiations and in tacit agreements struck during intense periods of argument. Beyond their generative moment, orders are constantly disciplined by the threat of exit. If a great many participants in a debate reject a set of concepts and measures in order to express their values and images of the world, the bridge of convention is weakened even if it does not fall. The number of "books" is multiplied, and sincere assent is replaced by ritualistic obeisance. People routinely speak ironically, signaling that words are not what they seem (Mandelbaum 1998). If they are alert and caring, bridge keepers respond to the decay of terms and the disaffection from measures with new organizing forms: the Bureau of Labor Statistics creates a new category of discouraged workers, the Census Bureau revises the definition of metropolitan areas, health officials broaden their notions of illness to include chronic as well as acute conditions.

In every open field, public orders are also disciplined and justified by tests of efficacy. You may note with relief that an agreement to bound an issue in a particular way breaks a "log jam." "This may not make sense to you," you explain to a skeptic, "but it 'works' for me." Don't scratch at that agreement, we warn critical interlopers. It may not be perfect, but it keeps us together.

It is tempting to think of these allusions to efficacy in evolutionary terms. With or without the apparatus of formal scientific experimentation, don't they signal an adaptive process in which our symbolic agreements change over time to fit the requirements of the "reality" of an external environment? The evolutionary prospect, however, is certainly elusive and may be illusory. There is no vantage point outside a symbolic order from which we can view that reality or act on it. We are bound to organize our understanding within an interpretive framework. Paradoxically, a rigorous scientific critique of our rough-and-ready evolutionary experiments only emphasizes how bound we are into our own premises, how likely we are to move back and forth between options that no process of argument can resolve, and how fragmentary are our conclusions about the discrete impacts of our collective decisions. Even the great formal policy experiments in the United States dealing with school and housing vouchers, preschool education, and a negative income tax were so deeply flawed or so partial that they could not—standing alone—sustain a new order reframing policy discussions. Only sustained and cumulative assaults on an established lexicon and an established conceptual array revise the terms with which we imagine and debate our collective options.

Procedural theories of social guidance—the subject of my extended fable—enter directly into the public orders. In various settings, we debate whether we should think of a problem within the framework of market adjustments or within that of public regulation and development. We agree to designate some arrangements as "centralized" or "decentralized" and then proceed to argue over alternative designs. We assume that we can measure "power" and operationalize "accountability" so that we need not stumble over fundamental meanings as we rank and blame. We put aside our philosophic quarrels over the meaning of justice and insist that we all want public actions to be "equitable," as if it were impossible to imagine or to speak otherwise.

Active practitioners in the guidance professions—planners, managers, policy analysts, and the like—are often ambivalent toward this subtle penetration of the language of theory into everyday practice. On the one side, they are engaged by their obligations to particular communities and with the ways in which those communities define and deal with problems. The professionals share with their communal colleagues an understandable skepticism about anyone who asserts that "local" practices can be understood—let alone corrected—by outsiders who arrogate authority to themselves in the name of theory. On the other side of the ambivalence, the professionals themselves assume that their claims to respect rest on the foundations of theory. Without theory, they are bound into local orders and cannot move from one community to another in order to plan, manage, or analyze; without theory, they are not a community. If theory fails them—if the library is too complex for ordinary use, if theorists speak incomprehensibly or appear to be involved only in themselves—then the practitioners feel neglected and threatened. They seek a reorientation of theorizing toward practice and a restoration of the faith that ultimately all differences can be reconciled through rational argument and scientific inquiry.

The myth of open moral communities suggests a quite different role for formal procedural theory and theorizing. In the face of contested words, deliberate ambiguity, and resistance to control, the limits of theory and theorizing are severe and their internal complexities profound. The set of tables imagined in the fable defy the best ordering temperaments. Indeed, imaginative synoptic efforts always seem to suggest possibilities that lie just outside their scope. Theorizing communities must be self-concerned if they are to mobilize and discipline the effort required to construct even portions of the tables. The communities' influence on practice is mediated through necessarily imperfect public orders and principles.

Communities of theorists, and the enterprise of thinking about things in general, operate within the field of moral communities as temporary settings for escape from conventional practices and as a resource in times of particular confusion. If ordinary terms such as "justice," "community," and "efficiency" have become so hollow that they interfere with conversation, formal theorizing provides a way of clearing the terrain and establishing a new set of meanings. If GOSPLAN collapses, theorizing provides a newly charged image of the Market as a substitute. If narrow contingency tables ("in case of this, do that") are framed oppressively, theorizing suggests alternative frames.

The image of theorizing communities as temporary and necessarily flawed settings for escape is not as grand as the vision of the scientific method as the cornerstone of a liberal society. It cannot match the soaring conception of Marxism as a theory of deep moral integration. The ironic rhetoric of public orders that are not quite what they seem is not as heroic as the perfected contract freed of coercion. It does, however, accommodate the dream of social knowledge to an intractable social pluralism.

6
Stories

Stories and Theories

As literary form and intellectual aspiration, theory has a very special place in the pantheon of knowledge. Theories shape our inquiries, marking domains of relevance, signaling when we have made a mistake, and occasionally rewarding us with the wonderful feeling that the elegant artifices of our mind work. Theories explain and anticipate events, and they allow us to shape the world and to understand the limits of our capacity. Could the pursuit of theory, I wondered, succeed in realizing the dream of a consensual social knowledge?

My answer was, simply, "No." Social theorizing cannot transcend the myths in which it is grounded, nor can theorists respond to just claims for attention without violating the sensible criteria of neutrality and brevity. This does not mean that theorizing is a wasteful enterprise; it means only that the products of theorizing are inevitably partial, fragmentary, and contested.

So it is with storytelling. Faced with collective choices or ethical difficulties, we usually struggle to make sense in the familiar ways: we distinguish "characters" and impute a range of human attributes to them; the stage is set; the plot begins and proceeds to a conclusion that fits the world that the story has created. Our uncertainties are framed by the narrative form, and our attention is commanded to them. We understand what has to be done to complete or correct a story when we realize that we don't know what motivates an important character, or that we are unsure about the beginning of the tale, uncertain where we are now, or unable to anticipate the ending confidently.

A global narrative that integrates all local and particular stories into a single drama is the counterpart of what I have described as a complete, general theory. All the arguments that were addressed to that synthetic theoretical aspiration are readily modified so that they apply to the narrative form. The stories told to establish the moral integration of a community or to justify its contractual bases are compelling only within the terms of the shaping myths that require them; a field of open communities can no more be pressed into the mold of a single narrative than it can be represented by the elegant prime table set by the most imaginative theorist.

Fair enough! There is, however, something very special about storytelling that cannot be understood by simply extending the critical analysis of the limits of theorizing (Chatman 1978; Kaplan 1986; Mitchell 1981; Phelan 1989; Ricoeur 1984).

The ordinary professional forms used to represent policy and planning arguments specify and measure competing interests, preferences, needs, wants, and values (Barry 1965). These familiar constructs (and others like them) allow us to decompose complex social statements into elements that can be calibrated and mapped. Conflict appears as a formal game or as a set of indifference curves sweeping across a multi-dimensional graph; arguments appear as a sequence of claims, warrants, and rebuttals (Stokey and Zeckhauser 1978; Dunn 1981).

These modes of representation characteristically ignore the narrative form within which most political arguments are couched, treating stories as only the raw materials from which arguments must be abstracted. There is, however, a very substantial content to the narrative form into which we craft the world as we contest with one another or seek moral guidance (White 1987). "Let me recount the history of the Exodus from Egypt," I tell my children and grandchildren, "so that you will never forget that once you were slaves and now you are free." "Let me tell you of my life, so that you will believe in the continuity of the Self and its accountability."

In the same way, in the offices of the World Bank, the Pentagon, neighborhood associations, manufacturing firms, and family therapists, guidance rests on the construction of images that describe the pattern of a desired world, who "we" are, and the ways we may move from here to there. In effect, we try to control potential events by telling stories about the future just as tell stories about the past. Developmental scenarios that are too rich to be tested as theories map chains of contingent decisions, the play of supportive and hostile responses, and the meaning and implications of success and failure (Hirschhorn 1980; Mandelbaum 1985; Roe 1994). The narrative form allows us to represent individuals and communities as agents capable of choosing among alternatives and of sustaining a moral order. Our conceptions of purposeful action require that chains of events have a beginning and an end, that events be connected in a way that fits the world as we imagine it, that we can tell what is important from what is not, and that we have an identity that allows us to distinguish between action in character and action out of character. We shape our lives by emplotting them retrospectively and in anticipation of events.

There is an awful power in these narratives when they are so complete that they appear to be beyond our control: what was must have been; what must be will be. These hyper-stories (often of intractable conflicts or invincible powers) close in on us, binding us to a fixed role within a script we cannot change (Cohen 1986). Theorizing and abstraction provide relief from these fully scripted scenarios. Skepticism about post hoc explanations and the exploration of counterfactual possibilities insinuate themselves into conversations otherwise controlled by stories that appear to mirror reality, helping us believe in the feasibility of alternative pasts and futures.

Relaxing the grip of verisimilitude by maintaining the tension between theory and narrative cannot, however, replace the pervasive process of imposing a narrative structure upon experience and expectation. We are bound into those structures even when we adopt the formal language of game theory or mathematical simulation: the "prisoners" faced with the classic dilemmas of trust learn to play tit-for-tat; the travelers shift cannily (but within inevitably frustrating limits) from one congested transit link to another, attempting to avoid the path that everyone should rationally choose.

Stories in Communities

I once thought that storytelling was a primitive form for containing social knowledge. In practice, of course, I observed (then as now) that people used theories as preliminary tools in the construction of narratives. The crafted stories were employed to guide action: establishing the existence of entities and the claims of membership, teasing out latitudes and disciplines, simplifying the acts of choice. I, however, knew better. Such practices were expedient but merely temporary. In a literal sense, they were unprincipled. Tomorrow, or the day after, the community of scholars would organize its collective knowledge of the world into theories capable of guiding the creation of the future. As "natural history" had preceded "theoretical" biology, so narrative history preceded a mature social science.

I long ago abandoned both that simplistic account of the dynamics of scientific development and my account of the forms of wisdom that await us at the end of the (alas, endless) rainbow. The distinction between ideographic and nomothetic discursive modes now often seems very muddy to me. Even when the line is clearly drawn, the modes appear as adversaries neither of which can survive or prosper in the absence of the other. My blood no longer quickens to the slogans of the war in which the proponents of one seek to drive out the other—theory displacing narrative or vice versa.

So much for the old war gone stale! I continue, however, to be intrigued by the repeated reminders that stories are not only salient but dangerous: multiple stories are more threatening to communities than multiple theories and harder to sustain.

Within the fable in the previous chapter, communities are constantly alert to the implications of the terms in which theories are cast. Fables are designed, of course, to allow for such exquisite sensibilities. In practice, attention is intermittent and selective. Communities are often indifferent to the proliferation of either theoretical cores or the propositions in a prime table; impervious to theoretical diversity. My family is barely touched by disputes among theoreticians of group dynamics. Tacit theoretical differences hidden in responses to events and in moral choices usually remain comfortably out of view. They are buried deeply enough to allow us to sustain agreements "in practice" despite our disagreements "in principle" and (unfortunately) despite our tendency to argue endlessly about particulars despite our "underlying" agreements *on* or *in* theory. Indeed, they are buried deeply enough to allow us (unfortunately) to suffer endless conflicts without appreciating their theoretical "foundations" and (fortunately) to settle matters practically despite our theoretical differences.

In contrast, competitive and irreconcilable accounts of the same putative event often damage social relations beyond repair. Members of complex communities may accommodate to rival theories and even relish them as a sign of intellectual vitality. Variety often is cast as a resource, sustaining an array of adaptive responses to environmental shifts. In contrast, alternative histories that challenge the boundaries of the group and its capacity for moral choice and instrumental effectiveness often seem to threaten the identity of individuals and the meaning of membership. A shared understanding of our "origins" and of how we have managed to survive to this point seems terribly important in establishing the existence of the communion and its moral claims.

Appreciating the ways in which we are threatened by competing stories requires treating narrative as if it were an unfamiliar and exotic form of speech rather than a tacit but universally understood convention. In that "unfamiliar" posture, consider the remarkable powers of the narrator. Whether as the explicit author, as a character in the tale, or as a spectral intelligence, the narrator is able to ordain when the story begins and when it ends, establishing at the outset how events are publicly concluded. The narrator fixes the identity of the relevant actors, affirms the competence of listeners by connecting events so that they make sense, and distinguishes between central and peripheral elements within the frame of the tale. With only bare suggestions, the skilled narrator allows the listener or reader to create a sense that reality has been captured whole rather than craftily constructed.

The disposition to encode experience in narratives does not, however, explain why we come to believe some stories and trust their narrators but respond to others only with suspicion and skepticism. Belief and trust appear to be intertwined. Believable stories engender trust in the narrator; trusted narrators endow the stories they tell with credibility.

Both belief and trust are shaped over time. Stories gain in credibility as they are retold and as they are assimilated into our actions and beliefs— as we live within their frames, invest in the sense and sensibilities of their plots, and accept the identification of actors. In this way, stories of a specific time and place are universalized as parables, archetypes, exemplars, and myths (Burt 1984; Walzer 1985). In these forms, they are capable of incorporating contradictory evidence without collapsing. We may forgive the temporary failures of trusted narrators without destroying our esteem for them.

However, when stories or narrators are new, or when we have not invested in them, trust is superficial and is vulnerable to tests of evidence and of coherence and to unforgiving measures of performance. We "trust" political candidates, news commentators, experts, and television evangelists, but most of us can shift easily from listening to one to listening to another without altering our fundamental conceptions of the world or of ourselves. We subject some stories to intense scrutiny but treat others as if they were immune to criticism. We recognize the devaluation of our investments in the imperious claim that all narrators must be treated equally: all trusted or all taken "with a large grain of salt."

When we argue within myths of community, we necessarily imply a collective capacity to create and sustain stories and narrators. Each of the three stylized myths I have described is associated with a distinctive narrative form. The contractual myth is principally maintained by tales of the making of promises and the ways they are fulfilled and broken; the myth of deep moral integration by accounts of the virtues in practice and the perils of dissolution, the open myth by struggles with moral dilemmas and the tugs of competing communions and loyalties.

All these accounts depend on narrators who simultaneously create communities and are created by them. In some settings, the narrator occupies an honored role and speaks within long-standing traditions that establish conventions for describing and recording the experiences of the group. In other settings, there are no institutional roles for narration, so the stories that unite people are composed from fragmentary personal or communal memories. In the latter case, there are no written texts and there is no continuity. A teenage gang, a neighborhood association, or a governmental agency with fluid participation and high turnover may, for example, have very little ability to recall anything but its most recent behavior or to emplot a future that differs substantially from its immediate past. Intercommunal fields often have no shared collective memory and no one who speaks for the pattern of relations between its elements. Segmented and polarized, the overlapping communities of Muslims and Christians in Bosnia lose their voices.

Sympathetic outsiders may attempt to extend the capacity of a community by writing its history or by projecting a new future: teaching the members of a union about the trials and achievements of the labor movement so as to connect personal experiences with a larger tradition, helping parents or neighbors to construct a developmental perspective that allows them to break out of the prison of their immediate memories and their stylized conceptions of the past and future, encouraging illiterate peasants or sophisticated engineering departments to place their current behaviors in an historical context. Until these narratives and the processes that generate them are internalized, however, they compete at a disadvantage with authentic albeit limited memories and projections. They remain, histories *of* but not *in* the community.

Communities of substantial size create and survive a great many personal and private stories without threatening the integrity of their collective narratives. Both highly stylized and informal processes of dispute resolution discipline these conflicts, however, so that the competing stories are cast in a socially manageable form. Whatever their initial phrasing, the rules of law impress upon legal tales a style and a substance that affirm the forms of collective narration, specifying the identity and responsibilities of actors, the sensible connection between events, and the beginning and end of chains of accountability. In some communities, for example, the behavior of previous generations is relevant to the adjudication of a current dispute: "You are a horse thief and a child of horse thieves." In other communities, past crimes cannot be mentioned in court. Everywhere, however, the idea of a morally sanctioned beginning structures the telling of stories.

Communities are threatened when conflicting stories can neither be forced into a disciplining mold nor synthesized without coercion or a serious loss of meaning. If you are trying to build a nation, your stories should focus on individuals as citizens and on the salience and integrity of the national space and its public orders. Time should be divided so as to focus attention on the central dramas of nation building. Precursors of nationhood should dominate the account of the pre-national past. Such stories— the stuff of nationalism—threaten the narratives of families, clans, ethnic groups, villages, or regions that speak of their own times, spaces, beginnings, identities, orders, and sensibilities. Those diverse stories, in their turn, threaten the overarching claims of the national account (Higham 1994).

In a common forum, these threats may be explicit and charged with emotion—the stuff of great constitutional debates, civil wars, and partitions. Threats may, however, be no less challenging if one group simply ignores the other: if you tell the history of the nation without discussing my religion, if my people are invisible until they are "discovered" by the imperial power, if my fellow women are seen only through the eyes of men.

Conflicting or neglectful stories are more threatening to a group than comparably divergent theories because the narrative form sustains a sense of communal sharing. When I tell my children a story about "our" family, the truth of the matter lies in our relationship and in the telling. A deceitful story is as meaningful an account of our relations as one that is sincere or honest.

In contrast, the authority of a theorizing account of the psychodynamics of families rests in an epistemic community and in its protocols for assessing the forms of speech and for radically excluding propositions that fail to survive the appropriate tests. The hidden authors are discouraged from making any authoritative claim based on personal trust and from evoking symbols of affiliation that would enable the reader or listener to identify with them. As a theorist, I never may say "Trust me; I was there and I understand you." As a narrator, that is the core of my claim even when I "observe" remote periods and places. When I am simultaneously a narrator and a theorist, I necessarily (though not easily) shift between creating affiliative claims and distancing myself from them. As therapist or a planner, I join my client in a narrative circle and then (jarringly) step outside it to protect my membership in another community, from which the client is characteristically excluded.

The presentation of reality also differs in narratives and theories. Theories describe actors as sets of attributes, always suggesting the possibility of alternative ways of specifying dimensions and of bundling them— of a variety of contemporaneous worlds, each with its own deep order.

Even with very sparse descriptive details, however, stories allow listeners and readers to invest them with a sense of reality seen whole, of things understood as they "really" are. Consider, as a thought experiment, a theory of human adaptation to stress that seeks to explain the relationship between levels of anxiety and the consumption of tranquilizing drugs. Compare with this "theory talk" any of the countless jokes that begin "This drunk moseyed up to the bar. . . . " No matter how richly conceived, the theorizing discourse neither achieves nor seeks the verisimilitude of "this drunk." The narrator says very little about the person and the setting but does not press the listener or reader to exclude any elements. (In contrast, either the excluded elements are irrelevant when we are talking theory or they indicate flaws in our construction of the world.) You have missed the point of the joke (at least any of those I have in mind) if you respond to the punch line with a question about the color of the walls in the bar. Your obtuseness is not, however, a threat to the narrator. You are free to see the bar any way you like—to embellish the story so that it is complete. Narratives evoke a sense that reality has been seen rather than constructed. This perception of authenticity interacts with the trust invested in narrators. When we decide to trust a narrator—whether the tale is of the past or of the future—we describe ourselves as realists and caution others to be "realistic." Trusted narratives close the past and confirm our competence as interpreters. A community that believes its own stories and trusts the individuals who tell them affirms its identity and the obligations of membership. Tales of the future may not be similarly closed, but the contingent possibilities are constrained if we keep the actors in character and retain the established frame. In the absence of any facts, being "realistic" about the future means accepting limited alternatives with the materials at hand: given the prejudices of rival groups, international conflict, materialism, or religious faith, only a few scripts are possible "realistically."

Multiple Stories

As of now, the stool on which I want to rest my argument has only two legs. Competing stories provide an opportunity for the members of communities to practice their shared communion: to ratify the authority of judges and guardians, to pray together for reconciliation and redemption, or to immerse themselves in rituals of affirmation. However, when the stories cannot be reconciled they are more threatening to a community than the clash of inevitably abstract theories. The third leg of the stool deals with the task of living with that threat. That task is salient in every large and complex community. Contractual or deep communities whose members believe that they must search out and extirpate every secret disagreement that violates the social contract or the integrative moral order consume themselves internally and freeze their responses to the external world. They survive only with the (episodic) emergence of reform programs of inattention or tolerance.

Narrative pluralism is an even more important matter for communities whose members represent themselves as participants in a field of overlapping communities. If we are simultaneously members of a family, a firm, a polity, a neighborhood, a labor union, a profession, and a church, whose stories are contingently in conflict, we must be able to sustain those differences without destroying the capacity for effective action. Since we act and relate to one another within the stories we tell, diversity would, as its critics attest, be terribly destructive if it wholly stripped us of our principal discursive guide.

How do open moral communities manage to balance diversity and competence? What difficulties do they confront? What are the standards of success? What are the marks of failure?

I presented an early version of this chapter at a conference at the Harvard Business School. In that unfamiliar setting, I personalized my answer to those questions by asking readers to put themselves in the shoes of a hypothetical Chief Executive Officer confronted with the appearance of diverse and competing stories within the executive suite of her firm. In this current version I have brought the CEO home, recasting her as the director of a planning agency in a large U.S. city. I am concerned, however, that something may be lost in the revision. We commonly expect that the leaders of business firms—particularly those large enough to have CEOs rather than mere "presidents"—will act decisively to resolve conflict in order to mobilize and sustain a hierarchical organization. There may have been something fresh (or at least unexpected) in an image of a firm as part of an open field of moral communities and in my rejection of the notion that successful "businesslike" companies are marked by organizational and discursive clarity and convergence.

We don't, however, make the same stereotyped assumption about public planning executives. We assume in the United States that their authority is limited and that they are bound to be more concerned with the maintenance and management than with the resolution of conflicting accounts of political struggles and public options. Planning executives (and those who write about them) may, quite reasonably, be underwhelmed to discover that they are eclectic pluralists. (They may be even less impressed to discover that they have "post-modernist" leanings.)

I hope that, despite the shift in venue, this account of five strategies for dealing with narrative conflict is not wholly unsurprising, and that I will not be damned by a comparison with Molière's prose-speaking gentleman. The incentives to represent the world with one compelling story are very powerful even in public planning agencies: if one way of acting is "better" than another, there must surely be a "best" way, and partial accounts of what "really" happened must surely give way to the "truth." My account of the five strategies may help all of us to defend ourselves against the sweet reasonality of this convergence.

Four Strategies of Convergence

I describe the first four strategies in order to establish the case for a fifth strategy as peculiarly appropriate to open moral communities. I don't, however, want to exaggerate the independence of the responses to narrative conflict. They usually are coupled as individuals seeking to control the talk and action of their communities play against one another.

The first response seeks agreement by suspending the explicitly interpretive and often passionate language of contesting accounts. Emotionally charged stories are devolved into lists of "facts" arrayed chronologically and described in a plain style. The meanings of the overtly neutral chronicle are argued fact by fact as if each item could be assessed independently without forcing agreement on the whole. The devolution of narratives into chronicles is the rhetorical strategy of mediators and managers attempting to negotiate a public order. (I will describe its uses and limitations in some detail in chapter 11 as part of my discussion of the MOVE encounter in Philadelphia.)

This strategy is simultaneously congenial and deceptive. Tired of passion and interpretation, we often welcome the reversion to "facts" as a way of both avoiding and transcending conflict. The plain style does not, however, create a distortion-free mirror of nature: like complex narratives, overtly simple chronicles are interpretations. Meanings reside in intentions, memories, and interactions that connect discrete events. Invested in the regime of fact, we may suppress alternative interpretations and meanings (ruling them literally and metaphorically out of court), but they periodically crack through the order we have created to control them.

The devolution of narratives into chronicles and the construction of a regime of fact is closely tied to a strategy that insists that, since there was only one historical reality, all disputes about the past are ultimately resolvable. No matter how deep the initial differences, rival stories (like competing hypotheses in the natural sciences) will ultimately be reconciled. In the long run, they will bend to the norms and dynamics of a community of disinterested or at least peculiarly public inquirers. Faced with conflict, we dream of a consensual resolution in which research and expertise will turn many into one. More commonly, we insist that only adversarial judicial processes can create authoritative histories. Until the Law has spoken, ascribing responsibility and either absolving parties or punishing them, cases are open and stories unresolved. (I will illustrate these uses in chapter 11.)

A third strategy seeks to resolve conflicting stories by synthesizing them. Neither research nor courts will choose between story A and story B. Patient inquiry will, however, provide some story C that will makes sense of the parochial differences in accounts and perspectives. A synthetic narrative enables a superordinate community to act as a dominant strategist. It may also, however, focus attention on a superordinate object though there is no competent strategist who commands it. Through this synthetic device, narrators have tried to reconcile conflicts among industrial workers by holding up for their approval the history of working people everywhere, and to reconcile conflicts among "narrow" interests by conjuring the development of the metropolis, the Judeo-Christian tradition, society, the ecosystem, or the world. No one, of course, is entitled to speak and act for the international working class or for all the adherents of the Judeo-Christian tradition. Without a commanding or legitimate strategist, these stories cast the narrator as a trustee for the latent community and the values imputed to it. Inevitably, this is a difficult role that is subject to abuse. It threatens communities by suggesting that in the "big picture" obligations to strangers must overwhelm the claims of members.

Faced with conflicting stories, the members of communities often insist that their communion is embedded in who they are and how they relate to one another *now* and in their intentions for the future. The past, the stories told about it, and the attempts to set them right do not matter. If you act appropriately as a Muslim, a family member, or a citizen, your knowledge of the past or your attitudes toward it are irrelevant.

This fourth—presentist—strategy may seem trivial or pernicious; it may appear to be not an argument within communal myths but one against them. It is, however, worth taking seriously, both because it is ubiquitous (as every critic of historical ignorance and cultural amnesia remarks) and because it has a moral content. Life is full of disputes, and we would be mad if we did not walk away from some, leaving others to fight *their* battles. Surely struggles over the past are sensible candidates for avoidance. Both psychotherapists and management consultants frequently encourage their clients to "let go" so that they are not dominated by the fantasy of resolving every conflicting story.

In some settings, however, urging others to disengage from contending tales is a way of disabling them. If they follow the advice, they are bound to the practical implications of living in one uniquely appropriate story. They are told, in effect, to abandon control of their memories to others. The paradoxical association of historical inquiry with political radicalism rather than conservatism stems from the repeated struggle against this advice. Radical aspirations for the future are imperiled when the past is represented as the unfolding of a single, seamless story into which today's choices must fit. Only in a history of varied possibilities, blocked options, manipulated cultures, and suppressed traditions can we free ourselves from the notion that there is one uniquely appropriate way to match our public choices and our character.

In other settings, disengagement has a quite different impact. Individuals are enabled by walking away from the contentious past, and it is the trustees of the community who are disarmed. If I deny the moral authority of stories, I free myself to shape the community as I choose. As long as I am a member, my actions define public norms. Citizenship means nothing more than the behavior of citizens, Christianity nothing more than the choices of Christians. The moral guardians of the community cannot sustain their authority by disciplining errant members. They may not even be able to expel deviants if membership is based on self-announced affiliation. If all that matters is practice and intention, the guardians cannot even effectively insist that they command a unique knowledge that entitles them to prescribe right action. Like Mr. Thompson, a victim of Korsakov's Syndrome described by Sacks (1987), the community may compensate for its loss of memory by inventing and reinventing its past. There is, however, very little stability, depth, or guidance in such ephemeral tales. There is no moral difference between the claims of the historic preservationists and the preferences of the proponents of modernist reconstruction.

The Fifth Strategy

The final argumentative strategy embraces controversy rather than seeking either to resolve or to ignore it. Again, as with disengagement, it is tempting to dismiss the acceptance of contesting stories as a strategy against myths of community rather than within them—a strategy denying the possibility of communion based on a common story and trusted narrators. Worse, it may appear to be not a strategy at all but merely the frustrating result of a badly argued case. When desperately fatigued parties to a debate "agree to disagree" before they collapse, it is difficult to credit their rhetorical concession with any virtue other than sheer survival. A judicial system we can trust does not boast of its record of repeatedly hung juries.

Neither of these dismissive complaints is compelling. The pluralistic strategy redefines the bases of communal identity but does not deny them. Although it may arise from a fatigued appreciation that some disputes cannot be resolved, it sets a strenuous program for integrating that sensibility into a communion.

The central and most difficult premise of this strategy is that stories are shaped in the interaction of narrators and interpreters. The dynamics of this interaction are usually described by beginning with a storyteller whose purposes and criteria inform the text. Once public, the tale is reshaped by interpreters and their communities. No text can entirely dominate the interpreters, forcing them to see it in one and only one way.

Some tales are, however, more powerful than others. Strong texts resist interpretation; weak ones belong to Everyman. The order of describing the interaction between narrators and interpreters may, however, be reversed, and the analysis of power and initiative may be shifted. "Purposes" fall away, a mysterious phantom of mind when all we really see are texts. They are replaced in this alternative telling by the norms of discourse and the adaptive processes we observe directly.

Start with a community of interpreters who shape the conditions under which stories are told, the forums in which they are heard, and the attention they receive (Fish 1980). Narrators respond to these opportunities and clues. Some are more acute in their perceptions or more skilled in their response, and they succeed. Very few narrators in any stable system of meanings are able, however, to alter the constructive choices of the inter-preters. If narrators could always force us to see the world in a new way, who would we be?

Stories may be faulted because the purposes or the discursive norms that guide their initial telling or their interpretation are trivial, incoherent, or self-destructive; they may be flawed because they do not serve our purpos-es or because they violate communal norms. The norm of "truthfulness" is important in virtually all communities, though it is not always specified in the same terms. Quite different stories about the same set of events or the same phenomena may, however, satisfy this norm. Many competing accounts of "Philadelphia" are equally true and variously useful for par-ticular purposes and for different narrators and interpreters. There need be no superordinate definition that reconciles the differences and no synthet-ic history of the city. The rival Philadelphia stories may be reconciled, of course, by indicating clearly that their subjects are different. You might, for example, construct histories of Philadelphia$_1$, Philadelphia$_2$, Philadelphia$_3$, and so on, noting each as pointing to a different entity. Differentiation is certainly useful in exposing specious disagreement or ill-founded consensus. It does not serve, however, when parties want to control a symbolic refer-ent—when they all claim the right to speak about Philadelphia (or "their" country, firm, plan, freedom, club, strategy, class, or community). Under those conditions, the terms of debate and the construction of stories are essentially contested and cannot be reconciled (Connolly 1987).

In every speech community, there are fewer distinct words than there are potential meanings. We each invest ourselves in words we cannot control, generating a trail of contested meanings in every encounter. Most of these contests, however, are easily dismissed or accommodated. Indeed, if we all owned our own words we could barely communicate. (So much for preci-sion!) The words that articulate the conflicting claims of moral communi-ties are not, however, likely to be either ignored or resolved. Because they constantly command our attention, it often appears that we are united by our symbolic battles rather than our agreements; by the stories we contest rather than those we share. These communities of ritualized conflict are denigrated or weakened only when speakers refuse to be drawn into battle. They are bound to one another as adversaries so long as they as they continue to argue over the meanings and the uses of the contentious symbols.

This rhetorical strategy sustains a symmetrical view of the narratives we construct about the past and about the future. When the frame of a history or its central terms are treated as real, albeit uncertainly known, the past often seems closed, its elements and dynamics frozen as if the plot we impose on people and events expressed an unfolding destiny. What was had to be. However, when we self-consciously construct the past and assume that our artifacts are both purposeful and contentious, we imaginatively free ourselves to see the actors in a world of possibilities just as we usually see ourselves in the futures we construct. Every frame and every lexicon of contested terms suggests an alternative narrative, every purpose a different story. If I write a history of "industrial society," for example, and describe the reaction of the "masses" to the new discipline, I provoke these critical queries: Who thinks of the world in those terms? Why, and with what implications? What happens to the history if I do not imagine the society as "industrial" or people as a "mass"?

The ability to realize and sustain these alternatives varies, of course, from one setting to another. If contending actors within an open community cannot all generalize their personal experiences into a collective narrative, the competition of meanings is uneven, one set being phrased with all the authority of prestigious figures and symbols and the others, clumsily, as cries of the heart or as nagging local complaints. If their stories are all told by professional narrators, members may be subtly cast as passive wards watching self-appointed trustees battle for them. Worse, they may find themselves largely ignored in conversations conducted in strange arenas and difficult tongues.

In the classic defense of a liberal society, John Stuart Mill argued in 1859 that open institutions (first among them free speech) protected us against error. *On Liberty* (Mill 1989) is framed within the terms of what I have described as the second rhetorical strategy. Competition within the marketplace of ideas would, Mill argued, inhibit our common tendency to worship our own values and conceptions of the world and to impose them on others. When we censor ideas, he insisted, we always risk suppressing truth or preventing its full realization in the response to challenge. Mill was particularly concerned lest informal social pressure and the demands of mobilized publics interfere with the freedom of intellectual elites. Society, he thought, depended on those elites to break the grip of those entrenched institutions and ideas (which he called "Chinese stationariness"). Only in a regime of freedom could knowledge and truth work their progressive way.

The fifth rhetorical strategy goes beyond the relatively simple and optimistic terms of *On Liberty*. It seeks to maintain conflict rather than merely to prevent censorship. That is not, however, a easy task. The uses of narrative diversity characteristically seem more compelling in the abstract than in practice.

Suppose you are the chief planner of a large city in the United States. Like any community, the agency you head engenders obligations and creates rightful entitlements among its members. Its communication channels are filled with talk about the virtues and right practice. As director, you depend heavily on the freely given loyalty of your staff, a gift that cannot be replaced by mere conformity or obedience. You may require that employees reside in the city or prohibit them from some forms of partisan political activity. For the most part, however, you are bound to accept that the employees (or members) of the agency participate in an array of communities. All those communions compete for the attention and energies of "your" staffers; some (such as the city polity, professional associations, and subunits of the agency) are directly concerned with your work program in a way that may sometimes complement and sometimes counter your program.

The story is even more complex. You yourself are engaged in the same complex network of affiliations, and you often recognize that you are of many minds on important issues. The boundary of the community you are supposed to lead is both open and contested. Other government officials, neighborhood associations, real estate developers, civic activists, bankers, and corporate leaders assume that they are members of your community, since you depend on them for resources, must attend to their views, and allow them to speak freely with your staff.

Not unexpectedly, you note (perhaps with apprehension) that even the members of your senior staff argue within competing stories of the city, of its external environments, and of the agency. The varied stories make sense of diverse experiences and of the complex and overlapping character of the field. If you follow the fifth strategy and don't try to exclude or suppress any of the stories, you preserve a rich repertoire of response that will be useful as the community and its environments change. At the same time, however, you are persuaded that the agency must make up its "mind" so that it can act decisively within a coherent conception of its past and its future. Without a compelling story, your program will be badly compromised if not thwarted as it works its way through the larger polity. You cannot act forcefully while maintaining a neutral posture in a field of contesting narratives. Your economic development program cannot, for example, be simultaneously premised on the notion that the city's loss of manufacturing jobs over the last two decades was an unavoidable result of massive changes in the global economy and (in the same breath) that it might have been avoided by better local policies—that the drama of future scenarios is driven by the search for a narrow path across a minefield of severely limiting and dangerous constraints or, alternatively, by the exciting challenge of unfreezing institutions and choosing among an abundance of new opportunities.

What are you to do? How might you mount vigorous action while maintaining narrative diversity?

I distinguish three stylized ways of balancing the two objectives:

• You might suppress all but one story (usually this is done by firing the "dissidents") but maintain an open channel between the agency and external critics. The outsiders—including the fired staff members—would preserve the repertoire of stories and policies, protecting the agency from worshipping its own temporary choices. This realization of the fifth strategy depends on the capacities of the outsiders and on your ability to continue to listen to them. The strategy fails if you cease listening, if the outsiders won't or can't speak, or if they are voluble but increasingly uninformed.

• The second stylized option complements the first. You might choose one set of consistent stories (excluding all or most of their advocates) but take great pains to record the climactic debates and the significance of the options. This preservationist strategy would be realized in a formal history and an information system that allowed the members of the agency periodically to retrieve and reassess paths not taken. Public memories would allow dissenters to revisit the past and to use it to break the frame of the present.

• You might try to preserve the alternatives as lively options within the agency while choosing among them. The staff would have to distinguish two domains. In the first, members of the staff—whatever their private opinions—would publicly support the position you had chosen. In the free space of the second domain, they would be free to articulate their dissenting opinions. As director of the agency, you would have to defend the first domain against charges that it was vapid and encouraged hypocrisy; you would have to defend the second against tests of loyalty to your own decisions. In your own soul, you would have to accept the notion that many members of the community felt fully honest, whole, and passionate only when engaged in the second domain. If you wanted those qualities in the first domain, you would have to either abandon the preservationist strategy or choose another (simplifying) way of realizing it.

These three stylized options are prototypes of the ways the fifth strategy is implemented in many communities, and they illuminate the difficulties that strategists encounter. Members of families, neighborhoods, cities, professions, churches and nations often face choices between organizational redesign and discursive accommodation. They struggle with the maintenance of significant but permeable boundaries, the construction of histories of the past and the future that protect against the worship of current choices, the articulation of two domains, and the tensions generated by the bifurcation of speech.

The image of a leader who has the power to choose one or another of the five strategies for managing narrative variety may appear to distinguish the organizational case from other cases in which there is no "boss" or (more to the point) in which the tacit strategies of dominant coalitions or institutional designs can't be altered by any single person.

I suspect, however, that the apparent differences mask essential similarities. In a field of overlapping communities, some associations will manage narrative diversity principally by relying on one of the five strategies. Each strategy, however, engenders a game against itself, so a pure type is very rare and the forms of communion in one part of the field insinuate themselves everywhere. Even in overtly hierarchical settings, the ways of coping with narrative diversity are likely to be varied, conflictual, and resistant to control. A planning director committed to the fifth strategy would quickly discover that she was vulnerable to manipulation. Every tale and every narrator would claim a share of the protective mantle. Every practice would be represented as a "culture" commanding respect, every lexical difference as a signal from an endangered stakeholder.

To play against these strategies, the director would have to deploy analysts who assumed (in their organizational roles and with the signatures of their professional self-images) that most differences would give way to the discipline of fact and authoritative rule, and that passion and deep belief would respond to their intellectual crafts. These technicians might complain that the director's "political" sensibilities interfered with their work, but politics and analysis could not be readily separated. Without the discipline provided by the first four strategies, the director would be overwhelmed; without the fifth, intractable and valuable conflicts would be forced into the uncongenial mold of "truth" versus "error."

The mix of strategies and their social expressions differs across a field of communities. In some communities, for example, "operatives" at the bottom of the social hierarchy are allowed to enjoy free critical space as long as they do their jobs, while the executive suite is held to a standard of complete loyalty. In others, the operatives are manipulated and controlled at every step. Free space is a resource only for the leaders and for a few dedicated servants or defiant souls. In many communities, the sometime war between politics and analysis is fought on a battlefield where the heights are held by the political proponents of the fifth strategy; in others, however, diversity is embraced only in the plains and must be protected against the volleys of critical analysis. Everywhere in this complex geography, however, the processes of telling and managing stories create and destroy moral communities.

7

Times

In the preceding two chapters, I argued that we cannot realize our dream of a cogent and consensual social knowledge. The literary forms in which we articulate our understanding of social worlds are implicated in our communal myths: the stubborn variety of stories and theories may be weeded and refined, but it cannot be compressed into singular accounts of social reality or moral meanings. Indeed, if we want to preserve a world of open and overlapping communities, we should cherish and sustain variety. Hence the fifth strategy.

The account of time in this chapter shifts attention from the forms of knowledge to its elemental units, but the sensibility that informs my argument is unchanged. Just as it is with theories and stories, the varied ways in which we represent and structure time are implicated in our communal myths. That sensibility should now, however, be both familiar and predictable. My major concern here is not with variety but with the ways in which it is managed and controlled. How do we compose and repair the public orders that allow us to imagine that we understand the times of our own minds and those of others with whom we speak? That question leads to a paradoxical answer: The close reading of "now" provides a guide to the construction of public time and an appreciation of its remarkable and ubiquitous difficulties.

Temporal Orders[1]

Whenever we argue with others or struggle with our own inner voices, we necessarily set ourselves in time: What is past and what is present? When must decisions be made? How long is the future that awaits us?

The ordinary experiences of everyday life alert us to three simple facts about these questions or (better) about our answers to them:

• Our personal responses to the questions differ across domains. Some ten-year-old memories are as immediate and compelling as today's newspaper; some are "ancient history."

• Our responses differ across time. On some days it seems that we will live forever, on others that the world will collapse tomorrow.

• People differ in the ways they frame the questions and in the answers they proffer publicly and in their own minds.

We are not, thankfully, forced to deal with this inconstant variety at every moment. Communities of all sorts provide incentives and disciplines encouraging individuals to stabilize their conceptions of time in order to get on with one another. If, for example, you and I have negotiated for a while and have developed a bond of trust, it would be outrageous of me suddenly to change my planning horizon by altering the duration of the relevant future, and it would be unfair of me to dredge up old wrongs as if they were current debts that had to be settled before we could proceed.

Communities also create public orders that allow a shared conception of time to be superimposed on the individual variations in a way that both legitimizes and limits them.

The psychological distances between members of a group may vary dramatically from one person to another and be quite independent of propinquity. The design of physical networks, however, imposes a common temporal metric on this variety: for everyone at site A it takes so many hours to reach site B by plane, and so many seconds to place a telephone call. This temporal map of location varies regularly and (for the most part) without personal distinctions within the cycles of days, weeks, and seasons: slower in rush hours, faster in off-peak hours, and subject to erratic interruptions in extreme weather. In the same way, social networks constrain us within relatively fixed communal calendars: times to work, to eat, to sleep, to rush, to relax, to indulge in (inevitably varied) memories, to live in the here and now, to budget resources, and to assess our performances. Beginning in infancy, we come to understand (or at least accept) the social structuring of even our most intimate body rhythms—to grasp (however dimly) when we are in and when we are out of public temporal orders.

The talk of city planners usually centers on the ways in which the patterning of space influences the character of communities. How, we wonder, does the spatial mix of groups influence the abilities of communities to sustain a moral order? If they exist at all, how do distinctive communal and public inter-communal places work and by whom are they controlled? How are spatial changes initiated and managed?

There is a comparable but less salient set of queries about time. How do communities cope with the rapid growth in the number of competing chronotypes engendered by tourism and global communication? (When is the city quiet when many of its residents are vacationers from elsewhere? When is bedtime when the World Cup is on TV at 2 A.M.?) How do families cope with the separation of the temporal rhythms of women and children, with graveyard shifts, and with the opportunities of markets in distant time zones? Can Mediterranean urban rhythms survive in a Europe dominated by a more insistent northern pace?

These practical matters are the meat of the politics of time around the world. Planners and publics argue about the hours during which stores and government offices should be open or planes allowed to land at airports; they worry about the forms and timing of TV programming and the scheduling of public rituals designed for tourists. These mundane arguments are often enveloped in memories and hopes articulated as chronotypes. The guardians of communities defined by great founding episodes configure time so that the sacred past is always contemporary and relevant. For them, being "up to date" means being in tune with eternal principles rather than with passing fashions. Historic preservation in its many forms is a moral imperative. (In contrast, chiliastic and revolutionary movements orient themselves toward a future event that obscures all differences in earlier time and experience.) Communities in which the lives of members have been structured by a powerful shared experience (war, migration, and depression are the examples that come most easily to mind) use that experience to create a consensual sequence that marks events as before or after the great moment, as leading to or following upon it.

Communities attempt to socialize new members into these temporal orders. If they are successful, novitiates come to accept the disciplines of the calendar and the meanings attached to it. Personal experiences are invested in collective memories and tasks, so that members see themselves as freed from Egypt, as fleeing with the Prophet from Mecca, as surviving the Great Depression, as betrayed at Yalta, as resisting the war in Vietnam, as validated by the agricultural cycle, or as energized by preparations for the coming season.

Each of the three stylized communal myths impresses its own intellectual forms and dilemmas on these temporal orders. The contractual myth depends critically on a narrative in which an agreement is explicitly struck or is imputed to social arrangements. Time is then calibrated in two complementary temporal sequences. The first marks us either as in the same period as the contractual moment or as in a new one. If background conditions are stable (if the moment is unchanged), our initial assent still obligates us: we cannot ethically "weasel out" of the deal. We are in a new period when we imagine that changes in those conditions are sufficient to free us from our obligations: the pact, we insist, is "obsolete." Without the possibility of occasionally using that release, promises are terrible prisons. In communities in which the creation of obsolescence is a way of life, there is, however, something frightening about the capacity of a new day to negate every legitimate social bond. The second temporal order within the contractual myth mitigates the terrible power of obsolescence. Within that order, time (after the bargain) is calibrated in periodic renewals and rites of reaffirmation: elections, re-negotiations of labor contracts, votes of confidence, "taking communion," pledging allegiance. The regular processes of renewal and reaffirmation build a bulwark against the corrosive intellectual judgment that we are free because "times have changed."

The complementary relation between the two orders constantly confronts us with dilemmatic choices between procedural commitments and intellectual judgments. We want simultaneously to write on a clean slate and to enjoy the advantages of familiar notions and comfortable protocols. The temporal routinization of renewal and reaffirmation of what is familiar and comfortable circumscribes the scope of new agreements by embedding them deeply in the terms of old practices. Ritualized (let alone coerced) assent—the pledge, the vote, the bowed head—rarely confronts the serious possibility that, indeed, a familiar arrangement is obsolete and that bonds of obligation are wisely loosened.

Stylized myths of a community integrated by a deep moral order struggle with a different set of temporal issues. If the community engages in a variety of activities and if its social organization is marked by stable divisions of labor, it inevitably creates distinctive temporal rhythms and realms. In order to sustain its moral integration, however, it must successfully mesh these differences so that they appear as elements of a single temporal order: deep communities must make one out of many. Members may differ in their social roles, but they are always bound to the rhythms of a common membership that is never far out of mind. When temporal demands conflict, they are resolved in favor of the integrated moral order: the faithful put down their tools at the call to prayer; citizens delay their personal plans to rally around the flag; tribes call scattered members back into their bosom.

The temporal dilemma within the myth of a deep community lies in the conflict between differentiation and integration. Resisting differentiation by suppressing temporal differences is difficult and costly. Increasing complexity, however, makes it progressively harder to hold everyone within the discipline of a single temporal order. Deep communities, struggling with temporal exceptions and differences, resist the erosion of communal rituals or seek to invent new ones to reinvigorate (and control) the common time of members.

Within the myth of a field of overlapping and open moral communities, we are all assumed to live in a variety of temporal orders. Navigating within and across communities, we constantly face temporal choices that test our identities and our ability to seek moral guidance and communal nurture. In the most common case, we are bound to the rhythms of both family and work communities and often find ourselves torn between them, unable to be at two different places or tasks at the same moment in time but switching between them mentally. We take the job home and vice versa. As we commonly observe about ourselves, our bodies are in one place but our heads are elsewhere. Though we are overtly on company or family time, we read the clock as measuring the rhythms of another world (Hochschild 1997).

For most of us, these conflicts can be resolved neither by making work and family one nor by rigidly bounding discrete domains so that mixing is somehow prohibited. For the most part, we must, instead, master the two rhythms (and all the others within which our lives are articulated) and then manipulate them creatively, responding as we go to revisions of familiar orders associated with aging and changes in gender roles, work and family responsibilities, retraining requirements, spatial location, health and disability. If we fail utterly to attend to a community in and on time, we cannot claim the benefits of membership: at the two extremes, we variously lose our jobs or our families.

The difficult choices faced by individuals within open communities are simultaneously a dilemma for the communities as social entities. The public orders of open communities must endow time with communal meaning and provide a bridge of understanding across substantial differences. If a religious group, a business firm, a family, or a city abandons its temporal perspectives by subordinating them wholly to another rhythm, it loses an essential element of its identity. If, at the other extreme, a community insulates itself wholly from the time of others, then it requires members to withdraw from their overlapping associations: either you conform to our time or you must leave. As communities struggle over the balance and the control of time, there are no cost-free solutions, no balance points that delight everyone.

Two Conventions

We can't act on the past—it is gone! We can't act on the future—it has not been! "Now" is that elusive moment in which we can characterize our world and act on it to shape our future. The ways in which we represent "now" and settle disagreements about its boundaries are central to the temporal orders that are evoked by each of the three communal myths and to arguments about collective choice that are articulated within them. Exploring "now"—when is it?—reveals the extraordinary complexity and limitations of the public orders that allow us to talk together about time. It is a wonder that we ever persuade ourselves that we understand our own minds let alone those of others.

Two conventions appear repeatedly in temporal arguments. The first, "objective" convention is associated with the rhetoric of historians. It orders events by distinguishing sharply between past and future. The second—call it "artificial"—is characteristic of the talk of planners and policy analysts. Through an elaborate process of design (hence the name), it shapes agreements on the definition of the present.

Everyone, I suspect, has had the experience of waking from a dream that merged past events and fantasies. In a daze, one temporarily cannot distinguish memory from anticipation. This personal experience is externalized when one attends a meeting at which people disagree about the order of events, inserts (in one's own view) imaginary happenings into the factual sequence, and confuses everything by speaking about the future as if it had already happened.

The objective convention of historians is designed both to make waking sense of personal dreams and to shape a public chronology within and across communities. Historians distinguish sharply among past, present, and future. The past is the domain of public, private, overt, and mental events. The future is the domain of contingent possibility. The present is an infinitesimally short moment in which possibilities are converted into events. Unlike the past, which grows by accretion, the present is constantly transformed, its old content slithering away in the very instant of contemplation.

The objective view is asymmetrical. The past can, in principle, be known; the future can only be forecast. The past cannot be changed; the future is peculiarly the domain of choice and is open to alteration. The words that establish this asymmetry—"event," "know," "change"—may on close philosophic inspection appear to be tautological. They work together, however, as a rhetorical concatenation built, as Gale (1968, p. 103) argues, of overlapping concepts of "causality, action, deliberation, choice, intention, memory, knowledge, truth, possibility and identification." The entire set of meanings must be turned topsy-turvy in order to insist in the face of this barrage that the past can be altered and the future known. No small adjustments will support coherent discourse. A community cannot be open if it does not accept the distinction in principle between knowledge of the past and forecasts of the future, or if it does not accept that we cannot change what has already happened. (Superman is such an intriguing hero precisely because he is not limited by this incapacity.)

Labeling this convention "objective" does not imply that it conforms to everyday experience. Confronted with the conflicting testimony of witnesses to an event (as in the Japanese film *Rashomon*), the reality of rival perceptions, memories, and speech diminishes the significance of the event itself. Since I do not know what really happened and hence cannot use it as a standard, it barely matters in understanding the witnesses' accounts. The simple fact is, of course, that the past that appears in such accounts is often changed. The objective convention counterposes a metaphysical insistence that events at one time cannot alter those at any preceding instant against the sensory evidence of history made and remade.

The insistence that the future cannot be known similarly runs against the sensory grain. Most of us are much more confident about our statements about the near future than we are about our images of large parts of the past. The confidence is usually not misplaced. I am more likely to have been correct in my surmise that my office walls would not change color in the next five minutes than in my estimate of the year in which they were last painted. Relying on a test of practical confidence, the past and the future are roughly symmetrical. Both are amenable to the light of inquiry; both, at any one moment, are only partially illuminated. The insistence that what can be changed cannot be known seems an overly fastidious or unrealistic creed.

The objective convention is rigid; that is, after all, the source of its compelling intellectual authority. By insisting that the future is only possible and never certainly known, the objective convention focuses attention on the character of contingent relationships. Why is it, in a trivial case, that my office walls will not suddenly be painted? Why, on more serious grounds, are the organizational and class relationships that provide me with a private office likely to persist?

The designation of past events as unchangeable distinguishes sharply between an initial act and the changing stream of perceptions, memories, and explanations that flow from it. My remembrance of what I said yesterday is not my statement but a distinct event. Its relationship to yesterday's speech is problematic. I may, for example, remember vividly what I intended rather than what I pronounced, or what the audience lauded rather than what it condemned or ignored. The difficulty in practice of establishing the content of my statement only emphasizes the importance of the in-principle inviolability of an event. If the past can be changed, there is no end to the ways in which it can be manipulated. If (as in *Rashomon*) all we have are alternative perceptions, then the death of one of the witnesses alters the past; the selective destruction of an archive by a revolutionary regime retrospectively creates a new reality.

The rigidity of the objective convention is complemented by its thinness. While it disciplines the construction of narratives, it does not determine their substance or force them into a single rhetorical mold. Accounts that are equally consistent with the convention may start at different moments and proceed at different paces, so that communities and individuals are not required to adopt identical conceptions of the origins of problems or of the significance of particular events. If the asymmetry of past and future is maintained, the convention will sustain competing theories and the rich intertwining of events and memories characteristic of both everyday speech and fictional narratives.

The power of the objective convention is illustrated in the discussions of the sale of U.S. arms to Iran and the transfer of the receipts to the Nicaraguan Contras that the press labeled "Irangate." The sale and the transfer may or may not have been consistent with the character of the American nation or with the letter and spirit of its laws. Opinions differed on those matters. Most everyone agreed, however, that lying about the sequence of events or altering the historical record was a serious attack on the capacity of the political community to function. Without a consensual chronology there would be no trust in the midst of conflict. The chronology did not, however, settle issues; it only focused them. President Ronald Reagan, for example, could not be blamed for failing to alter events of which he was unaware. Unlike Superman, he could not reverse time's arrow. He could, however, be held to account for his ignorance. Denying that knowledge was within his capacity would step outside cherished myths of the presidential role and of human agency.

The evanescent present is the great gap in the objective convention. Without a definition of an extended now, it is very difficult to specify the relations between events and future actions so as to bring them to bear on collective decisions. Within the framework of the convention there is—in a literal sense—no time in which the connection between event and possibility can be forged into a public assertion. Suppose that, before I act, I sensibly inquire "What are things like now?" That simple question poses enormous intellectual difficulties, but it is answered every day in ordinary speech. Within the objective convention, however, there is no way of disciplining those answers or of shaping a public order. Now cannot be the present that is gone in the moment it is noticed. To what past, then, does the question refer? Why should anything that is past matter in deciding now how to act later?

The gap between past and future is filled in the artificial convention with an extended moment that incorporates events and contingent possibilities. This artificial present is the implicit temporal referent for a variety of common phrases: "current conditions," "in today's world," "this is how things are now." The rules people use to specify these referents are not, however, immediately obvious. The notion of now must incorporate both historical evidence previous to an evanescent moment and the discounted value of future possibilities. How much of past and future should be incorporated? When does the present start in the past? When is it finished?

In February of 1987, Senator Daniel Patrick Moynihan spoke to a reporter from the *New York Times* about welfare policy. The interview (published in the *Times* on February 19) is a rich example of the forms in which we specify the present. Moynihan argued that "we have a child support system that's medieval." The historical reference is a value judgment: the system currently exists, but it is neither practically nor morally appropriate to this time. The "original welfare program" was formed in a period "before washing machines and refrigerators and vacuum cleaners" when the family "was seen as an arrangement where the husband went out to work and the woman stayed home and kept house and raised the children." "Now" began when high female participation in the labor force devalued earlier assumptions and institutional designs: "You looked up one day and women were working." (If, of course, you believe that those assumptions specified a preferable social order, then they remain in the present, ready to be mobilized against an ephemeral or pernicious trend.)

Looking to the future, Moynihan insisted that a revised welfare system would have to "get rid of disincentives," though he doubted that welfare recipients should be required to work as a condition of receiving benefits. "The experience of workfare," he insisted in the historical present, "is always disappointing. Partly it's because the big bureaucracies can't handle it." This characterization of disincentives and the incapacity of bureaucracies relied necessarily on historical evidence. The period from which the evidence was drawn was not specified in the interview, but we know that, in contrast with the era in which "the original welfare program began," its social dynamics have not been rendered obsolete. It is part of the present, and it is presumed to be continuous with the future. It was certainly not defined by any particular rate of female participation in the labor force. There were, it appears, at least two presents in the senator's mind.

The objective convention is well known to historians and to philosophers. It is employed widely and self-consciously in public debates to control arguments by placing them within a common chronology. A barrage of overlapping questions about what can be known and what can be changed distinguish past from future, memory from anticipation, history from speculation. Applied retrospectively, they establish a unique public sequence of events that dominates all private orders. Our personal memories may be jumbled, but (in public, at least) the legislation, the administrative rules, the meetings, and the speeches of 1963 always precede those of 1964.

The artificial convention that facilitates the public specification of a usable present out of the sort of complexities that are apparent in the interview with Senator Moynihan is not likely to enjoy the same recognition. I have patched it together from bits and pieces of observation of policy arguments and of methodological debates among analysts and planners.

In broad strokes, the convention works by specifying elements of both future and past that can be treated as contemporary. The future boundary of the artificial present is marked by a planning horizon. Within that horizon, it is possible and wise to act now to shape the flow of contingencies. Beyond it, high uncertainty and the extreme hazards of mistaken choices suggest that nothing should be done for the moment. (Confidently anticipated but very small future benefits may also not be worth incorporating into the present.) When our confidence is high, the current value of long-term benefits great, and the risk of failure modest, or when we refuse (out of obligation to unborn generations) to discount the future, then of course the boundary of the present may extend across millennia to come.

Contingent possibilities beyond the planning horizon are part of a simple future that may justifiably be treated as irrelevant in policy discussions.

The boundary between the artificial present and the simple past is not quite so easily described. All the relationships and resources that may influence the course of a policy must be currently present at the moment of initiation or must appear over its lifetime. Nothing that is not present or prospective can act over an interval. The sensible planner is concerned only with images of the present state of the world and of its potential paths. If, for example, I expect to open a day-care center that markets its services to parents, I want to know what parents like now; I will then estimate what they will like tomorrow. Yesterday's preferences are, in principle, stale news.

The in-principle clause cannot, of course, be implemented in practice. There is no way of knowing the state of the economy or of my personal feelings at the instant at which a policy judgment is made. (The same limitation applies if the judgment is made and remade over an extended period of time. At each instant of decision, one cannot know the world in a fleeting present.) Past observation must serve as a surrogate for a present measurement. Every empirically based statement about the capacity of institutions or about their current state incorporates a past into an artificial present. A great many of the incorporated events lie in a zone that Cottle (1976) called the "near past." A market analyst describing yesterday's measurement of the attitudes of parents toward day care would not hesitate to characterize the report as "current." Recency is not, however, the sole or even the necessary criterion or the delineation of the boundary between the past-in-the-present and the simple past. An event in a seemingly remote era may be appropriately considered as a measure of a current phenomenon; in another circumstance, a recent occurrence may be rejected as a surrogate.

The test of appropriateness rests on the conception of a "system." Planners and policy analysts employ a considerable technical apparatus in imagining how interactions constrain and guide linked elements; others employ a more rough-hewn notion of connected entities. Whether sophisticated or crude, these images all involve conceptions of hierarchy, control and what is metaphorically described as "structure." Only within the context of such a stable structure can the record of past behavior or causal propositions serve as surrogates for present measurements or models.

The knowledge we derive from a study of England in 1480 may replace a contemporary measure if the controlling patterns of interaction at that time and place were substantially the same as our own. If they were different, then that fifteenth-century history describes a part of a simple past that cannot tell us what we are now and how we might react tomorrow. No matter how long ago it occurred, the overflow pattern in the last "100-year storm" is a measure of the current potential of a river if new embankments, ground cover, and channels have not altered its hydrological dynamics.

The artificial present—in summary—is distinguished from the simple future by a planning horizon and from the simple past by the limits of replacement. Four judgments are required to design an artificial present: specification of its future elements, complementary specification of its current dimensions and structure, justification of a planning horizon and a discount rate, and selection of a surrogate past. The cycles through these judgmental tasks are repeated so often and in such complex patterns during the course of policy arguments that for many purposes it barely matters which task initiates a sequence of deliberation. That is not, however, the usual perception. Individuals or communities concerned that they are adrift or that innovation may be disruptive are apt to argue that the first step is to get right with the past; others invoke a rhetoric of hard-headed realism to insist that discussion begin with a diagnosis of the current situation. Advocates of change, eager to unfreeze institutional designs and to expand the array of imagined alternatives, start with the future: Who are we, and what do we want? Only when an infinite buzz of possibilities is transformed into a set of discrete choices, can the attributes of systems and time be jointly specified with any confidence.

Articulating these initial biases may soften them. Whatever the beginning, all arguments over collective choices cycle through the four design judgments. Any anticipatory mapping of the sequence of choices will reveal a process of repeated moves back and forth across time. Eventually, of course, some of the participants will succeed in calling a halt to that searching movement back and forth across time. We should, therefore, be sensibly alert to the identity of those who are able to limit search and to the character of the stop rules (i.e., discussion-ending rules).

Suppose, for example, that a discussion starts with the desired future. A projective sketch leads to the selection of a discount rate and a planning horizon. The conventions of discounting among economists and bankers barely scratch the surface of the rules implicit in these judgments: Should individuals be allowed to discount their future incomes? May anyone discount the income of children or of unborn generations? How are social discount rates appropriately calculated? Answers to these questions lead back to a systems sketch and only then—at the end of a cycle—to the search for surrogate measures in the past.

Of course, conversations are not so tidily ordered! Each step in constructing an artificial present loops back through experience before moving forward. Any judgment that may be justified by reference to events may also be self-consciously informed by historical inquiry and argument. Once I tie an image of an artificial present to a conception of the past, a protagonist (e.g., a political rival, a therapist, or my conscience) may press me to confront the record of events. In that confrontation, the statements with which I began and the organization of memory are placed at risk.

The same vulnerability complicates the sketch of a system. There are a great many collections of phenomena that someone would like to call "system." Some collections, failing to demonstrate attributes of stability and control, clearly do not merit the designation. However, if one system model fits a set of phenomena, it is likely that others will also fit. The choice of a model depends on the purposes of the analyst: Which scale seems relevant? Which differences matter? Which elements are controllable? As an analyst alters his or her purposes or reevaluates the opportunities for effective action, models and temporal perspectives shift.

The variation in the testimony of witnesses to an event is usually imputed either to deliberate lying or to unconscious biases in attention, perception and memory. The differences in the choice of a system model, in contrast, are intentional and legitimate. A model that is correct by the most severe operational tests may be rejected as inappropriate or useless. The central characterization of a current reality depends on normative assertions of what should be and on assessments of what might be practical. The loops through time within each judgmental step and the varied sequence of steps vastly complicate discussions of collective choices. The artificial convention specifies the items on an agenda of discussion but not their order. It cannot prevent debaters from talking past one another. Indeed, it cannot even prevent intrapersonal confusion. Our individual planning horizons vary broadly across issues; the specification of a surrogate past depends on the characteristics of the future we are concerned with at the moment. We envelop ourselves in an individual array of artificial presents without either the constant necessity of rendering them coherent or the means of doing so.

In some times and places, arguments are tightly controlled. The chair of a legislative committee, a therapist, or a judge may force parties through the cycle of choices so that they always know where they are and where the next step leads. Even in such unusual conditions, the discipline of the artificial present is so deeply embedded in other orders that it cannot independently constrain the play of arguments. Advocates of alternative policies may sometimes resolve their differences when their attention is focused on the justification of their planning horizons or on historical research that bears on the potential behavior of a current system. Diverse goals and values influence the construction of a present so profoundly, however, that the triumphs of public convergence are characteristically modest, albeit precious. Values enter in the first specification of the future and of a planning horizons. They are not, however, confined to those steps, nor are they easily traced. Even events in the simple past may enter the present through the window of the idealized future. We should understand events in the simple past, I may argue, so as to increase our repertoire of behavior or so as to transform the system in which we are engaged. When we represent our communities as either deep or contractual, we usually focus this search for a prosthetic past on our own collective experience: our covenants, our contracts, our moral order. The image of an open field encourages a greater eclecticism. The specialized historical and anthropological imaginations make it possible to learn the lessons of pasts in which a community itself is not engaged. Ethnographies tracking the political practices of the ancient Greeks, the adolescence of Samoan villagers, or the lack of coercive authority among the Fox Indians enter into the artificial present as sketches of policies for the future.

The way we incorporate the past into the present hinges on the ways we define our ethical terms. Suppose, for example, that I insist on a standard of social justice that requires that every person receive his or her "due." That straightforward requirement has been interpreted variously to imply respect for rights, deserts, or needs (Miller 1976). However, many rights and all deserts are justified only by a record of behavior: rights are conferred; positive or negative deserts are earned. Even a largely ahistorical conception of need may require a history to establish the identity of a person or community entitled by need to dignity or self-respect. The histories required by such alternative definitions of justice may not, however, incorporate the same past into the present. Rights and deserts may originate in different periods; equally significant, they may age at different rates and for different reasons. In the absence of coercion, right claims, most of us believe, diminish if they are not exercised. They are not otherwise rendered obsolete with the passage of years: if I own my house legitimately, my possession is not diminished (without a notion of a communal jubilee[2]) because I have held title for a long time. Positive and negative deserts, in contrast, do diminish with the passage of time, so that the retribution for past wrongs and the rewards for old virtues ultimately fade out of the present. We are certainly not entirely agreed, however, on the rate of attenuation across the full range of potential circumstances (Sher 1987).

Conceptions of attenuation are embedded in images of a moral entity. Suppose, for example, that economic theories grounded in the experiences of the 1950s no longer explain or predict the behavior of the U.S. economy in the 1990s. If we imagine that a moral entity—say the "nation" or the "market"—persists across the structural change in the economy, then the obligation to repay debts incurred in the 1950s is not diminished even though our theories are "out of date." A revolutionary regime that disavows the debts of its predecessor denies the existence of such a continuous entity or distinguishes sharply between the obligations incurred by the abiding nation and those incurred by particular regimes. If they contest the disavowals, the creditors cannot rely on empirical judgments about the stability of social structures and about the continued cogency of historical propositions as surrogates. Like the revolutionaries, they must argue about the wisdom of a future in which certain classes of contracts are absolutely binding. (Not by accident, the construction of the past hinges on aspirations for the future.)

Words and Relationships

The protean character and the responsiveness of the convention that locates "now" in time serves, paradoxically, to explain ubiquitous (and often intractable) temporal misunderstandings and to shape shared meanings. The construction of an artificial present requires a set of interlocking judgments that is so complex and so dependent on normative assertions that misunderstanding must be the norm and effective communication a rare triumph. Attempts to expand understanding are easily swamped by the interdependence of the relevant judgments. Correct a model of a system and you confront differences in moral and reformist notions of the past.

Draft a statement on what was and you must somehow accommodate variations in aspirations for what might yet be. Settle on one time frame and you face another when the subject of discussion changes (often unobserved).

The artificial convention provides a lexicon of necessary terms and a map of arguments and rebuttals—a guide to rhetorical warfare and to persuasion. The rhetorical construction suggests ways in which the organizational design of argumentative settings may influence the process of setting a public order in place. If a political arena does not allow for iterative cycles through past, present, and future, then temporal perspectives and the images they sustain are frozen in their initial positions. If the cycles are opened and negotiation is permitted, new possibilities for agreement emerge. If the protocols of correct speech in an arena inhibit the examination of temporal differences, we are likely to mistake our disagreements and to assume that there is assent where none exists.

In each of the three communal myths, the hope of locating a semi-solid trail through the swamp of temporal confusion rests both on the qualities of words and speech and on the forms of relationships. The effective simplification of choice and the implementation of rules stopping discussion or shifting its focus depend on deference in one of its many forms: personal trust, fear, communal affiliation, respect for expertise or authority. Deferential relationships are validated by discursive practices: trust, for example, rarely survives repeated lying. However, deference is effective in sustaining agreement only when it protects against and limits the regime of words, focusing critical attention and negotiations in some areas while necessarily cloaking others in the mantle of convention and tacit assent. When everything is discussable—when relationships don't limit words—communities collapse.

8

Tools

The Promise of Tools

'Theory', 'story', and 'time'—the subjects of the last three chapters—are words in ordinary language. This does not mean, of course, that we all use them in the same way. Indeed, common words are likely to be ambiguous, conjuring layers of contested meanings. Augustine's reflection on time—he knew what it was as long as he didn't have to put his knowledge into words—captures the experience of being momentarily left speechless, or the somewhat rarer experience of having words suddenly seem to lose their meanings. Words are "common" because we share those pragmatic difficulties. The lexical difficulties do not belong to any single occupational group or class.

In this chapter, I am particularly interested in the way in which the word 'tool' is linked to a technological sensibility that marks the identity of planners, managers and other professional schemers. There are two elements in that sensibility: a willingness (or, better, a passion) to represent the world as a series of emergent problems that must be addressed and, at least for a moment, solved; and a belief that professionals can create, reproduce, and improve problem-solving tools and carry them successfully from one setting to another. It is not a particular theory, story, or chronotype that distinguishes scheming professionals; it is a mastery of the tools of their craft. Strong tools leave very little room for professional discretion: there is one and only one way to use them. Other tools require a great deal of discretion, substantial training, and a supportive environment. If, for example, polities and their institutions do not respond to measures of aggregate well-being, the tool of cost-benefit analysis solves no problems and is barely worth transporting from site to site.

It is the process of diffusion that particularly interests me. How deeply, I wonder, can tools impose common practices and negotiated public orders on a variety of communities? Can tools and toolmakers resist the pluralism that impresses itself so strongly upon theories, narratives, and chronotypes? If we distinguish (as is common these days) between *decisions* and technical *decision-support systems,* how deeply can the professional tools constrain idiosyncratic political choices?

The two elements of the technological sensibility sustain one another. On the one side, problems justify toolmaking; on the other, tools embolden professional planners and their kin to present themselves as both problem makers and problem solvers. (Without a stream of constructed problems, there wouldn't be many careers to be built in solving them. Imagine the voices: "We are running low. Make some new problems!")

The notion of the world as a series of problems is so familiar that it is easily taken for granted. We are all necessarily fatalists about most of the elements of our lives. We act—"naturally," we say—without treating external phenomena or our reactions to them as problematic. That ordinary and essential fatalism contrasts with the demanding practice of constructing problems by marking off domains, subjecting them to critical inspection, estimating their plasticity, and commanding attention to prosthetic possibilities. We do not, of course, live in a simple world in which one mind defines the array of collective problems. If your problem cannot survive in the world as I have represented it, we are bound to struggle over problem definitions even before we have fairly begun to talk about solutions.

The notion of a tool is similarly both familiar and confusing. We employ a great many instruments to solve the problems we create. In my lexicon, an instrument is a tool only if users are able to distinguish and reproduce its design and performance attributes. I may not know how a telephone works, but I know how to use it. I can train novices so that (rather quickly) they will be master callers capable of carrying their skill across borders and using telephones wherever they find them. In contrast, "talking things out" is an important planning instrument but it becomes a tool only when conversational practice follows a distinctive protocol that is replicated over time and across settings.

My restrictive definition of 'tool' is not intended to sort phenomena into boxes, as if by that semantic tactic I could construct compelling comparisons of the performance of instruments that are tools and those that are not. I am, instead, interested in the social processes through which tools are constantly being constructed and denied. Lifting the lid on the (mythical) planner's tool kit, I see in one compartment instruments that may (or may not) become tools; in another I see tools that (tomorrow or the day after) may no longer command agreement as to their shape, performance, or relevance. Read as a text, the kit is an account of countless arguments and layered symbolic adjustments. The same overt tool takes on one form and meaning if it is understood as an aid to negotiations and is hedged about with warning labels, quite another if it is presented as a uniquely authoritative and rational way to replace the messiness of ordinary politics.

Tools are made by crafting agreements that fit problem definitions to the form and the capacity of apposite instruments. This iterative process—back and forth between problem and instrument—moves through cycles of simplification and cycles of expansive integration.

In what I suspect is the more common practice, we turn thick relationships into thin ones, simplifying problems or decomposing them into discrete elements so that they are within the scope of a tool in hand. If I have only a hammer and nails in my kit, it is foolish (at least for the moment) to imagine structural problems that require screws or miter joints. If a mathematical model can handle only two players, three variables, and certain knowledge of the future, the problems to which it is addressed must fit within that procrustean bed.

That is, of course, too static an image: the technological sensibility is grounded in the confident belief in a progressive developmental path. It would, after all, have been quite amazing if the first computerized information systems had been used for anything grander than printing checks and reconciling accounts, or if the first geographic information systems had engaged anything other than static constructions of spatial addresses. Belaboring the simplicity of a problem definition presses toolmakers into a defensive posture and distracts them from their labors.

A simple problem and its associated tool creates an ordered enclave within a larger and uncertainly manageable setting. In such enclaves, toolmakers insist, they refine their instruments in order subsequently to extend their reach.

Decomposing the complex problems of our minds so that some of their elements are amenable to our tools defines by implication a set of worlds that cannot be controlled within the terms of our technological consensus. Endangered by those worlds or unwilling to forgo their opportunities, toolmakers sometimes reach for the stars. Persuaded that they must and can reshape the structure of a city, a region, or an economy, they seek to create tools that will tame their grand problem by simulating the system's structure, anticipating its performance, and assessing strategic interventions. This ambitious focus on the structure of a system and on the ways we frame the most general social problems characteristically depends on the willingness to accept subordinate but loosely coupled domains in which actors rely on tacit knowledge and idiosyncratic judgment. The thin science of fiscal and monetary policy or transportation networks gives way to the thick "business sense" of experienced entrepreneurs and managers.

A great deal rests on the character of the coupling of the macro complex of tools and problems with their micro complements. At one extreme, the two complexes may be so loosely connected that the consensual macro world is right "in theory" and wrong or sensibly ignored in every detail. ("The model is a great achievement and beautiful but, alas, irrelevant.") At the other extreme, the coupling is so tight that it can be maintained only with an intense and destructive discipline that requires that every choice be governed by a rule in a coherent and internally consistent set of rules. This grand strategy is never trivial or boring: its malaise is a surfeit of attractive nonsense and destructive pride.

Risks and Dangers

The struggle over the coupling and the costs of all choices radiates across the processes of making and breaking individual tools and the transformation of the professional tool kit. I have selected a single probe into those processes: a class of instruments that are, were, or may yet be tools for representing in the present the form, the magnitude, and the distribution of future dangers.

The creation of shared images of *risk*—the present representation of future dangers—plays an important role in the intertwined processes of designing markets, organizations, polities, inter-organizational fields, temporary associations, and stable confessional communities. Naming and calibrating images of prospective dangers make it possible to divide those dangers between parties and to buy and sell insurance that will compensate us when our fears are realized—to accept some risks as the price we must pay in order to reap the benefits of our enterprise while hedging against or avoiding others. Regimes that are designed to mitigate or to collectivize risks depend on shared representations of both aggregate and individual dangers to guide their behavior. How many people will probably be unemployed, injured in industrial accidents, hospitalized with an acute disease, murdered, or poisoned by toxic wastes in a given period? What are the chances that any particular individual or group will suffer those assaults? There is a certain charming innocence in the blind faith that only good things will attend our efforts in a wholly beneficent world. Most of us, however, expect collective choices to be informed by a more calculating prudence in which we consider *now* the implications of future hazards.

The talk of physicians, lawyers, planners, engineers, policy analysts, managers, and (above all) actuaries characteristically assumes that inchoate or merely personal apprehensions can be disciplined and compared; that our varied risk assessments can be grounded in a shared public conception (or, as it sometimes seems, a shared professional conception) of the form, incidence, magnitude, and legitimacy of the dangers we will face. Even if the full realization of that dream is delayed, the development of tools for the public representation of risk will surely narrow the bases for normative disagreements and facilitate consensual collective decision making.[1]

Through most of the nineteenth and twentieth centuries the representation of risk has principally depended on the historical observation of hazards experienced by a large population, the construction of patterns from those observations leading to their extrapolation into the future and then, in the critical step, to a representation of present risk. The nineteenth-century construction of actuarial tables exemplifies that mode and the optimism it generated. The tables were the most visible expression of a complex of institutional and intellectual innovations, supporting and disciplining what Zelizer (1979, p. 43) describes as a "general movement to rationalize and formalize the management of death." Across the North Atlantic Basin, an idiosyncratic actuarial craft of narrow scope was transformed in fits and starts over the course of the nineteenth century into a confident public order

wrapped in the mantle of statistical science and legitimized by professional associations, formal training programs, state regulation, and an
"avalanche of printed numbers" (Hacking 1990, p. 2).[2]

The table as a representational tool was initially designed to inform the
assignment of insurance premiums and annuity payments. By the middle
of the century, however, it had already assumed a larger role, providing a
baseline for the assessment of social practices and of public interventions in
hygiene, nutrition, medical care, housing, and the control of deviance.
Knowing the "normal" patterns of death, allowed analysts to represent the
future dangers of polluted water, contagious disease, poverty or over-
crowding. The surface form of the actuarial table as tool was stabilized by
1850, though the data sets it contained were progressively enlarged, the
number of subgroups increased, and the methods of analysis and extrapolation became more sophisticated.

Death, however, is a fairly simple danger and does not pose very difficult
representational problems. It happens only once. It is irreversible and uncal-
ibrated—no corpse is deader than another. (It was also unambiguous until
the miracles of contemporary medicine complicated its definition.) Other
dangers that are represented as risks are much more elusive. It is much harder to develop a social consensus on the measurement of illness, accident, or
battery than to develop one on the measurement of death; much harder to
pattern business failure, crime, or unemployment than mortality; much
harder to ascribe a form to poverty, abuse, or chronic depression. The effort
to create consensual public representations of the risks of these elusive dangers has often been frustrating. Nevertheless, at the end of the twentieth
century the talk of professionals remains suffused with optimistic belief in
the promise of public representation. As in the nineteenth century, the symbolic construction of risk relies heavily on the patterning of historical observations and the extension of those patterns into the future. The array of
complementary tools has, however, been enhanced over time. Animal testing and double-blind random field trials of new drugs allow us to craft and
control the histories we observe, and meta-analysis allows us to make sense
of a variety of uncoordinated studies. The mathematical and iconic simulation of complex systems permits us to "observe" sequential generations
and rare phenomena without waiting for events to take their normal course.
Fault-tree analysis permits us to ascribe probabilities of failure to compo-

nents of systems despite great gaps in our knowledge of how the system as a whole will operate.

The Worlds Created by Risk

In my account to this point, no tools have been broken. Indeed, the progressive effort to represent future dangers has been an enormous success. In the nineteenth century, the great environmental and health hazards—polluted water and air, infectious disease, riot, war, fire, explosion, spoiled food, famine, plague—were tightly linked to clear and present dangers. In the last half of the twentieth century, however, policy communities have been absorbed with images of the counterintuitive implications of our attempts to improve the world, with catastrophic collapses not preceded by gradual accumulation of difficulties, and with dangers in futures so remote that we cannot calibrate them in the life spans of our children or our grandchildren. Around the world, cosmopolitan elites have adopted a discourse in which these remote dangers appear in the present as risks that justify political attention and allocation of public resources. Large publics in many nations are similarly accustomed to the notion that personal and collective behaviors that present no discernible danger in the short run should prudently enter into their present calculations.

Yet, for all those signs of success, a note of self-doubt has entered into the optimistic talk of the professional communities concerned with risk. The shadow, as I understand it, is a suspicion that the representational tools are so essentially contested that they cannot provide a consensual grounding for the politics of risk without major institutional innovations. The tools are not so much broken as they are reframed as elements within a new or potential set of social relations. Absent those relations, the words and tools of experts are not sufficient for the construction of public orders.

In a great secular shift, the symbolic meaning of risk has subtly but surely changed over the last century. The term continues to indicate dangers we *take* in order to increase our income—the hazards of place and markets that are the price of opportunity and fortune. The entrepreneurial meaning is now, however, dominated by risk as a representation of dangers we and our successors endure involuntarily: we are *at risk* as victims of circumstances we did not choose and cannot readily control without collective action.[3]

In the nineteenth century and early in the twentieth, the symbolic change was articulated in the governmental assumption of the risks of reduced income and reduced well-being associated with urbanization, old age, unemployment, and industrial accidents. At the end of the twentieth century, the shift is most apparent in the broadened public assumption of the risks associated with technological innovation, long-term environmental degradation, and predictable accidents (Cox and Ricci 1990).

We have created a shadow world of risk populated by some old dangers and many new ones (Smith 1990). The density and the temporal range of that world have been enhanced by our growing scientific ability to apprehend hazards whose presence we may not even be able to measure and by our moral reluctance to discount the well-being of future generations. Our ubiquitous images of future dangers influence deeply the ways in which we represent even the simplest attributes of current phenomena. The dangers we anticipate are scattered across the future, but risk is the contemporary of every assertion of a current fact. A geographic information system locating phenomena in space is transformed by risk into a map of time and contingency. We sensibly wonder about the magnitude and incidence of accidents in the network portrayed in an ordinary street map, about the possibility of crime or social conflict just below the surface of the most banal presentation of demographic data, and about the sustainability of the ecosystem captured in an aerial photograph.

The shadow world of risk has become so dense that it is now subject to all the intellectual and institutional difficulties of complex collective action. There is no reason in principle that various dangers, taken one at a time, cannot be publicly represented in a distinctive code and embedded in a unique narrative. In this mode there is no reason to compare risks; we should just do what is right and necessary, one risk at a time (O'Brien 1989). In a world dense with apprehensions, we no longer have that luxury: in order to shape public choices, we are bound to develop a common metric that allows us to aggregate and compare risks within and across domains. It is not surprising, however, that the most compelling candidates for that simplifying role suffer from all the familiar difficulties associated with the singular conceptions of "costs" and "benefits" as evaluative measures. The prospective incidence of cancer or of lost days of work doesn't quite capture all that we apprehend as dangerous. Simplifying the narrative in which hazards over time appear as current risks, we neglect the dangers evoked by our own representations and mitigating efforts: the deaths caused by asbestos removal or by the condemnation of industrial brownfields awaiting complete restoration, the pain centered in the intermittent rhythm of chronic illness, the frustrations of failed therapies.

The complexity of this dense world of intimations and apprehensions has divided the community of toolmakers. In the policy circles in and around the federal Environmental Protection Agency, for example, the "softs" have argued for a framework that facilitates the comparison of environmental risks without adopting a single metric (US EPA 1987, 1990). The "hards," in contrast, have repeatedly emphasized that "sound environmental policy making is mostly an analytic, rather than political, enterprise" (Hornstein 1994). Risks—as they are relevant to public policy—are usefully described as expected losses of income and are "sufficiently fungible as to be compared, traded off, or otherwise aggregated by analysts wishing to produce the best environmental policy" (Lash 1994).

Both positions reveal the limits of the toolmaker's craft. In the world of the softs, consensual representations of risk may encourage agreement in risk assessments and in strategic choices. The discipline of a compelling representational mode may even encourage civility in political discussion. The attempt to develop shared representations is not, however, likely to succeed in the face of secrecy, ignorance, distrust, and deeply embedded differences in communicative competence (Gundersen 1995). The hards bear a quite different burden. To control the political debate, they must engage a broad range of evaluative dimensions in a simple and compelling representational form. In the terms of a 1995 request for research proposals issued jointly by the EPA and the National Science Foundation, "systematic and credible" valuation of environmental goods and bads that speak to policy making concerned with ethics, legitimacy, equity, and procedural justice must "illuminate the psychological, social, cultural, and moral dimensions of value" (National Science Foundation 1995, p. 5). The metaphor of illumination tacitly recognizes that no simple representation of value (and, it follows, of risk) will bend the political process to its rhetorical constraints. A fly cannot swallow a trolley car.

Tools and Institutions

Toolmakers are a hardy lot buoyed by a deep professional commitment to their craft and their aspirations. While they continue to devote a great deal of effort to the improvement of representational tools, faced with the dense shadow world of risk they have subtly shifted their attention to the design of institutions—to protocols and principles that depend heavily on murky individual judgments that drip with contested normative meanings.

I distinguish four themes in this turn to institutional design: the politics of trust, the creation of markets, the rhetorical turn, and the lure of consensual groups. I describe them here very cryptically to illustrate the ways in which tools and toolmakers respond to a pluralism they cannot wholly contain.

I was first attracted to the idea that the tools for the consensual representation of risk could succeed only if they were supported by major institutional innovations by Stephen Breyer's Oliver Wendell Holmes Lectures (Breyer 1993) and by Robert Pollak's critique of those lectures (Pollak 1995). Breyer argued that the political relations among Congress, mobilized publics, and administrative agencies systematically distort the assessment and the mitigation of health hazards in the United States. At the center of his argument were the familiar contrasts between expert and public assessments of health risks and between expert assessments and the allocation of risk-mitigating dollars. Scientific knowledge cannot break this vicious circle, Breyer insisted, unless it is institutionalized in a deeply competent bureaucracy that the Congress entrusts with broad discretionary authority. Pollak responded skeptically, wondering whether the "scientific" component of risk assessment can ever be made compelling enough to engender the trust that Breyer's regulatory regime would require. Breyer concluded with a plea for a "Socratic notion of virtue" in which regulators whose leadership actually improves public health might, step by step, cultivate trust where there is now suspicion and skepticism. Pollak's riposte was a gentle suggestion that Breyer seemed "a bit naive." Like all long-term forecasts, expert risk representations and assessments cannot readily be validated by ex post tests. "Instead of lamenting the public's lack of trust in experts, bureaucrats and politicians," Pollak proposed, "it may be more fruitful" to imagine better "mechanisms" to ensure that the regulators are not captured by the industries they are supposed to supervise and that they respond to persistent public images of risk even if they find them misguided.

The exchange between Breyer and Pollak points to a loosely coupled but very complex set of debates over bureaucratic discretion, the conditions of trust, the comparative assessment of risk perceptions, the balance of aggregative and integrative political claims, and the privileged role of expressed preferences in a utilitarian calculus. These debates, like those surrounding the artificial present, are so complex that they fairly beg for simplification. Enter the cultivation of markets. The extension of market processes to environmental and health policy and management are expected, in theory, to reduce the need for consensual representations of risk in collective decision making. If pollution rights are traded freely, public officials acting within a broad framework of environmental goals and constraints do not need to know how each individual or firm imagines risks. If individuals choose from a diverse menu of health-insurance options, or if old-age pensions are voluntary, then collective risk assessments are needed only to define a (presumably high) threshold: only in extremis will individuals be protected against their own mistakes of judgment, maladroit performance, or simple bad luck.

I have drawn my illustrations of market simplifications of risk from recent policy arguments in the United States, but the use of markets to represent risks extends well beyond these matters. Around the world, individuals imagine that they may be harmed by crime, conflict, personal abuse, political oppression, or downward social mobility (to name only a few of the ills to which we are prey) and act to avoid or mitigate the anticipated dangers. They buy (or attempt to buy) safety by building walls, joining in coalitions, hiring guards and teachers, praying, changing their locations, and either excluding or converting the threatening others. Each of these diverse markets begins with a tentative, inflected, and contingent construction of a private domain in which individuals and firms may do as they please. The public constructions of private domains are, however, constantly subject to conflicting and often dilemmatic demands for realignment: e.g., insisting that private discretion be constrained by public rights, that latitude in one area can be protected only by limiting free transactions in another, or that the "bubble" within which trading is permitted should be redrawn. No matter how the balance is struck, markets (whether for pollution permits, for development rights, or for personal status and security) are dangerous settings that evoke apprehension and a stream of new and politically salient risk claims. Expansion of markets alters but does not eliminate the collective problem of representing those claims.

It is, of course, the diversity of representations and not their sheer volume that makes collective action so difficult. In the policy circles concerned with crime, health, and environmental affairs, a good deal of the talk centers on the differences between the ways in which experts and lay publics represent and assess the hazards they jointly face. Why is it, experts wonder, that people who "should know better" continue to smoke, overeat, underexercise, drug themselves out of their minds, and drive recklessly? Why do they support enormous public expenditures to clear a few sites polluted by toxic wastes or to incarcerate criminals while more serious hazards are relatively unattended? Why do they persist in habits of consumption that will impoverish their children and endanger the future of civilization? How might these publics be persuaded to correct their misrepresentations of risk and their flawed comparisons? There are, of course, similar conversations on the other side: How is it that the experts don't appreciate our fear of children with AIDS in our classrooms, our willingness to live in earthquake zones and flood plains, or our resistance to incinerators and halfway houses in our back yards? What would it take to persuade the experts to correct their distorted representations?

In a 1992 essay, Paul Slovic argued that in the fields of radiation and chemical technologies that he had studied closely these acrimonious disputes over risk reflected a "breakdown of trust" in "scientific, governmental, and industrial managers." According to Slovic (1992, pp. 151–152), research on the "nature of trust" is needed if we are to "develop social and institutional processes for decision making that restore and maintain this vital but fragile quality." Trust was so important in Slovic's mind, I suspect, because his own work and that of others concerned with "risk communication" suggests that the differences in the ways in which risks are represented are both valuable and intractable. Pressed to estimate informally the incidence of fatalities from various hazards, ordinary citizens make judgments that do not differ greatly from the data recorded in official actuarial tables. That is not, however, the way in which individuals characteristically represent hazards as risks when they are not forced to speak in the thin, comparative terms adapted for collective decision making. Free of that rhetorical discipline, experts and laymen alike represent risks in a complex matrix of values and practices. We embed risk in contingent narratives that assess the varied faces of blame, volition, legitimacy, and justice.

The epistemic communities concerned with risk have developed a battery of tools to understand these matrices and stories. Unfortunately, as Slovic observed with disarming honesty, risk managers trying to use this understanding to shape their decisions face a difficult task. None of the proposals generated by the toolmakers to "insure that social and psychological factors are incorporated into technical and economic analysis" have been "developed to the point of application" (Slovic 1992, pp. 151–152). With good reason! It was not "obvious"—even to Slovic—how to aggregate and compare these complex representations in a way that would bring them to bear on decision making.

The final theme in my quartet responds to difficulties of communication by attempting to alter patterns of interaction. Large polities depend on a division of labor among agencies and between governors and citizens. Constantly renewed and extended, that division is the source of persistent misunderstandings and of prudent mistrust. Breyer and Pollak engaged those structural difficulties within the frame of republican theory and its dilemmas. Leaders must be wise, Breyer affirmed, and must be graced with both the formal authority and the cultural mandate to act in the absence of consensus. At the same time, Pollak warned, they must be regularly accountable to an electorate.

Alas, accountability and wisdom war with one another unless the electorate appreciates its own interests in the commonweal and distinguishes between individual judgments and prudent statecraft.

Social engineers cannot, of course, stop the practices and the institutional dynamics of large polities while they sensitively tune or redesign the elements of intelligence, accountability, and authority. New regulatory careers cannot be protected against suspicion until the politics of trust is robust enough to overcome the vicious circle.

However, simple (and, characteristically, small) polities *sometimes* offer more congenial settings for the cultivation of an uncoerced, consensual representation and assessment of risk. These simple polities are temporarily isolated from the larger institutional system in which they fit in order to settle environmental disputes, to manage land use and behavior in residential settings, to resolve nagging labor-management battles, to allow neighbors to join public authorities in the co-production of facilities, to assign guilt or blame in legal controversies, or to craft agreements that will survive protracted and contentious development. The domains in which they operate are usually bounded in a way that makes logrolling difficult and that rewards (and, in some cases, compels) constant attention and ultimate unanimity. In order to cultivate consensus, the simple polity as an *arena* for decision making must take on the qualities of a *forum* in which the participants come to understand themselves and one another and to open themselves to persuasion while they attempt to persuade others (Slovic 1992, pp. 151–152).

Many planning theorists, practitioners and politicians (across the political spectrum) are now intrigued by the possibility of multiplying simple polities so as to reduce the level of coercion in collective politics and to increase the discipline of moral communities. Others hold out the more ambitious hope of using consensual processes to reform even the core practices of complex polities.

I will address these arguments in chapter 13. Here my point is another paradoxical observation. There is a child's story that starts with the question "What happens if you give a mouse a cookie?" The answer, in summary, is that one thing leads to another until the mouse takes over your entire life. There is some of that in the attempt to thicken measures of risk in order to reduce the level of political coercion. The representational practices of toolmakers in complex polities marked by erratic attention, shifting and segmented participation, hierarchy, logrolling, compromise, and a declarative rhetoric intended to mobilize and threaten rather than to persuade do not work well in simple collaborative polities. In those contexts, representations must engage the matrices and narratives in which the participants imagine hazards. If the level of aggregation in a geographic information system or even in an old-fashioned map is too large to capture the moral concerns of the collaborators, it is difficult for them to express and compare their worlds. Maps confuse and contaminate the conversation when boundaries are wrong, distance doesn't capture location, social conflicts are misread in the language of space, or protean processes are deceptively frozen in time. Professional representations are rejected as irrelevant or pernicious when they do not engage the experiences and moral judgments of the collaborators.

Engagement is not, however, a simple craft. Opportunities to act together create uncertainties for the participants in any polity. As they work through those uncertainties and argue with their collaborators, they both discover and create themselves (Bryson and Crosby 1992; Kingwell 1995). There is no genie in their heads waiting to reveal their representations of risk to anyone who owns a lamp or knows the appropriate PIN. Indeed, the first voices in an interagency task force, a jury room, or a neighborhood meeting often express conventional measures and apprehensions imported from the complex polity. The new voice permitted and cultivated in the simple polity emerges over time and moves through a series of transformations that test the adaptive capabilities of the toolmaker, the system for storing and retrieving information, and the patience of the participants.

The stages of deliberation alter the demands for information: an actuarial table, a display of comparative risks, or a map of hazards must be appropriate to its moment. Boundaries, dimensions, developmental scenarios, and levels of aggregation simple enough to begin a conversation comfortably may be too simple for a middle game. As a group works toward convergence, however, the complexity of the middle game may retard closure if it is not shed. The divergence of the brainstorming session must give way if consensus is ever to be achieved.

The technology for shifting from one stage to the next may vary widely. We have learned to run and rerun mathematical simulations with new constraints and data, thereby allowing individuals to play out their options within the modeler's world. It is much harder to sustain multiple models and scenarios simultaneously—impossible if the toolmakers see themselves as creating a stable foundation of "fact" or if the deliberative process is not robust enough to support a conflictual conversation of incomplete intimations and uncertainties (Marris 1996).

Tools, like castles, are not built in the air. The processes of "making" are embedded in communities, institutions, and cultures. There is not, however, much latitude for design if the toolmakers' worlds are too much with them. For this reason, toolmakers act to create free spaces within which to ply their craft and to bend institutions to the logic (and the promise) of their creations.

Once offered to the world, tools sometimes succeed and sometimes fail. Occasionally the "breakings" are spectacular, but usually flawed tools, like old soldiers, simply fade away. In the more interesting cases, failure and success are intertwined. Struggling with their own tools, the toolmakers extend their reach into the redesign of institutions, trying to shift the norms of interaction to address problems that formalized methods of analysis or routinized instrumental sequences cannot solve: a new bureaucratic corps, a market, a sensitive communication protocol, a consensual group. Each new reach creates its own difficulties, each new tool a game against its controlling influence. Tools cannot transcend the intellectual difficulties that hold theories, narratives, and chronotypes in the world of communities.

9
Cities

The Talk of Philadelphia

Arguments over collective choices often are grounded in differences in the labeling of social entities. My "loyal friends" become a problem in your eyes when you stigmatize them as a "gang." The struggles of my "nation" are diminished when you label us as "tribal." Even the use of identical proper names—General Motors, France, Shanghai—does not protect us from an intractable interpretive variety. A name masks differences in the ways we bound the entity and describe its elements and environment. Are GM's bankers part of the firm, or are they assigned to an external environment? Are "migratory workers" part of the French nation? Are political exiles part of a Chinese city? We tell competing stories grounded in one or another of these alternative representations, and we then live within those stories in a way that invests them with reality. Even when we agree on a policy or an action within a story, we cannot lightly assume that the objects of our efforts are identical. Your tax proposals and mine may be the same, but are the economies that they overtly address the same? All of this is to say that the intractable plurality of social entities is a predictable implication of my account of stories in chapter 6. It is similarly linked to the notion of the diversity of social times. In order to form a social entity (or, indeed, a person) in our minds, we must first collect and then integrate a stream of historical observations and future possibilities into an image of a current structure. China exists in the here and now because we imagine that it has been in the past and will persist into the future. When we freeze the flux of events in this way, we carry the design of an artificial present into our conception of an entity and its environment. Only in that moment is it possible to connect intentions, resources, constraints, action, feedback, and response to create an abiding social unit that stretches across time. The entity of our minds incorporates within it the often contested histories of the past and the future that allow us to live in the present.

Happily, we are not required to argue repeatedly over the structure of every social entity any more than we are bound to challenge the meaning of every "now" in ordinary speech. Our worlds are populated by units to which we attach names, practices, and values as expressions of settled conventions that both sustain and survive ambiguity and conflict. How do those conventions work? How do people manage to talk with another about these units without repeatedly coming to screeching (or screaming) halts, staring blankly at one another? Those questions are the subject of the following account of a civic conversation.

In the period 1980–1982, hundreds of Philadelphians were engaged in a project—called Philadelphia: Past, Present and Future—that encouraged discussion of policy issues in virtually every aspect of life within the extended urban region.[1]

As they talked about particular issues, the participants in P:PPF frequently asked themselves and others these questions: "What would be good for Philadelphia?" "What can Philadelphia do?" "What can be done with Philadelphia?" "What can be done in Philadelphia?" Philadelphia, as it appeared in those questions, was variously an object of strategy ("good for"), a strategist ("can do"), an instrument of strategy ("done with"), and an arena for action ("done in"). The city that appeared in those four roles was rarely the same social entity. The Philadelphia polity as a strategist might, for example, use the instrument of Philadelphia as a spatial order in order to benefit the city defined as a set of persons—the same word, but not the same referent.

Philadelphia did not, of course, always appear in all four roles. Some speakers treated the city only as an object, others only as an instrument or a strategist. Action in the city need not be directed to Philadelphia as its object, nor need it imply that the city is either an instrument or a strategist.

Some people carefully limited their use of the term "Philadelphia" so that it always referred to a social entity within the political boundaries of the central city of the region. Others varied their usage, shifting readily from city to region to suit their immediate purposes. Some talked of "Philadelphia and its region"; others carefully avoided the possessive pronoun or even dropped the city's name in favor of the less contentious environmental image of "the Delaware Valley." Most of the P:PPF talk, however, focused on the "city" rather than the "region," and I have adopted the convenient device of treating "Philadelphia" and "city" as ambiguous but identical terms. It is well to remember, however, that when speakers talked about labor markets, infrastructure, transportation, communication, and the environment they often pointed to the region as an arena, an instrument, an object, or (less securely) a strategist.

It was difficult to confine meanings narrowly. If only to avoid the risk of accidental self-destruction, strategists must always treat themselves as moral objects; they must always command some instruments if they are to be capable of acting collectively and if they are to sustain the belief that their choices matter. The instrumental repertoire of strategists and the criteria against which they assess moral objects shape their self-definition. They become what they care about and what their capacities allow. Philadelphia could, therefore, never be only a strategist, even when speakers described the welfare of the nation as the object of local action or focused on taxes, subsidies, and regulations as the instruments of policy rather than on anything as grand as a "city" or a "region."

Meanings also converged when discussion focused on the city as instrument, object, or arena. For example, when debate turned to desegregation or to equality of opportunity, Philadelphia often appeared as an instrument of the broadest social goals and as a moral object testing the commitment of the nation to justice. Thinking of the city as an instrument or an object belies the noisy agency that radiated through P:PPF. Philadelphia as a spatial envelope was barely interesting until it was transformed into a *place* by investing it with meaning as a moral object, filling it with memories and anticipations, and populating it with the human interactions of strategists.

The line that distinguished "city" and "region" also drew meanings to it, encouraging convergence. If the region was a moral object but was incapable of acting as a strategist, wasn't that a signal that something was wrong? Shouldn't moral objects be empowered to act in their own behalf? If the region (or a resource system such as the watershed of the Delaware River) was an instrument but no one cared about it as an object, didn't that similarly signal the need for a new set of moral accounts?

The People of Philadelphia

Many of the participants in P:PPF overwhelmed these difficult distinctions and contingent relationships by repeatedly evoking the image of two groups of stakeholders who (somewhat uneasily) combined to form "the people of Philadelphia" and to define the city. "Stakeholders" was a fashionable term in the early 1980s, particularly in circles interested in the links between public and corporate strategic planning. Successful planning or negotiations—so the argument went—had to engage all the persons whose fortunes (or "stakes") were affected by collective choices, even if they did not formally belong to the planning organization, were not initially well organized enough to claim a place at the bargaining table, or (like future generations) could only be represented by a trustee. This fashionable usage echoed an older tradition that allowed individuals and polities to alter settled social relations or environmental conditions only with the approval of those who were harmed by the change or, in a slightly different version, who had received fair compensation for the harm they had suffered.

One group of stakeholders was composed of all the "residents" of the city. A stake defined by the simple fact of political residence encourages the counting and aggregation of individuals rather than stakes: so many residents want X, so many want Y. "Stakeholder," in contrast, signaled a variety of relationships. Downstream water users, Canadian investors in a Center City hotel, suburban commuters, temporary renters, long-term homeowners, and the University of Pennsylvania were all stakeholders in Philadelphia. However, some stakes were larger than others, and some stakeholders were narrowly at risk whereas some were broadly vulnerable across many domains.

The difference in the ways that residents and stakeholders were counted made the "people of Philadelphia" an incommensurable combination of individuals and relationships. As potential voters, current residents of Philadelphia owned the symbols of local democratic governance. External stakeholders were, however, also often residents of Pennsylvania or the United States and citizens of polities capable of legitimately shaping the future of the city. Quite apart from voting, the claims of both resident and nonresident stakeholders were articulated throughout the processes of governance and were particularly sustained by courts that attended to "due process" and "compensation." Differences in form—so many voters against so many diverse stakeholders, some of whom could vote and some of whom could not—were resolved every day in the political practices of overlapping communities. The rules of aggregation were, however, certainly not those of the census enumerator.

The symbolic construction of "the people" of Philadelphia was a significant political practice rather than a "mere" conversational practice. In a city that was losing jobs and residents, a good deal of the talk of the project centered on the claims of current and prospective persons: Should the economic development program promote the retention and expansion of current firms, or should it attempt to promote new investment by new investors in new industries? Should employment opportunities and educational resources be targeted at current residents or used to lure newcomers? Should social service and housing programs be used to discourage the in-migration of poor people and, indeed, encourage their dispersion outside the city limits? Each of the many conflicting answers to these questions implied a set of accounts, a history, and an array of institutions and communities. If, for example, it is not ethically acceptable to make the city better by encouraging the poor to leave, then exiles must remain part of the unit no matter where they live. That issue was usually articulated in rejecting the idea that gentrification supported by subtle tax policies or by explicitly coercive demolition and reconstruction improved neighborhoods by forcing poor people to go elsewhere. The exiles, many speakers insisted, would have to stay on the books rather than disappear in the obscurity of other neighborhoods. If that was a morally commanding accounting convention inside the city, it certainly applied to inter-jurisdictional moves; if it applied to residents, it should also sensibly cover stakeholders (including nonresidents) whose investment was diminished or displaced by the explicit policies or the tacit neglect of the polity.

How would the distinction between voluntary and involuntary migrants be established? If we follow the taint of coercive public policies into the web of individual decisions, no choice is entirely free. Even within the most generous liberal polities, the protocols for compensating displaced residents and stakeholders cover only a modest portion of the most direct "takings." If, however, only forced deportation at the end of a bulldozer and egregious pollution counts and all those coercive cases are covered by fair compensation, then in the ordinary circumstances of a liberal polity there are no exiles among either residents or stakeholders. The merchants clustered in the central shopping street of a city or a town are not morally "dispossessed" by public support for a large shopping mall along a highway, and my children are not "exiled" if current zoning virtually ensures that they will not be able to afford a home in "our town."

If, however, uncompensated exile is a morally compelling notion, how should we assess the causal chains and tally the accounts? If relocation harms individuals, should their distress detract from the aggregated welfare of the people of the city? If they benefit from relocation, should their success enhance our estimate of the general welfare? Should bads count more than goods in order to impress upon a liberal polity a version of the Hippocratic Oath, as if its first obligation were to avoid doing harm?

Who would keep track of displaced stakeholders and residents to manage these books? In terms rather like the fable in my account of theory building, imagine a group of demographers providing a periodic census of Philadelphia exiles scattered around the world and merging them into a "state of the city" report on the ancestral homeland (and, presumably, on all the tribes and their homelands). Would the taint of the past wrong ever be extinguished as long as the exiles were in diaspora or as long as they identified themselves as Philadelphians? (Should, indeed, the accounts be preserved to rouse the exiles even if they had forgotten their homeland?) For whom would the scattered tribe appear as a moral object? Could the exiled residents and stakeholders ever be organized to act as a strategist speaking in their own behalf?

Set within the framework of the American federal system, these are fanciful or even foolish questions. Around the world, however, they have a more compelling meaning. Jews and Palestinians speak of a diaspora and an accounting in precisely the terms I have employed. The playful image of demographers at work with a moral arithmetic resonates with serious memories of the partition of the Indian subcontinent, the displacement of peoples in Africa, the travails of the "overseas Chinese" along the Pacific Rim, and the demi-world of many migrant workers. Even within Canada, the United States, and Mexico, they describe the claims of "native" peoples and their "nations" for an accounting that is not articulated within the ordinary spatial divisions.

All of which is to say that what seemed so simple and so tangible in P:PPF—as if we could certainly point our finger at the residents and stakeholders of Philadelphia—was difficult, contested, and, ultimately, dependent on the norms of overlapping polities.

The definition of Philadelphia was even more difficult, contested, and dependent when potential residents and stakeholders were represented in the artificial present of P:PPF—i.e., when current residents sought to enhance the attractiveness of the city to investors, organizational and individual migrants, and (above all) to their own children and grandchildren.

Future residents and stakeholders are, of course, always an ill-defined, emergent group whose transformation into actual residents and stakeholders with names, faces, and preferences is strongly influenced by the actions of the city itself. If Philadelphia attempts to send its garbage and wastes far beyond its borders, it creates (or at least mobilizes) external stakeholders; if it cleans and recycles within its own boundaries, the potential group is never realized. Similarly (in a more optimistic vein) with investors and migrants.

The future residents and stakeholders would be even more difficult to organize as strategists than the scattered Philadelphia tribe. Suppose, however, that their imaginary bodies could breath deeply enough to select trustees for their varied interests. Who should they select?

The preferences—let alone the interests—of the potential residents cannot be precisely measured, since their identities cannot be specified well: indeed, some (individuals and firms) are not yet born. Whoever they are, however, they must share a common concern that the city (as arena) be open to them: as residents, they will require appropriate housing, environmental amenities, and the ability to sustain themselves economically; as stakeholders, they will require institutions that will allow them to create an interest and protect it.

An arena's being open to me does not, of course, require that the arena be open to you. Indeed, it may preclude it! Potential residents and stakeholders (in this elaborate hypothetical politics) should seek trustees who will guard the door and the arena, allowing them to pass into a congenial setting but blocking the way to unwanted others. The more uncertain the specters are of their emergent identities and interests, the greater the catholicity they should seek in the trustees. If I want to manufacture a particular commodity, my designs on the future site are specific. If I know only that I am eager for good business opportunities, I will ask only for a generically friendly climate for new enterprises.

The current residents and stakeholders in Philadelphia are, of course, also potential residents of Philadelphia Future and of a great array of other jurisdictions. Looking outside their current city of residence to cities in general, they are appropriately eager to ensure that worlds are open to them, though their image of what that requires may be quite vague. When, however, their imagination is provoked by a proposal in Philadelphia—"widen this street," "increase that tax," or "close that school"—their future takes on a grain and a grounded bias that it would lack anywhere else in the world.

Paradoxically, the potential Philadelphians who might anticipate depending on current residents and stakeholders to ensure the future should be wary of trusting them: they know too much, want too much, and are too readily engaged by their own internal conflicts and cooperative bargains to serve outsiders faithfully.

In an expansive moment, the paradox would be irrelevant: the city would be able to act as a club coopting the residents and stakeholders it desired. (This is the spirit of suburban growth management and of the constitution of cooperative apartment houses and homeowners' associations.) For Philadelphia in the early 1980s (and the late 1990s), however, that image was both impossible to sustain and impossible to abandon entirely. It flourished in a pervasive notion that neighbors could or should be able to control their immediate social environments. For the city as a whole, however, the world of exclusive municipal clubs was part of a hostile regional environment in which the city was not competing very successfully.

The notion that the complexities of defining Philadelphia could be simplified by looking at "the people" and by testing policies and potential futures against their preferences and their interests ran deeply through P:PPF discussions. Indeed, it is at the core of the democratic component of all liberal polities. It was, however, remarkably difficult to specify the names and purposes of the peoples of Philadelphia—to describe who spoke for whom, who was an appropriate trustee, and who could be held to account for a false representation of the population. No one, of course, really tried to employ "the people" in these ways. The people were evoked as a moral object and as a strategist; however, when the conceptual difficulties of the construct emerged in debates over development policy, other terms entered into the conversation to avoid the conflict between present and future Philadelphians.

Economy, Community, and Polity

Three institutional images were commonly used in P:PPF discussions to define the city: *economy, community,* and *polity.* The three institutional terms framed a public order in which arguments could be articulated and in which speakers could subtly shift attention from one set of relationships to another. They were not three faces of the same underlying entity; rather, they were three distinctive and often conflicting symbolic constructs that, nevertheless, reinforced one another.

"Economy" often appeared to be the most influential and (where tough-minded talk was valued) the most practical of the three institutional definitions. The verbal construct was reinforced by aerial images of transportation networks spread across a vast region and of the ground-level experience of daily commuting, so that the regional economy seemed almost palpable. It was easy to fall into representing the agglomeration in the valley of the Delaware River as if it were a single firm in which the fates of all the residents and stakeholders were jointly engaged. Regional accounts could measure the well-being of the economy as a moral object. Individuals and groups who worked to increase production and profits became the synecdoche of the entire web of economic relations; when they spoke, they gave voice to the region as an economy.

Public orders are interesting and important because of the way they accommodate arguments and contain challenges. We can always create a set of regional economic accounts by laying an arbitrary spatial grid over an open system, assigning a name to each cell, and attributing income and productive activities to them one at a time. Such arbitrary cells cannot, however, serve as moral objects, nor are they likely to be compelling strategists or instruments: they are porous spatial envelopes in which propinquity is of very limited importance. It hardly pays to argue about the future of each cell.

The image of Philadelphia as an economy used repeatedly in P:PPF discussions contained the compelling but insidious suspicion that the city or region was just such an arbitrary cell: so open to external influences that it could not control its own fate or even usefully measure its collective well-being. Philadelphia had to be constructed as an economy in order to sustain its competence as a community in which propinquity and common tasks created mutual obligations and expectations—as a polity in which citizens were minimally justified in taxing the economy and, more broadly, were capable over time of influencing if not fully controlling it.

However, the public order that connected the three images was not tightly integrated and could be employed only by shifting rapidly across referents. The economic image was characteristically applied to the region, not to the city. The region was, however, not a formal polity, and it was rarely described as a community. This asymmetry generated a repeated plea for regional comity ("We are all in the same boat") and for increased cooperation between political jurisdictions. The prosthetic appeal revealed, however, that the public order called "Philadelphia" was incomplete or flawed.

The breaks in the order were also apparent in discussions that began with community rather than economy. From the outset, the designers of P:PPF were eager to elicit the cooperation of "community leaders." We used that term in two conventional ways. It designated, first, a group whose members, although they lived across the region, directed the major economic, cultural, and philanthropic organizations of the core city. These (mostly) men and (a few) women were commonly described as leaders of the "Philadelphia community."

The community called "Philadelphia" that they led was defined initially by widely shared status aspirations: a great many people, we assumed, wanted to be CEO of a major corporation, a partner in a large law firm, president of the United Way, or director of the orchestra. The set of persons who now filled those high-status roles *were the Philadelphia community*. Within that community there were leaders, distinguished by the personal respect they commanded and by their sustained attention to inter-organizational networks, rather than by their particular institutional offices or their personal wealth. That elite community was virtually invisible to most of the people of Philadelphia. Nonetheless, more than a few P:PPF hours were spent worrying about its structure and its performance: Was it recruiting new members from distant suburbs? Were senior managers in the

Philadelphia branch offices of major firms captured by its philanthropic discipline? Would the community concert its economic resources and political influence to reform public education or to reorganize the port or the regional transit authority?

We also distinguished a second and quite different group of "community leaders." They had risen to distinction in the world of neighborhood, racial, labor, ethnic, and religious associations, principally in the core city. Like the elites, they were loosely bound together by networks and coalitions of various sorts and were "led" by individuals whose judgment they trusted and who had invested in building bridges between them. We would never have suggested, however, that the community was composed of the eligible association leaders. The aspirations and the self-images of these leaders were more expansive than those of the elite. This group spoke for "the community" as an emergent necessity that expressed the common predicament of the entire people of the city and the moral imperative of "brotherly love."

That expansive populist image of "the community" played an important role in the talk of the project: indeed, it was probably the most important meaning assigned to "Philadelphia" in the evocation of an abiding entity that was "past, present, and future." The image was, nevertheless, fragmented and contested. The conception of membership in residential or self-consciously "minority" associations depended on the articulation of boundaries, exclusion, and intimacy and on the specificity of obligations and loyalties.

Though it was often described as a "city of neighborhoods," no one imagined that Philadelphia was itself a neighborhood. It was, perhaps, an "alliance," bringing together residential and non-territorial associations. A great many civic rituals evoked a shared regional identity in which distinctive communions were provided a stage upon which they could be acknowledged and merged into a larger cast: festivals on the parkway that connects City Hall to the Art Museum on Fairmount and along the newly refurbished esplanade on the banks of the Delaware River, sports events at the complex of athletic temples in South Philadelphia, the Flower Show marking the beginning of spring and the Penn Relays its full blossoming, the Mummers' Parade along Broad Street on New Year's Day. The rituals celebrated the seasons, confirmed the bonds of camaraderie with food and music, and engaged Philadelphia in the wonders of common loyalties and competitive games against other cities.

In a similar and complementary way, newspapers, radio, and television repeatedly told Philadelphians that they shared the primal identification of the same weather, bound together by their vulnerability to calamity and sustained by acts of mutual compassion. Television in particular provided a set of shared fictions that were integrated into conversations across the region.

The participants in P:PPF, however, rarely spoke about civic rituals, and if they had they probably would have dismissed them as distracting circuses. The mass media were often discussed, usually to inveigh against their flaws and their detachment. Philadelphia as an alliance of neighborhoods was not constituted by waves at Veterans' Stadium, by tales of fires and snowstorms on the evening news, or by coffee-break talk about television heroes and heroines.

But a conversation focused on housing, transportation, education, crime, and the like left little room for a Philadelphia community that was distinct from the polity and its institutional processes—bureaucracies, legislatures, voting, taxation, citizenship, Law, police, prisons, courts, politicians, competition, conflict. An uneasy accommodation between communal and political images ran through P:PPF. Its most obvious forms were the frequently expressed suspicion of government, the evocation of "community people," and the experience of working with "community people" as the ultimate source of a consensual moral authority. "Community" as a populist faith sustained pleas for heroic transcendence of the ways we ordinarily conduct our lives. Appropriately empowered, the communities of civil society promised to unfreeze institutional forms and to permit the expression of passions that could not be contained by the ordinary rhetoric of urban politics.

Like all such faiths, community as a populist faith was a loose rhetorical cannon. It was only partially controlled by confining talk of community to neighborhood associations working largely outside the formal polity to create systems of mutual support, affiliation, and obligation: building houses, providing job training, patrolling the streets, tutoring schoolchildren. It was, however, impossible to talk for very long about action in the small without defining a moral perspective on the city as a whole. The need for such a perspective became more compelling and the conception of a large community more problematic when neighborhood groups asked for governmental support or were created in response to public programs. They were then implicated in the invidious political processes that targeted one area rather than another and struggled with the balance between the welfare of "the neighborhoods" and of the city "as a whole."

For some participants in P:PPF discussions, the political image of the city as a corporation in a competitive market was enormously compelling. That image provided both a discipline and an excuse that allowed decent folks to make difficult decisions. For other participants, however, it was a cloak for narrow business interests and for a flow of dollars to Center City rather than to the neighborhoods where "the people" lived.

The responses to the corporate image sustained one another. The image required cold-hearted "public servants" and warm-hearted "communal leaders." (Polity is cold, community is hot. Polity is "system," community is "life.") The polar positions in that dialectic are, however, unstable. Mayors find it difficult to be cold and to leave compassion to community advocates.[2] They cannot resist a warm rhetoric they cannot fulfill. The community advocates find it difficult to accept the city government's stylized incompetence. They press their public counterparts to share their concerns, their modes of speech, and their construction of the relationship between community and polity.

Forms of Reconciliation

Social entities, like social time, are symbolically constructed within stylized communal myths. Our constructs simultaneously allow us to articulate our differences and to understand one another well enough to engage in collective activities. Arguments proceed and contestants struggle within public orders because the contesting images overlap and re-create one another over and over again. The complementary relationship between alternative conceptions of Philadelphia depended on the ability and willingness of individuals to speak ambiguously and to avoid tightly disciplined choices between alternative cities of the mind.

I would, however, misrepresent the P:PPF discussions if I were to leave the impression that everyone appreciatively embraced the notion that

Philadelphia was a symbolic construct or the idea that the variety of city images might be irreducible and essentially contested. It would, indeed, have been very strange if these densely linked city definitions had entered into public debate without engendering a way of talking that reconciled them so that there was only an appearance of conflict. The most common tactic of reconciliation justified switching from one definition to another as peculiarly appropriate. Cities, it was often said, could be understood only from an "inter-disciplinary" perspective. Each of the symbolic constructions conveyed a part of the essential truth about "Philadelphia." This eclecticism provided a way of asserting the existence of an entity whose dimensions could not be directly observed but which was nevertheless "real." The alternative definitions were points of view that could only be synthesized in the mind of a God-like observer who viewed the city simultaneously from every perspective. What appeared overtly as a genial acceptance of diversity and ambiguity was, instead, a legitimization of the moral claims of the detached observer who could see the whole behind the symbols. As one might expect, that version of the idea of a consensual social knowledge was troubling only in the rare moments when someone sitting at a P:PPF table presumed to speak with the voice of God.

10

Plans

Planning and Knowing

Human beings cultivate an amazing array of ways of choosing between alternatives so as to construct the future. They visit priests who read entrails, put themselves in the hands of Chance, seek buyers in the market, and craft complex schemes requiring mountains of blueprints. In some settings they rely on hierarchies to "command and control" the flow of alternatives; in others they rely on egalitarian consensus and improvisation. Sometimes they coerce assent with machine guns; sometimes they reject any choice that is influenced by even a hint of physical threat.

Planning practitioners and theorists are often reluctant to describe all these diverse practices as "planning." In contrast, I am suspicious of restrictive definitions of planning as peculiarly scientific, rational, self-conscious, or future-oriented. We know enough about the influence of informal processes in organizations, about tacit knowledge, and about folk wisdom to be wary of deliberately blinding ourselves to communal crafts that do not satisfy the rituals of professionals.

I confess, however, that, despite my catholicity, I am especially fascinated by the public plans created by professionals–by images of how a site, a program, or an organization will appear at a future time if some specified set of actors follow a prescribed series of steps. I am intrigued by two qualities in these histories of the future. The first is that they deal entirely in a world without facts and hence without the discipline that shapes the historian's construction of the past. The more elaborate and innovative the fiction or the closer it comes to the border between the artificial present and the future, the harder it becomes to assess the workings of its places and practices (Little wonder that the familiar exerts such a powerful gravitational attraction.) The second attribute is the complement of the first. Some significant set of readers must believe in the necessity or the wisdom of the history of the future in order to endow its authors or promoters with the capacity to follow the appropriate series of controlling steps.

The ways in which plans mobilize publics are, however, quite varied. Some plans will be realized if only a small group is persuaded; others require very broad consent. Some are persuasive on first reading; others are acquired tastes. Some are persuasive only when they are implemented; others ("great in theory but terrible in practice") are persuasive only until they are realized.

The qualities of a plan that elicit the commitment of its readers to its image of the future and its controlling steps often have very little to do with the cogency of its instrumental calculations or with the rhetorical skills of its authors. Schemes are adopted in the face of the likelihood of failure because they fit an organizational culture or satisfy the claims of envy, and authors are trusted or distrusted not because of what they have said but because of who they are and how they are likely to respond to the anticipated flow of unanticipated difficulties. I tend to believe plans that explicate the ways in which a scheme may be reshaped over time, the uncertainties attached to it, and the modes of failure. Others believe that those pessimistic qualities erode the confidence of readers. Plans, in their view, should be optimistic, surefooted, simple, legible, and (paradoxically) comfortably ambiguous. They should leave room for development but no room for failure.

The pluralism of a field of open moral communities resists the dream of a consensual social knowledge and forces us to resolve competing truth claims with limited and often ironic agreements. Those agreements are imported into plans and play an important role in validating instrumental judgments. Plans are not, however, truth claims. What has not yet happened cannot be observed or analyzed. Rather than resting on knowledge, the formal plans that intrigue me seek to bend the world and its contentious interpreters to a text. The plans work by focusing attention, shaping constraints and opportunities, parceling out incentives, ordering sequential actions, learning from surprises, and correcting unwelcome failures. In their strongest guise, plans create "imaginary facts" that are so compelling that they erase memories of what was or what might have been. The authoritative plan is not so much "true" as it is necessary. Once realized, the new places and practices appear as "natural" features of everyday life—as "real facts" that can be altered only at great cost.

Writers of plans struggle to create imaginary facts and to order them. Once a plan has been launched into the world, however, the writers give up control of the text to readers who shape a political world in which claims are tested. Even in command economies, the writers of ambitious five-year plans are vulnerable to readers' strategic interpretations and tactical responses. In liberal polities, readers expect to possess plans by spinning a rich web of meanings and associations around them.

Reading Plans

In the spring of 1988, the Philadelphia City Planning Commission issued a document titled The Plan for Center City. Even before the formal publication date, I started to sketch in my mind a scheme to help residents of the region read the text. That intention was strengthened when I actually saw the document. It was 176 pages long, handsomely produced, and richly conceived in the urban design tradition, synthesizing policy arguments, histories, and graphic images of three-dimensional space. I easily recognized the Plan as a literary text that might be illuminated by the craft of critical reading.

I failed to implement that scheme, so I can report on neither its successes nor its failures. This account deals only with the ways in which I thought the residents of Philadelphia should read the new text.

I started, simply enough, by asking myself how I read plans. Later I realized that I was posing a question to an introspective reader who was implicated in the Plan. I knew that I would walk those Center City streets and share in either the triumphs or the failures of the proposed schemes. "Would I read in quite the same way," I wondered, 'if the plan were old or the city far away?"[1]

From the first, I called my scheme "Reading Plans." Even before I had actually seen the text of the Plan, my title evoked a set of insidious social stereotypes and secrets cloaked in irony. Talk of helping people "read plans," my critics insisted, was infantilizing. Worse, it smacked of an imperious class attitude that might be barely acceptable in a high school English class or a literacy program for adults. Outside those instructional settings, it grated against ordinary democratic sensibilities. Neighborhood associations might need help in getting a plan they wanted or in writing a plan that would satisfy the rhetorical demands of professional planners and lawyers. They would have no trouble, however, "reading" the plan in front of them, though they might be well served by a program helping them to "interpret" it. If reading and understanding the "plain sense" of a text is difficult, that is a sign that the writing is flawed, these critics argued. Better to devote my attention to the writers than to the readers.

I assumed, however, that there is no reading without interpretation; no "plain sense" that requires only that the reader pay attention, decode accurately, and "get the message straight." I persisted in my original title because I wanted to emphasize a practice of reading as interpretation that might be shared by those who easily decode the symbols on a page and those who stumble badly as they pronounce the words, by those who easily follow complex syntactical arrangements and those who often lose their way in the branches of dependent clauses and semicolons, and by those who have mastered the lexicon of planning and those who regard a professional document as a minefield of unfamiliar terms.

I was affirmed in my choice of a project title by jocular chiding: I was welcome, friends said, to spend time encouraging people to read the Plan, but I was clearly swimming upstream: "No one would read the Plan!" ("I have enough trouble," one laughed, "getting my colleagues and staff to read memoranda.") The Plan was published with a set of videotapes that featured a narration based on the text and interviews explaining its meaning. The executive director of the planning commission described and defended the Plan before scores of groups. As far as I could tell, however, the elaborate effort to spread the word orally did not lead into the text but substituted for it.

Of course, everyone knew that some people would read the Plan. My friendly critics assumed from the outset that neighborhood activists, developers, and developers' lawyers would closely check at least those portions of the document that related to their areas or projects. Within a few weeks of publication, it was obvious that these expectations were correct. New requests for project approvals were justified as conforming to the prescriptions of the text.

The insistence that "no one reads" also ignored, of course, the thousands of people who must have at least scanned both the substantial newspaper accounts of the Plan the day after it was published and the editorial comments and letters in the week that followed. The joking betrayed a characteristic reluctance to invest much importance in newspaper reading despite the aggressive effort to elicit press coverage. The newspaper accounts were inevitably ephemeral. (What is as old as yesterday's news?) Even in their fullest versions, the stories and summaries were embedded in a barrage of competing messages that could not help but distract readers.

As they joked, the planners described a serious view of reading and writing as the practice of insiders. Only people with very special interests would engage the text over which the professionals had labored so long. Creating a document such as The Plan for Center City might simultaneously serve many different purposes. It could be designed either to legitimize a planning process or to protect it by obscuring its inner dynamics and dilemmas, and either to mobilize a dominant coalition with a "vision" or to immobilize opponents by offering them the promise of (perhaps illusory) future rewards. Whatever the generative purposes, it was a mistake to assume in advance that the authors of a plan expect or want a substantial group of readers to read their text with care.

Indeed, several canny professionals who read an early draft of this essay wondered at my failure to understand that people don't read because, after all, plans are not intended to be read. How does this perception affect the authors of plans? How are they affected by the knowledge that their handiwork will be read in bits and piece and in arenas where men and women fight to win, rather than in forums where they try to understand? I can't answer that complex question with great confidence. Broadly, however, I assume that planners as writers are guided by their expectations about who will read and by the settings and modes of reading. If "no one" will read so as to grasp the "whole," good sense calls for a defensive prose that is careful in its details but obscure in its framing assumptions and strategic choices and that avoids signaling uncertainty or warning of future hazards. A plan should be designed so that it can be decomposed and affirmed section by section without forcing assent to the whole.

Readers and writers interact. A text written to be read in parts encourages readers to skip the generalities and to focus on relevant details. The reader, in effect, is impressed into the model of citizenship assumed by a writer who believes that the whole is less than the sum of its parts.

Authors and Readers

Planners may, of course, protest with good reason that it is they who have been forced into the model of citizenship in the minds of the readers. The relation between readers and writers, I readily admit, is embedded in the dynamics of political communities. Citizens who do not read cannot command the attention of planners as writers. (The fervent support or opposition of the nonreaders may, of course, attract a great deal of attention no matter their literary practices.) That is why it is so difficult for either party to alter the dance of readers and writers unilaterally and suddenly.

There is, however, some latitude for step-by-step alterations in reading and writing behavior, allowing readers to grapple with defensive plans that were barely meant to be read outside small and intensely interested circles and allowing planners as writers to encourage reading without dramatically challenging conceptions of what should not be said in print. I began to explore this latitude and the large question of the ability of plans to encourage consensual agreements with a simple but powerful assumption in mind. Everyone, I thought, should read plans in the same ways that I read them. (It followed, intriguingly, that planners as writers should compose their texts to encourage reading in my style.) I was—and still am—alarmed by the imperiousness of that assumption and my unanticipated turn to toolmaking. The sting is somewhat reduced, however, by the recognition that I am not entirely sure how I read. My introspection is much tutored, and I may exaggerate the coherence of my reading practice in order to conform to the normative guidelines proposed by literary theorists and teachers of rhetoric. With that disclaimer, let me try to describe my reading modes and their implication.

When I read a plan, I start with the text before me and the world of readers and writers it creates. Within that world, I identify and locate myself. Starting with the text is neither a simple nor an uncontroversial beginning.

Everyone who has dealt with complex plans will recognize, I suspect, a common tendency to put the text to the side: "What does this really mean?" "How will the scheme really be implemented?" "Are the important actors really committed?" Only when these contextual secrets have been revealed in face-to-face speech may it be worth attending to words on a page. That assumption and the practices it engenders are, of course, part of that frozen dance in which readers and writers are locked. Reading texts seriously is the only way to unfreeze the dance.

Starting with the text, I suspend my ordinary knowledge that men and women of flesh and blood created the words, figures, and pictures on the page. I shift to the sometimes startling convention that the text constructs both a real and an ideal author. The real author constructed by a work of new fiction may be a name, a photograph, and a brief description of a life in progress. Works of nonfiction, in contrast, often begin with a preface that seeks to establish that the author is the sort of person who is touched by the love of a spouse, grateful for favors and advice, or too tired ever to consider another bout of tedious number crunching. As a reader, I am grateful for these little hints of humanity. They allow me to believe that reading and writing are continuous and related acts; that I too may create texts. The creation of real authors in public plans has a similar impact on me. The image of the author tells me whether the plan is open or closed to further change, whether implementation is likely or unlikely, whether the text is to be trusted, and who may be held accountable for arguments and rhetorical strategies. When a text doesn't describe its author or its authorial process, I am mystified; I am forced to invent clues in order to orient myself within the polity.

The Plan for Center City illustrates one moderate form of mystification. At the bottom of the attractive cover appear the words "Philadelphia City Planning Commission." The same attribution of responsibility for the text does not appear on the title page. Instead, on the back of that page (where one might expect copyright and bibliographic information) is a list of the names of the members of the commission, its executive director, and her deputy. The mayor's name appears at the top of the page, much as it would be exhibited on a billboard in front of a construction site. Should I assume that the mayor is the responsible author, or is he the primary audience to whom the text is addressed?

The prologue does not address that issue directly. It describes an authorial process in which the commission moved from community views and consultant-gathered "facts" to a plan:

In January 1985, the Philadelphia City Planning Commission began work on a new plan for Center City. The process started in community meetings in every neighborhood in Center City and progressed to city-wide forums. Consultants began to gather facts, special tasks forces began to review them. The members and staff of he Planning Commission synthesized the facts, the ideas and the issues in newsletters and speeches and finally, in the autumn of 1985, in working papers. Many hours of feedback later, the commission began to write this plan.

The account is remarkably vague about the duration and flow of activities between the autumn of 1985 and the spring of 1988 when the Plan was published. The back-of-the text credits are fuller, but they are hardly more explicit on the role of the mayor or on the dynamics of the collective authorial mind. As a citizen-reader, I am confused about my own identity when the account of the authorial process doesn't tell me who took initiative, how conflicts were articulated and then resolved, and who if anyone held a veto. At the simplest level, not understanding the author, I couldn't tell whether the Plan was a binding legal prescription or a statement of aspirations.

Real authors are characteristically creatures of title pages, jackets, prefaces, and acknowledgments. Texts also create ideal or fictional authors who appear on every page. These authors don't get tired and don't buck for promotion. Their beings are absorbed in the worlds of their texts. In many works, of fiction and of nonfiction, these ideal authors have magical powers: they enter into the heads of characters to tell us what they are thinking, and they nimbly skip back and forth across time and space. The capacities of the ideal authors of public plans are usually more ordinary, though magic is not entirely excluded. The ideal author of The Plan for Center City, for example, appears in some places as a vision hovering outside the document, generating the plan and setting its terms. In other places, the author is a peculiarly confident narrator who knows that Philadelphians are the sort of people who are guided "forward" by a "vision." Their affection and pride for Center City will be the "one resource:" that will "determine the success of the plan," though the future "will depend on many separate but related factors." The narrator assures us that "growth" can occur without destroying or even compromising what is "unique" and "best" about Center City.

Ideal authors construct ideal readers. The authors of some texts create readers in their own image: they should understand the plan and act on it. The ideal readers of other texts may be designed to endorse a plan without really understanding the text. Whenever I read, I attend closely to these idealizations. When reading a novel, I extend poetic license to the magically empowered ideal author. The authors of plans, however, receive no such gift from me. I wonder with a studied skepticism whether the real author could approximate the knowledge of the ideal, and whether I want to assume the mantle of the ideal reader. Suppose, for example, that I think of urban development as an endless game in which shifting groups of actors play with and against one another. Am I willing to drop this strategic perspective in favor of a heroic idealization in which action in one jurisdiction elicits no significant external response, success is determined by will and commitment, and (if we only think comprehensively) we can overcome ideological dilemmas and trading across precious values? If I refuse to become the ideal reader, will others be less persuadable, or more so? If heroic exhortation meets with universal skepticism or is ignored, how will that affect the real authors and their plan?

Reading the Core

If my engagement with a plan were to stop once I was satisfied that I understood the construction of authors and readers, I would miss a great deal of the meaning of the core of the text. I would miss its images of the world as it was and as it might be, and of the modes of maintenance and repair.

I approach the core in one or more of three complementary ways: as a policy claim, as a response to a design opportunity, and as a story. When I first started reading plans, I tended to match my reading mode to the style of the text. I read analytic arguments and budgets as policy claims, architectural plans as design opportunities, and organizational narratives as stories. Now I have freed myself from the control of the text. Indeed, I cherish the insight gained by reading against the grain of the textual style: treating an urban design plan as a policy analytic argument, reading a budget as a theatrical narrative, or transforming a policy argument into a design opportunity.

The Policy Claim

When I read a plan as a set of policy claims, I start by imposing a conceptual and temporal discipline on it. Some phenomena are designated as inputs, some as system and environment, and others as outputs and valued outcomes. This conceptual frame designed for command and control allows me to interpret a text as a set of instrumental relations between policies and outcomes.

There is, of course, a serious danger of misreading a text by imposing such a tightly disciplined template on it. Some economists reading The Plan for Center City insisted, for example, that it depended critically on a highly specified demand for office space. If that forecast were unwarranted, the Plan as a whole was unjustified. That dismissal was not, however, consonant with the rhetoric of the text. The Plan provides no closely argued projection of flows and stocks in related systems and no decision trees; it offers only an image of vectors of activity and pictures of physical spaces and actors within and about them. It resists summary and testing as a small set of discrete policy claims.

In order to penetrate the Plan's structure, however, it is useful to examine how it is bolstered by a large group of loosely coupled and vaguely specified claims embedded in both pictures and words. Consider, for example, these two sentences:

The Plan envisions a city that combines the best of a dense high-rise American center with the grace, delight and serendipity of a lower-scale European city. The quality of the urban environment must not be compromised as Center City grows and develops.

These sentences are obviously incomplete as a policy claim. They don't tell us what is "best" about a high-rise American center; only that the best is not "grace," "delight," or "serendipity." No evidence is marshaled, no theories are presented, no reason is offered for thinking of the environment in a way that justifies an absolute prohibition on any policy that would reduce its "quality." No experimental design is proposed to distinguish the effects of culture and scale on that quality. The fragmentary form of the argument does not, however, prevent me from reading alternative versions of the missing terms into these sentences, drawing potential meanings from other sections of the Plan or from my own intellectual armory. Emancipated by the ambiguity of the sentences, I do that freely, reading in a concern with juggling employment, consumption, and residential goals and policies that are at times conflicting and that are difficult to balance even though they all seem principally to benefit upper-income groups. In a bold stroke, I rewrite the sentences in my mind:

Some people are worried that, as office employment grows, Center City will be a less attractive place to live, dine, shop, and take pleasure in both the good things of life that are free and those that are very expensive. Trust us! This plan illustrates our ability to balance conflicting goals and to imagine attractive resolutions.

My revision points to the same planning frame as the original but is politically quite different. It locates values in people rather than in the symbols of urban design theory or environmentalism. (Indeed, it gently mocks those symbols by hinting that the pleasures of Center City often come dear.) Both statements plead for trust, the first by promising that one global value ("the quality of the urban environment") will not be compromised in order to achieve other values and the second by asking for a critical assessment of difficult choices.

The Design Opportunity

I do not want to put too much weight on this particular revision or to suggest that I methodically resolve every plan into a long list of unambiguous policy claims. ("Ambiguity," after all, is not a disease and cannot be eradicated.) Long before I reach that point in reading any text, I shift into a second interpretive mode. In order to assess what is important in a plan, who the clients are, and what constitutes a cogent argument, I read a plan as a response to a "design opportunity."

The Plan for Center City describes its provenance in this way:

In 1984, the proposal to construct One Liberty Place, the first building ever to exceed the height of William Penn's statue atop City Hall, prompted questions that previous plans could not answer. What would be the impact of a building taller than the statute? What could we lose? What could we gain? In the year 2000 what would Center City look like? What would it be like? The questions were asked not only in boardrooms and government chambers but in homes and restaurants and on street corners. Philadelphians wanted a vision to guide us forward. It was time for a new plan.

It would be a mistake to read this history as if the decision to violate the informal height limitation were independent of the planning process that responded to it. A highly professionalized planning apparatus in Philadelphia crafted the development pressure into an occasion for pattern planning. It is not difficult to imagine settings in which the same break would have been treated as an opportunity for studied deregulation or for a continuation of a long tradition of ad hoc decision making. (Arguably, the latter is the dominant Philadelphia tradition.) Philadelphia would not or could not have acted that way in the world created by the Plan. In that world, Philadelphians had always "believed in the power of a plan to inspire action and to shape the city's future." In that world, Philadelphians "wanted a vision to guide [them] forward."

A plan first creates design opportunities and then responds to them. As I read, I try to reconstruct the processes of creation and response. Suppose, for example, that a plan proposes a policy that seems both anomalous and wrongheaded. Reconstructing the process that generated the policy, I may, however, recognize it as a fairly struck compromise within a diverse polity. Indeed, I may come to suspect that no other policy was possible within the rules of collective decision making. My reading allows me to understand the policy and limits the terms and forms of my opposition.

Most readings are, of course, not so determinate, and most do not have such compelling practical implications. Poets rarely tell us about their cognitive processes. Planners are likely to be more expansive about parties consulted and interests considered, but synthesis characteristically remains a mysterious art that is beyond explication. Readers of both poems and plans must struggle with the text, digging out design clues, sketching interpretations and ending with conjecture.

Readers who aren't writers may think that the uncertainty surrounding their conjectures is wholly theirs. They may assume that, even though authors may not tell us about the opportunities and dynamics of design, they certainly understand in their own heads how they decided on each element of the text. Writers know better. Planners as writers recognize that even overtly simple design opportunities—e.g., approve or reject a zoning variance or a new bus route, balance maintenance and new construction in the recreation budget—reshape us in strange ways the moment we attend to them. More complex opportunities, such as the preparation of a plan for the center of a city, are great muddy sinks. Values and linkages appear out of nowhere and then are transformed in the process of planning. Each choice creates a circle of clarity and coherence at the cost of uncertainty somewhere outside the light. We run to settle one issue only to create another in an endless chain, appreciating in our maturity that the world cannot be completely fixed and that we live by creating problems.

The process of alternately creating uncertainty and coherence leaves its mark on the language of a plan. Consider this sentence from The Plan for Center City: "How much Center City grows will depend upon its ability to adapt its physical structure, its workforce and its image." There are at least two anomalous linguistic devices in those 20 words. Why, to begin with, does the author seem to make a simple stylistic mistake in the use of 'adapt'? The sentence should read "upon its ability to adapt to [something]." The omission of that something allows the argument to proceed as if the requisite changes were acts of will within Philadelphia's control. There is no external drummer.

Twelve pages later, the same sentence appears in expanded form, with the mistake corrected:

> The economic future of Center City will depend upon its ability to adapt to the needs of a new economy based not on the manufacture and sale of products, but on the generation and exchange of ideas, information and services. Center City will have competition from within and outside the region for the business investments and office users of this new, office-based information and service economy. To compete successfully, to realize its future potential in this economic transformation, Center City must adapt is physical structure, its workforce and its image.

Even here, however, the text turns quickly away from the character of the competitive environment in a confident (though patently problematic) assertion that Center City is the region's "ultimate place of interchange" and its "most efficient and effective economic center." The call to Center City "to realize its full potential" conjures up images of the way we assign rights and obligations to individuals without regard to social structure: everyone is entitled to reach his or her "potential" and bound not to squander it.

My sense that the author is conflicted about the way in which the city's control over its own future should be imagined is strengthened by the second quirk in the original sentence. The text describes Center City as both a strategist and an object of strategy—as if it could act on its own physical structure, workforce, and image to adapt them to competition within and outside the region. Even at first reading, I paused at the sentence, wondering why the author didn't indicate that growth depends on *our* rather than *its* ability or that we were concerned about *our* potential rather than with *its* current workforce. What would be changed, I mused, with the seemingly straightforward and correct assertion that the Philadelphia polity is the relevant strategist to whom the Plan is addressed and that Center City is one of its many strategic objects and instruments?

Again, the language betrays an unresolved and perhaps unresolvable conflict in the design process. The Plan for Center City was part of a (still incomplete) series of plans for each section of Philadelphia. The device of dividing the city spatially for planning purposes is sometimes justified as encouraging local responsibility—neighbors caring for one another and for their shared streets, parks, and schools. And indeed it may encourage such responsibility. At the same time, imagining the city as a collection of neighborhoods presents both local and city-wide decision makers with serious conceptual and normative problems at virtually every corner and in every section. The image is particularly difficult when it is applied to the central business district and its surrounding neighborhoods. In one of the few passages in which the Plan directly addresses conflicting political views, the text asserts that Center City is a fragile citywide resource, a source of jobs rather than a drain on "the neighborhoods." Development in the center, it warns, should not be subject to linkage fees on behalf of low-income housing or job creation in other neighborhoods.

The authors of the Plan cannot, however, shift unambiguously to treating Center City as an object or an instrument rather than a strategist without impugning the conceptual and organizational frame that divides the city into sections and then undertakes to plan them one by one over an extended period. I am bound to accept and to interpret seriously the ambiguity of the text. The major problem the Plan addresses—the reconciliation of the desire simultaneously to increase the attractiveness of Center City to employers and to middle- and upper-income households—may, indeed, be best addressed by encouraging employers, developers, and current residents to believe that they own the area and that they must resolve land-use conflicts with very little intervention from the city's political leadership. If there is no recourse to a superior power, their negotiations may define a frontier along which the best possible deals for all parties may be struck. The text, of course, holds out no such program. Its dominant language is that of control, not that of game theory, conflict, and negotiation. Its core is rich with proposals for physical design interventions presented as encouraging growth and protecting residential amenities. The Plan suggest one major organizational innovation, a downtown management corporation (DMC) "modeled after the management philosophy of private malls and office parks." The DMC would strengthen "management standards" in the "streets, buildings and public spaces" of the commercial areas of Center City. (Indeed, a decade later the DMC is widely thought to have fulfilled those promises and is being copied in other areas of the city.)

Reading the play of language against itself is a tricky business. There are no clear standards to distinguish specious from sound interpretations. If I assume that texts are coherent and ultimately consistent, I can dismiss readings that fail those demanding local and rhetorical tests. If, however, I make no such assumption, I must supply my own standards of interpretive cogency. I certainly can't depend on asking even an easily accessible author what he or she "truly" meant in a particular passage. The completion of the work and the reader's query "What does it mean?" transform an author into a new person who may be an interesting interpreter but not a uniquely privileged one. When the authorial process has wound its way within and across groups over an extended period of time (as in the preparation of The Plan for Center City), I feel on even stronger ground in denying the special authority of an individual participant's interpretation of collective meanings.

Writers may be dismayed by the way in which interpretive authority is given over to readers once a text is published. Even as a reader, I feel adrift until I can set critical standards to discipline my own interpretation. How can I tell, for example, whether I have provided a cogent or a vacuous reading of the failure to specify the something to which Center City must adapt? Pondering a line from *Hamlet,* I may turn for guidance and validation to an interpretive community. Reading a new plan, I create that community—those communities—in my mind even before I have had a chance to share my interpretation with anyone.

The Narrative

The third mode of reading is the one in which I struggle toward those interpretive standards by imagining actors ascribing meanings to a plan and then acting within them. In this mode I read texts as narratives that the author has imposed on the continuous and messy stream of life. As I have already described in chapter 6, stories, unlike life, have beginnings and endings; they are embedded in characters whose relations in a setting are formed into a plot by a script. Even a budget in which the only characters appear as labels in the headings of columns and rows may be illuminated by transforming allocations into stories of relationships (e.g., taxpayers will send in checks in April and janitors will be paid in June; we will support five site visits by regulators this year).

I read two sorts of stories in plans. One sort deals with particular projects or policies and is simply another way of approaching policy claims. The Plan for Center City, for example, suggests that "nothing above ground should count as part of a building's gross floor area." As a policy analyst, I articulate criteria, array anticipated goods and bads stemming from that policy, and compare them against the alternatives. As a storyteller, I start with the recommendation and move forward in time. In such a story, architects, developers, and various users and competitors act within and against the accounting convention over an extended period. Constructing a story around the policy claim allows me to explore alternative assessment criteria within the social setting provided by the story rather than as disembodied standards. In the second and more important kind of kind of story, I assess my own reading of ambiguity and conflict in the process of constructing and responding to design opportunities. These stories begin with the characters and relationships created within a plan. The stage is populated by developers, homeless panhandlers, the mayor, the city council, the press, and the planners—a long list of players, some with major parts and others with only bit roles. These characters receive the text that created them, responding to it and to one another. "Is my reading of the text in all its ambiguity," I ask myself, "consistent with the ways in which the authors would address the players and with the ways in which character would unfold into plot?"

Under the best of circumstances, it would be difficult to read a plan as the beginning of a play and to follow its characters through its coils. For those reading public plans, the circumstances are, however, rarely propitious. Planners as writers do not usually convey a rich sense of character and plot. They tend to adopt a protective rhetoric that rarely sets the stage sincerely. In their texts, publics are never fickle and short-sighted, civic leaders never confused and uncertain, bureaucracies never incompetent or ignorant. If the dramatis personae is disingenuous, I can't rely on it to test the cogency of my reading. I am forced to supply characters and to judge the fitness of my reading within a story that I bring to the text. Paradoxically, partial stories and plaster-saint characters—devices to reduce conflict—multiply private interpretations and enhance both the power and the uncertainty of readers.

Conclusion

The six chapters in part II have dealt with the creation of public orders from the diversity of conflicting claims. The accounts of theories, stories, time, tools, and cities have dealt largely with truth claims. Plans, however, are different. Although inevitably touched by he pluralism of knowledge and the character of the resulting orders, they stand largely on their ability to shape the world into a desired form. That difference shapes the ways of reading. Even readers following protocols quite different from those I have professed ask questions of plans that they would never ask in forming and assessing truth claims: Will the planners command the resources necessary to impress their will upon a world? How will others attempt to frustrate our aspirations? Is that what we really want to do?

The reliance of plans on authority and power does not, however, tame the pluralism of an open field. Both in the plan and in the deed, new places and practices are enveloped in the same variety of ascribed meanings that characterize our social knowledge. In both the plan and the deed, they require the same crafts in fashioning a public order that is partial and ambiguous even when it is set in concrete.

III
Moral Claims

11
MOVE and the Poetics of Redemption

Passion sometimes cracked through the sedate forms of policy analysis and advocacy during the Philadelphia: Past, Present and Future discussions. The moments of high emotion were, however, exceptional. The rhetoric of the participants, shifting from one representation of Philadelphia to another, was rarely strained by intense feelings or ethical imperatives.

This chapter and the one that follows describe events and feelings that could not be so easily contained. I am concerned here with the emotional range and the ethical capacities of the stylized myth of open moral communities rather than with that myth's import for the dream of consensual knowledge or for the construction of public orders.

We commonly observe communities repairing themselves by evoking the contractual myth to renew or revise the bargain that holds them together. Do they (in a comparable though less ordinary way) sometimes redeem and correct themselves by reaching into a deeper and more passionate communion? Do severe breaks in social relations require us to drop our overlapping identities and the rhetoric that supports them in favor of more ecstatic expressive modes? Do deep ethical failures respond only to strong mandates that rearrange an open field so that we can all (at least temporarily) either do what is right or suffer for our sins?

After May 13, 1985

In the early morning of May 13, 1985, officers of the City of Philadelphia attempted to serve arrest warrants on four members of an organization called MOVE living at 6221 Osage Avenue. The day-long effort to force the four to surrender and to permit a search of the house culminated in a decision to drop explosives on the buildings and to allow the resulting fire to spread. At the end of the day, six adults and five children in the building were dead (there were only two known survivors) and 61 adjacent dwellings had been destroyed.

This chapter explores the search for redemption after May 13—a search that simultaneously was contained within and constructed alternative myths of the city as a moral community. There is a bias in my account of this search. The events of May 13, 1985, as they were remembered and imaginatively reenacted, reached into countless private realms and face-to-face conversations. I have not, however, tried to capture those personal experiences or the processes of redemption within intimate circles. I am interested here in the search for the restoration of a public moral order. Inevitably, I have relied on transcripts of talk within the formal settings of courts, commissions, and election campaigns—on texts designed to be read (or watched) at arm's length rather than engaged immediately in intimate circles. Though I have, I think, seen all the major television documentaries produced about MOVE and listened to a good deal of local talk radio, this account is overwhelmingly a report of redemption on the printed page; of emotions poured into the literary forms and disciplines of written English.[1]

Secular policy analysis and social science rarely deal with themes of evil, violation, tragedy, or expiation.[2] Even heated political debates that reach into the guts of social relations usually are dominated by talk of justice and rights rather than redemption. There cannot, however, be a moral order of substantial range and duration without ways of acknowledging sin and tragedy; without ways of restoring individuals and groups into the fold. If a community cannot imagine that good men and women may act badly or that horrific results may flow from justifiable deeds, then it is trapped by a fragile perfectionism. If it cannot blame itself, confront the possibility that its legitimate structure is diabolic, and assimilate indictment, punishment, and forgiveness into its memory, then it can neither use nor be free of its past. It is hobbled by the unlimited demands of guilt.

Christianity provided a language and a protocol for civic discussions of redemption after May 13. Sin could be forgiven and sinners redeemed within the familiar terms of the dominant religious discourse if the wrongdoers accepted responsibility for their deeds, asked forgiveness from those they had harmed, offered penance, reformed their practice, and sought with love to restore the damage they had caused.

Philadelphia is not, however, a deep Christian community united by a common faith or a canon of sins. No one could hold the parties to the forms of religious redemption. Ramona Africa, the lone adult survivor of the residents of the MOVE house, did not seek forgiveness from those she had harmed; nor, in the days after May 13, did the mayor or other city officials beg her to pardon them. Nearly a year after the bombing of the MOVE house and the devastating fire that followed, Mayor Wilson Goode publicly cried over the deaths while responding to questions during a radio interview. For the most part, however, he sought vindication for his good intentions and sympathy for the emotional scars he promised to wear for the rest of his life. In his 1992 autobiography he asked for forgiveness from MOVE members and their supporters but cast himself as a tragic Christian hero: without malice, accepting formal responsibility, but essentially betrayed by his subordinates: "The MOVE incident was the darkest hour of my Christian experience. . . . I too was a victim of May 13." (Goode and Stevens 1992, p. 201)

The city's Managing Director and its police commissioner resigned without public professions of contrition. The administration of private relief and the implementation of the mayor's promise to rebuild the ruined homes were both quickly tangled in charges of deception, as if bureaucracy and ordinary politics were incompatible with intense or passionate restitution. The promises of reform were clouded by the ambiguity or vapidity of the acknowledgment of error. In the most lucid moments of political debate in the mayoral campaign of 1987 (in which Mayor Goode was reelected), the rival candidates' analyses of evil and tragedy were either trivial or self-serving.

At her criminal trial, Ramona Africa described MOVE as a deep community, a "family" committed to an integrated way of life and to a compelling vision of the Right. She viewed the surrounding society as equally coherent and intentional—a deep but malevolent and immoral "system." Other actors in the MOVE drama sometimes spoke as if they accepted this view of two deep and antagonistic Philadelphia communities, though they reversed Africa's terms. What she saw as clean they viewed as dirty, and vice versa: natural as polluted, life-loving as suicidal, orderly as chaotic.

The more usual image, however, was of a more pluralistic and less intentional social order integrated by what the commission appointed to investigate the events of May 13 described as a combination of "laws, customs and contracts" rather than a nested set of consistent ethical claims or distinctive domains (Philadelphia Special Investigation Commission 1986). Rights often seemed at odds with laws, and laws with customs. Contracts seemed not only plural (in the commission's revealing phrase) but opposing. The rights and obligations of neighbors were not neatly incorporated into those of citizens. Children subverted every order that threatened to exploit their vulnerability or to violate their innocence.

These complex communal images did not sustain either a consensual conception of the virtues or a completely satisfying redemptive path. One was not possible without the other. Moral condemnation without physical punishment did not satisfy the outraged or repair the order that had been breached, because there were so many communions in which sinners could find both solace and justification.

Within a landscape of open moral communities, Philadelphians did, however, search for redemption after May 13. I distinguish three themes in this search: the assertion of communal competence, the construction of a public order of explanation, and the authoritative allocation of blame. These themes overlay the religious framework and dominated it: blame and punishment were more important than forgiveness, and control and accountability limited the domain of love and penitential offerings.

I wrote a fragmentary version of this chapter in the autumn of 1985, and I revised it several times subsequently. At each revision, however, I resisted completing the text, waiting (as I told myself) for the story to be finished. My procrastination violated my own understanding that endings are artifacts of the narrative form. Life is endless: only the tales we manufacture are equipped with conclusions. Certainly, absent authoritative absolution, there would never be a time when redemption sought could definitively and forever be either won or denied.

By the spring of 1990 my (flawed) excuses had largely vanished, and I completed a draft for publication. I thought (mistakenly) that the process of legal blaming was almost concluded. In the spring of 1988 a local grand jury decided that, although city officials were guilty of "morally reprehensible behavior and "incredible incompetence," bringing criminal charges against them would be "cathartic but improper" (Report of the County Investigating Grand Jury of May 16, 1986). Two years later, the U.S. Department of Justice, resisting appeals from several members of the Philadelphia Special Investigation Commission who had been appointed by Mayor Goode, allowed the statute of limitations to expire without charging any officials with federal offenses.

The process of penance was also coming to a close. Although some civil suits remained to be adjudicated, in June of 1990 the city agreed to pay $500,000 to the estate of each of the five children killed on May 13. Their violated innocence—the common ground that united virtually all the interpreters of redemption—had been given a price in the bargaining between those with a proprietary right in the status of the victims and those who might have been judged as violators in an open trial.

Even the stubborn nut at the center of May 13 was softened. In 1978 another MOVE house (this one in nearby Powelton Village) had been assaulted by police. An officer had been killed. Nine MOVE members had been tried in 1980, convicted of third-degree murder, and given long prison terms.[3] The Osage Avenue conflict had been precipitated by MOVE's efforts to influence the mayor and the governor to intervene on behalf of the prisoners. In the two years leading up to the Osage Avenue incident, the mayor had refused, insisting (as he later publicly argued) that guilt or innocence was not his to judge and that he could not interfere under pressure with legitimate judicial processes. By 1989, however, the impossible seemed both feasible and necessary. In December, Managing Director James White announced that he had asked the State Parole Board to release the prisoners. Until they are free, he pleaded, "as a community and as citizens . . . we will never be able to have the peace that we all seek" (*Philadelphia Inquirer,* December 10). Though the mayor would not explicitly endorse release, he accepted White's essential premise: that "there is no way ever to resolve the issue of MOVE until the people in jail are paroled" (*Philadelphia Inquirer,* December 12).

I did not publish the free-standing essay in 1990, though the five-year anniversary of the Osage Avenue encounter might have provided a period to my account. When I returned to the essay in 1994, what once had seemed on the verge of closure was still unfinished. The Powelton Village group had not been paroled, and their case had not been reopened.

Ramona Africa had been released from prison in 1992, but her suit in federal court against the City of Philadelphia and major officials was still pending. The suit was not heard until the spring of 1996. In June of that year, the jury awarded $1.5 million to be divided between Ramona Africa and the estates of two of those who had died in the MOVE house. (Birdie Africa, the other survivor, had already received $1.66 million from the city.) The jury also ordered the police and fire commissioners to pay symbolic fines of $1 a week to each of the plaintiffs for 11 years. The judge dismissed those fines in August, arguing that the officials had not shown "willful misconduct." It was the *city* that had used excessive force; the *city* that was legally accountable for its sins.

There is no great consensual redemptive myth that unites the Philadelphia polity: no Exodus, no Resurrection, no Revolution, no Quest. From the outset of the MOVE encounter, many Philadelphians argued that, ultimately, the courts and only the courts could heal the breach in the moral order. They were wrong. The protracted litigation and the final cash payments did not provide an emotional or a moral conclusion to the drama. The redemption Philadelphians sought after May 13 is finally embedded in the irreducible plurality of public stories about an abstraction—the city— and in the transformation of personal memories into conflicting but, nevertheless, shared traditions. The Law did not suffice.

Communal Competence

The creation of domains of competence is an essential part of the construction of moral communities, and the denial of competence is an essential part of their diminution or destruction. Without competence, communities cannot make credible promises, engender obligations, or sustain expectations and identities. They may be objects in a moral drama, but they are not intentional agents worthy of either praise or blame.

Competence is sometimes conceived as an all-or-nothing quality. Rarely, however, is any community free of external discipline and lord of all it surveys. Within fields of open moral communities, competence is limited by boundary and by circumstance. An open community is able to perform some tasks but not others: It can initiate action within a domain, but it cannot protect itself against external vetoes. It can veto actions, but it cannot initiate them. It can edit texts, but it cannot create them. A community competent to act under ordinary conditions may collapse in a crisis; incompetent under ordinary circumstances, it may discover unrealized capacities within itself in the face of an imminent disaster.

The MOVE encounter threatened the competence of Philadelphia as a polity. That may seem a strange way to tell the story. Most observers would, I suspect, say instead "The encounter exhibited the incompetence of city officials—an incompetence so appalling and so structurally determined that it may be described as a mark of the city's failing rather than that of particular individuals."

My wording—competence threatened rather than exhibited—speaks to events after May 13, not before.

In the federal system of the United States, cities play an important role in managing the relations between individual rights derived from membership in national and state polities and the claims of small social groups (e.g., the occupants of an office building, groups of teenagers in a playground, neighbors surrounding an overtly public street) to control "their" spaces. Over a broad range of cases, conflicts between rights and local claims are dampened and contained by a decentralized and temporizing managerial style. The police don't usually contest local control in what Suttles (1972, 1990) has called "defended communities." Instead, they often welcome and support its predictability and security. In contested spaces they are content to create corridors along which strangers may pass through foreign territory. Asked to intervene in local disputes, city bureaucrats respond warily, apprehensive that they may be overcome by the unwelcome burden of constant mediation.

Some conflicts and some contestants resist management by indirection and avoidance. Over several years, city officials acted as if the differences between MOVE and its neighbors would work themselves out if City Hall did not visibly intrude to magnify local disputes. The city government was, however, a major protagonist rather than a bit player in the Osage Avenue drama. MOVE hoped that its neighbors, simultaneously angered by the loudspeaker blaring from 6221 Osage and persuaded by what they heard, would press the mayor and the governor to reopen the convictions of the members of the "family" imprisoned after the 1978 siege.

At her own trial and in her subsequent suit against city officials, Ramona Africa wrapped MOVE in the mantle of the First Amendment. As she described events, the group had used the classic devices of political protest in a necessarily unsettling but nevertheless legitimate way. It had attempted to shock its audiences into recognizing that familiar assumptions about judicial fairness and the sanctity of a home were unfounded, pressing them to undertake unexpectedly radical actions. Even before the first shot was fired, MOVE's rights had been violated by the massing of military strength to inhibit free speech and political protest.[4]

The neighbors, the mayor (speaking in his own defense), and the Philadelphia Special Investigation Commission articulated a conflicting view: MOVE had violated a sanctuary, shattering the customary and contractual distinction between vulnerable public spaces and protected private spaces. We are all legitimately at risk of being discomfited and even coerced by the varied forms of guerrilla theater in public plazas and business streets. But not at home! May 13, however badly managed, had been a justifiable attempt to preserve a domain of privacy.

After May 13, virtually everyone in Philadelphia indicted the city's failure to grasp the implications of its central role in the drama scripted by MOVE: the city had temporized for too long and then violently imposed its will upon the contested territory. The consensual indictment obscured deep disagreements. The disagreements did not, however, threaten the competence of Philadelphia as a moral community. That threat stemmed, instead, from the possibility that the polity would not be allowed to redeem itself—that the city's evident incompetence before May 13 was so profound that the city could not be trusted to heal the moral breach.

Hard on the heels of the devastation of May 13, Mayor Goode appointed the Special Investigating Commission. The creation of the PSIC was challenged on two grounds, each resting on one of two concepts of "interest" that would have seriously limited the domain of Philadelphia's competence.

The first concept associated disinterest with fairness and objectivity: the PSIC could be trusted only if it were disinterested, and it was tainted by the very fact that it had been appointed by the mayor and by the ties that bound many of its members to the day-to-day business of running civic affairs. Many critics insisted that only a judicial process could be trusted to establish the truth and to assign blame. A polity acting as a moral community must nurture and legitimate networks of "professional citizens" who are engaged in political affairs even though they hold no formal public office. If this political society cannot be trusted because it is interested, and if only judges are treated as dependably fair then the normative public order of the community is wholly defined by coercive law. If, however, all reprehensible public acts must be illegal, then either the domain of the polity is very narrow or the law in a pluralistic settlement must be oppressive, investing tacit, ambiguous, and contested conventions with formal authority.

The second concept treated objectivity as a fantasy: trust must rest on the representation and balancing of interests, not on their suppression. A commission could be trusted only if it included representatives of all stakeholders: Republicans and Democrats, MOVE members and their Osage Avenue neighbors, Philadelphia residents and individuals far from the city who saw themselves as harmed by the MOVE encounter and as therefore entitled to play a role in its resolution. "In our community, among black leadership, we are totally outraged," Representative John Conyers Jr. of Michigan announced on May 19. Conyers proposed a congressional investigation into the constitutional questions raised by "the most violent eviction notice that's ever been given in history" (*Philadelphia Inquirer,* May 20, 1985). Jesse Jackson—whose voice was amplified by his national presidential aspirations—elaborated on the same theme. Only a congressional investigation, Jackson insisted, could prevent police across the country from emulating Philadelphia's response to MOVE. He compared the MOVE encounter to the bloody restoration of public control at the New York State prison at Attica in 1971. Both cases of "excessive force" revealed "a kind of impatience by the executioners and such terrible miscalculation that lends itself to human tragedy" (*Philadelphia Tribune,* June 7, 1985). May 13 demanded a national response because it heightened "fear and anxiety in every community across the country" (*Philadelphia Inquirer,* June 5, 1985)

The polar notions of disinterest and representation established a powerful rhetorical field. Observers of the "political spectacle" are characteristically attuned to the dangers of hidden connections and selfish advantage under the guise of social status and professional citizenship. They expect a vigilant press to reveal a truth that is compelling because it is secret. Anything else seems either naive or self-serving. They similarly insist that those who are harmed by public actions are entitled to be heard in settings that are not at the outset either indifferent to their pain or biased against them. The people of Detroit, alarmed by May 13, would not be served by a Philadelphia arena in which they had no part.

Without directly confronting Jackson or Conyers, the mayor and the PSIC challenged their major assertions. The mayor allowed that anyone was free to investigate the events of May 13, but he defended the independence of the commission he had appointed. It would be impossible, he argued, to choose a distinguished group in which no one had contributed to a campaign. William H. Brown III, the chairman of the group, played on the same theme: "Look around you. Look at the people who are on this commission. You have to make the judgment and the public has to make the judgment, are these the kind of people who are likely to compromise the kinds of standards that they established for themselves through their entire lifetimes? I don't think that they are that kind of people." (*Philadelphia Inquirer*, May 23, 1985)

The commission encouraged the public to think of its processes as exemplary. Over five weeks, more than 144 hours of testimony from 90 witnesses were broadcast live over the local public radio and television stations. Extensive excerpts from the transcript were published in the two metropolitan daily newspapers. "By the time the hearings concluded," the final report claimed, "the public had been presented with all the principal facts known to the Commission."

The fabrication of a factual order was a crucial step in the assertion of communal competence (PSIC 1986, pp. 1–3):

After the staff work and the testimony were concluded the commissioners began "sifting through all the facts, weighing what its members had seen and heard, attempting to resolve the contradictions and discrepancies. . . . Every major relevant question was examined, every key issue explored. Strict standards of fairness and impartiality were followed as the group unanimously agreed on 66 of 68 findings, conclusions and recommendations. On the remaining two conclusions, ten of the 11 Commissioners agreed.

Could any other group—could any community—demand less of itself than fairness? Could any community hope for more agreement in a diverse world?

The report was greeted with approval on almost every side. Suspicions that the PSIC was "fixed" were put aside. "A whitewash is what the critics expected," the *New York Times* noted editorially (March 8, 1986). "A withering denunciation is what the commission has now produced." The report provided the city with a "benchmark" and a "springboard," the *Philadelphia Inquirer* concluded (March 4, 1986). "Here is the mayor's commission rejecting his story, judging him reckless." The commission provided a model for a new politics; a conscience of the community "in a city that in its most desperate hour, could find no conscience to heed."

The commission originally expected to release its final report by Labor Day of 1985, but the final report was not actually released until March of 1986. Though the drama was by no means completed, the challenge to the city's competence had been thwarted. There was no congressional inquiry, and the U.S. Department of Justice decided to monitor local actions rather than to initiate an independent inquiry. (Ultimately, as I have already noted, no federal charges were filed.) Ramona Africa's criminal trial and the grand jury investigation of the behavior of city officials were based in the local courts. For better or for worse, May 13 belonged to Philadelphia.

Understanding and Control

A city that was competent to describe and to interpret what had happened on Osage Avenue ought to be able to restore its damaged moral order. Within myths of deep community, understanding comes when sinners acknowledge their deed, recognizing what they have done in the light of the shared standard. Brethren may pray for themselves and for others, pleading for an illuminating flash of understanding. The stylized image of an open field replaces the metaphor of sudden illumination with an image of detailed negotiations fabricating a public order in a rhetoric dominated by objective facts. The report of the PSIC provides a particularly telling illustration of the uses and forms of that rhetorical style. The group crafted a text designed to achieve internal unanimity and to command broad external assent. Rather than present a narrative of the MOVE encounter, it opened its report with a "chronology," as if the series of discrete events did not require a narrator whose perspective informed the account. The body of the text is composed of 31 "findings," each resting on two or more behavioral observations, causal imputations or normative assessments.

The rhetoric of a chronology and a list of findings focuses attention on the truth of statements as if they could be validated in isolation from one another. There is, however, a content to the chronological form and an interpretive pattern in the overtly independent series of findings. The content and the pattern are particularly apparent in how the commission represented MOVE, ordinary urban governance, and the relation between innocence and racial victimization.

The Nature of MOVE

The commission's first conclusion was that "by the early 1980s MOVE had evolved into an authoritarian violence-threatening cult." This statement was supported by four findings (PSIC 1986, p. 11):

John Africa and his followers in the 1980s came to reject and to place themselves above the laws, customs and social contracts of society.

The members of MOVE saw themselves as the targets of persistent harassment by regulatory agencies, unjust treatment by the courts, and periodic violent attempts to be suppressed by the police.

John Africa and his followers believed that a catastrophic confrontation with "the system" was necessary, if not inevitable, because of the campaign by "the system" to force MOVE to conform to society's rules.

MOVE's last campaign for confrontation began in the autumn of 1983, and was predicated on (1) the unconditional demand that all imprisoned MOVE members be released; and (2) that harassment of MOVE by city officials cease. The stridency and extremism of individual MOVE members escalated during the first years of the Goode administration.

The meanings of these findings and of the conclusion that MOVE was by 1985 a "violence-threatening cult" rested on one of three powerful assertions:

• a denial of the correctness of MOVE's perception that it had been harassed by public officials and treated unjustly by the courts

• a more complex procedural claim that, despite the correctness of its perceptions, MOVE was not entitled to protect itself by fortifying 6221 Osage or by imposing upon its neighbors in order to mobilize them politically in its defense

• a defense of public suppression of "violence-threatening cults."

None of these assertions as interpretive premises was either explicated or argued. Rather than treat MOVE's perceptions of harassment and injustice as responses to its specific experiences, the PSIC treated them as attributes of its character or philosophy and of its very broad indictment of the "system." Charles Bowser, a member of the commission, explained the choice not to assess this indictment and its ideological premises (Bowser 1989, pp. 129–130):

> The racial differences on the commission were not strong enough to supersede the common commitment to the perfection and the enjoyment of American liberty and justice. That common commitment . . . meant that MOVE's version of liberty was inconceivable. . . . The hearings could have examined the teachings of John Africa and compared his versions of the truth to those truths represented by everything the commissioners believed in. That inquiry could have taken months, maybe years. It would have required acrimonious debate and painstaking historical research. It would have required opening minds and testing sacred values. It would have required questioning the unquestionable foundations of American society. There was neither the time nor the inclination to initiate such an analysis.

The factual order of the first set of findings was thus an affirmation of the values that the commission articulated as the framework within which it might "heal the wounds and remove the blemish from liberty and justice" (ibid., p. 128). The choice between a virtually impossible assessment of MOVE's broad social critique and a scrupulously factual characterization of its self-perceptions displaced the feasible but communally divisive articulation of any of the three missing interpretive premises. In particular, the commission did not assess the fairness of the conviction and sentencing of MOVE members after the Powelton Village siege. Such an assessment would, in effect, have granted MOVE's primary demand—blasted profanely through the loudspeaker attached to 6221 Osage—for a public inquiry that might exonerate their "brothers and sisters." Placing such an assessment at the center of the commission's work, no matter the conclusions, would have assimilated MOVE into the tradition of legitimate political radicalism.

Within that tradition, the adults in 6221 Osage Avenue would have appeared as both sinners and victims in a complex and contentious script. The consensus-seeking moral order of the report, however, rests on a tacit martyrology that emphasizes the status of the Osage Avenue neighbors and, even more significant, the MOVE children as the sole victims of the drama. The first set of findings and its factual rhetoric laid the foundations for this order.

Normal City Government

The consensus-seeking discipline of the rhetoric of fact is also apparent in the sharp indictment of the mayor. In its third conclusion, the commission argued that "Mayor Goode's policy toward MOVE was one of appeasement, non-confrontation and avoidance." Three findings were presented to justify that conclusion (PSIC 1986, p. 11):

The Goode Administration assumed that any attempt to enforce the law would end in violence. MOVE-related issues thus became "too hot to handle" and the Administration pursued a do-nothing and say-nothing policy. Avoidance of the problem was so pervasive that city officials did not even discuss the issue among themselves.

The Mayor attempted to mollify neighbors with claims that a proper legal basis for action was being sought, and with superficial actions that were designed to diffuse neighborhood frustrations without addressing the crux of the problem.

With this policy of benign avoidance, the Mayor hoped that the problem might dissipate on its own, particularly, that MOVE would weary of unanswered challenges, modulate their confrontational behavior and/or relocate. To a great extent, then, MOVE effectively paralyzed the normal functioning of city government, as it applied to MOVE and to the Osage neighborhood.

The commission completed this narrative of failure in the next three conclusions, asserting that the city administration had left the problem to the police and discouraged responsible groups from mediating despite "compelling evidence" in the spring and summer of 1984 that its policy was "doomed to fail."

The central interpretive proposition in this narrative is the assertion that city government normally does not manage conflict by avoidance and superficial mollification of aggrieved parties. The response to MOVE was, therefore, an unusual and unjustified paralysis. Suppose, however, that the mayor was operating in the ordinary way until the few days leading up to May 13, 1985. He treated MOVE just as he did drug pushers, street criminals, and errant landlords.[5] Unable to mount an all-out battle on any front for very long, he fought an episodic or ritualistic war of attrition. When he asked the neighbors to work out their relations with MOVE by themselves ("black on black"), he was expressing the practical wisdom of city life and urban governance. That tacit wisdom warned that no one should take peace for granted and no one should sensibly rely on the city for anything other than weak and occasional assistance in the resolution of disputes. The Osage Avenue neighbors were either politically naive or reprehensibly passive. Unwilling to use force creatively against MOVE, they had pressed the city to violate its normal mode of managing conflict, and they should bear some responsibility for the resulting devastation.

I have no difficulty articulating this scripture and fitting it to a familiar world. My text may be read as a defense of institutional slack and of personal and small group responsibility rather than as a cynical rejection of comity. Even with its most compelling face, it is, however, virtually unspeakable within the frame of authoritative political discourse. Within that disciplinary frame, a government that cannot maintain the rights of its citizens and its own rules, then it forces them to live in chaos. Chaos may be ubiquitous, but it cannot be accepted as a fact leading to normatively compelling conclusions or policies. The PSIC argued that MOVE had violated the "basic rights of those living in the Osage Avenue neighborhood." Since claims to rights must be protected by a moral polity, attention to them must be the norm of government behavior. That moral expectation becomes a descriptive fact upon which the consensual condemnation of failure is grounded.

Race and Racism

In the rhetoric of fact, arguments that build on the recognition of a pattern are severely controlled. It is ethically inappropriate to blame individuals for the sins of a class to which we have assigned them. However, we all necessarily perceive, understand, and judge events within our cognitive frames and prejudices. Even the anomalies that surprise and confuse us are created by the orders that make sense of our worlds. Interpreters of the MOVE episode tried to tame a surrealistic collage by reshaping it so that it would fit a larger and more familiar pattern. Their explanatory stories moved from context to internal chronology and back again. In "Osage Is Burning," a television documentary first broadcast on the regional public television station on July 2, 1986, the meaning of the May 13 incident was understood as one of many days in many places in which a violent "municipal power" imposed its will on a "community."

The members of the PSIC could not escape their own minds in order to isolate May 13 and its actors. Even more significant, they could not play their redemptive roles if they ignored the ways in which Philadelphians structured the day and were confused by it. If a white mayor had guided a set of events in which eleven blacks had been killed and 61 homes in a black neighborhood destroyed, a great many Philadelphians would have imagined, rightly or wrongly, that they instantly understood what had happened. They would have located a redemptive path—an end to racism—within that understanding.

Wilson Goode was, however, the first black mayor of Philadelphia. The managing director was also black. The sense of tragedy was exacerbated by the frustration of hopes for a new regime under black leadership: the sense of confusion was enhanced because ordinary categories and explanations didn't seem to apply. The world and its words were in order when whites attacked blacks; however, this seemed another war, and a much-muddled one.

Many black and many white analysts attempted to reestablish the expected script, emphasizing that the police or the hidden forces behind the facade of black leadership were white or insisting that the blacks in power must be white under the skin. A nationally televised film, "The Bombing of West Philly," expressed this effort to make sense of events in a familiar pattern. May 13, according to the film, was the result of a "blood feud" between MOVE and the largely white police.

Stanley Vaughan, who had vainly used a bullhorn to plead with MOVE members on the afternoon of May 13, elaborated on the same theme. The attack on MOVE, Vaughan argued, was "an act of perpetual racism on behalf of the Philadelphia police and Philadelphia firefighters." "Previous mayors," he explained, "were always found to be out of town when a Black organization was scheduled to be raided by the police! This left the police commissioner completely in charge with the authority to do whatever he chose without interference. In the MOVE situation, the mayor did not vacate the city but it was like he was not around. He became invisible to the policemen and firemen in charge, specifically subsequent to the bombing, and soon after thousands of citizens in this country witnessed mutiny once again as they have seen in the past." (Harry 1987, pp. 201–205)

Other analysts, including Ramona Africa, were not content with the image of a racist mutiny that excused the mayor as merely negligent. May 13 revealed to them the subtle but pervasive power of white racism. Blacks were divided among themselves. On one side of that struggle were those (including Mayor Goode and the Osage Avenue neighbors) who thought that they could be empowered within the system; on the other side were those who rejected any such accommodation. Unless blacks who "wanted in" could demonstrate their willingness to use public power to suppress rebellion, they would never be trusted by the hidden rulers. The mayor's inept pose was a studied deception intended to limit his culpability for the predictably disastrous results of his suppression of black radicalism.[6]

If the PSIC had not addressed these racial explanations, its whole carefully sculpted interpretation would have collapsed, its "chastening words" hollowed of their redemptive meaning. Without consideration of race and racism, the report would necessarily have confused and disappointed many Philadelphians.

The commitment to the rhetoric of fact and truth made it difficult, however, for the commission to adopt any of the patterns that others imputed to events. Absent evidence of explicitly racist speech on the part of city officials, none of the reconstructed racial narratives or the patterns that critics perceived in events could be either affirmed or denied within an objective public order. Constrained by that rhetorical discipline, only one of the 31 conclusions and the supportive findings spoke in any way about *white, black, race,* or *prejudice.*

The commission was very open about its quandary. At the very end of the report, the members announced (with one dissenting vote) that they felt "obligated" to add a comment that did not conform to their "factual standards." The dissenter, Bruce Kauffman, accused his colleagues of indicting the mayor of racism "without a scintilla of factual support," relying only on "surmise, conjecture, speculation, and suspicion."

The commission's comment is organized in four paragraphs (PSIC 1986, p. 27), which I have lettered here to facilitate close reading:

(a) Despite the progress which has been made in recent decades toward achieving greater equality, the sad fact exists that racial and other prejudices remain in our society.

(b) Black and white leadership accordingly must recognize that the decision-making process, both public and private, may consciously or unconsciously be influenced by race, socioeconomic conditions and the lack of political power. Such recognition dictates particular sensitivity, caution and patience in analyzing and developing appropriate responses to crisis situations.

(c) In this context, the commission concludes that this city's administration failed to approach the Osage Avenue situation with sensitivity and care.

(d) The commission believes that the decisions of various city officials to permit construction of the bunker, to allow the use of high explosives and, in a 90-minute period, the firing of at least 10,000 rounds of ammunition at the house, to sanction the dropping of a bomb on an occupied row house, and to let a fire burn in a row house occupied by children, would not likely have been made had the MOVE house and its occupants been situated in a comparable white neighborhood.

It is easy to dismiss the characterization of residual prejudice in (a), the cautionary advice in (b), the indictment in (c), and the elaborate counterfactual in (d) as very weak tea, hardly worth losing Kauffman's support or meriting his tirade. It would, however, be a mistake to sneer at this weak tea. Struggling to interpret these paragraphs—particularly the strained prose of (d)—I tried my hand at two versions of a bolder restatement:

The peace of the city rests on the commitment of decent, ordinary blacks—whether you call them "middle" or "working" class—to the social order. If they are not treated with special regard then the foundations of Philadelphia are shaken. The willingness to risk massive harm to the Osage Avenue neighborhood was, on its face, a failure to treat their aspirations and city itself with appropriate care.

More dramatic:

My God! If you treat decent folks that way, you won't have a chance in hell of controlling unemployed black teenagers or "street" toughs.

I don't know whether either of my paragraphs captures the intentions in the mind of any particular commissioner or describes a shared understanding of an obscure collective text (Moran 1987). I present them only to highlight the commission's own rhetoric. My paragraphs, however "realistic," are not appropriate vehicles for communal affirmation and healing. They represent individuals and groups as schemers whose moral commitments are contingent and calculating and who are, therefore, appropriately manipulated to sustain a fragile social order. In contrast, the carefully crafted commission text constructs integrative ties by evoking universal (though ambiguous) values of equality and the end of prejudice; by praising prudential virtues of "sensitivity and care" that are unassailable after decisive, risk-taking action (often highly valued) has resulted in disaster. The subtle suggestion that white neighborhoods that were poorer or less stable that Osage Avenue might also be subjected to reckless public action conjures an alliance across racial lines.

Most significant, the commission's text is not about calculating schemers but about victims and the ways in which innocence frames redemption.

Most critics of racial bias in the MOVE episode speculated about a central counterfactual scenario: How would the city have behaved if the MOVE adults had been white? Would it have expended more effort in negotiations? Would it have brought more to the table? Would it have assaulted the house so violently, used a bomb, or allowed the resulting fire to burn? The added comment did not, however, address that issue. It is the Osage Avenue neighbors—not the MOVE adults—who are represented in (d) as the victims of the insensitivity and lack of care indicted in (c) and speculatively attributed to conscious or unconscious biases in (b). The strong idea running through these paragraphs (and, indeed, through the entire report) is that healing depends on an acknowledgment of the suffering of the innocents and a reaffirmation of a putatively shared commitment to protect them. In that frame, it is the neighbors, not the MOVE adults, who matter. It was the obligation to speak to the pain of the neighbors that evoked the breach in the commission's commitment to "factual standards."

Innocence is an even more compelling theme in the treatment of the MOVE children. The symbolic representation of the children is the emotional center of the commission's effort to understand May 13. Whatever may be said about the complicity of MOVE or even of the neighbors, the children were certainly innocent, and it is their loss (and our collective loss in them) that must be redeemed. City officials are indicted for gross negligence because they failed to separate the children from their parents and guardians. As long as there were children in the MOVE house, the "operation" should have been halted. While it was not clear whether any use of force that placed the children at risk was justifiable, certainly 10,000 rounds fired in 90 minutes was (variously) "excessive," "unreasonable," and "unconscionable." The deaths of the five children—but not the MOVE adults—evoke the redemptive possibilities of formal legal blame and punishment. The contrast in treatments is stark:

29. Five children were killed during the confrontation on May 13, 1985. Their deaths appear to be unjustified homicides which should be investigated by a grand jury.

30. Six adults also died as a result of the May 13 confrontation.

This representation of the children as victims was incorporated into the final comment. The children were not, however, allied with the neighbors as victims of racial or class prejudice. Their status and their rights were distinctive: individual adults and their collective institutions are obligated to refrain from putting children at risk or directly causing them harm because children—all children—are innocent, impotent and vulnerable. That construction of childhood is a strong mandate[7] that simultaneously promises to correct and to disrupt the alignment of interlocking communities. The PSIC and other commentators spoke harshly about Irene Pernsley, the commissioner of the Department of Human Services, who before May 13 had failed to respond to a hint that she should (surreptitiously if necessary) protect the children by removing them from the care of their parents and guardians. However, Commissioner Pernsley acted within a socially conservative and widely shared set of norms. Those norms dictate that healthy, well-loved children who have not been abused or neglected not be removed from their families for reasons of state. Within those norms, the PSIC's first findings about the character of MOVE might have justified responses in the worlds of adults, but they didn't sanction taking children into custody.

If she had asked, Commissioner Pernsley might, of course, have discovered that the operation planned for May 13 endangered the lives of the children. She might then, however, have argued consistently that she could not morally (or legally) take the children, and that the city government could not morally place them at risk by using force to serve the warrants or to inspect the house. The worlds of adults may, indeed, be held hostage to the rights of children.

There is, however, a serious moral alternative to the priority of children: children fit within adult communities and can neither control nor transcend them. There is literally no place for an innocence that is not implicated in the communions of adults. Ramona Africa, for example, insisted that MOVE could not be forced to submit its offspring to the custody of a hostile system. Similarly, Commissioner Kauffman provided an archetypal account of the subordination of children to the competitive dynamics of adult worlds. He rejected the idea that the police were morally bound to limit their self-defense in order to protect the MOVE children once the battle was joined and (in his narrative) the officers found themselves under attack.

The representation of the children is the most compelling element in the public order and the redemptive path crafted by the commission. The passion associated with the image of the children cracks through the rhetoric of fact and the strained presentation of racial and class prejudice. The most touching moments in the commission hearings centered in the sensitive and careful discussions with the lone surviving child. Even the bold presentation of the children as the primary victims of a tragedy did not, however, succeed in subordinating the contested worlds and words within which redemption was sought; it succeeded only in temporarily obscuring them.

Blame and Punishment

In the myth of deep community, blame and punishment are barely distinguished from understanding. Confronted with the evidence of wrongdoing, a community renews itself by punishing the sinner. The sinner is called upon to understand his or her deeds in the process of acknowledgment, penitence, forgiveness, and restitution. The personal understanding may be enhanced by communal sharing and prayer, which help everyone recognize the character of sin and the power of redemption. Public contrition (even at the moment of death) renews communal bonds.

In the stylized myth of an open field, blame, punishment, and understanding are only loosely coupled. We believe that we can understand without blaming, blame without understanding; we can punish the victims of social oppression for their transgressions even though we do not blame them, and we can blame individuals or even large groups for their behavior even though we are incapable of punishing them.

When punishment does not follow blame, the process of redemption remains open, mirroring the moral orders toward which it is directed. Three forms of legitimate public punishment were available to Philadelphia after May 13: administrative, electoral, and judicial. None of them closed the breach or concluded the redemptive process.

The administrative domain was simpler than the others, allowing individuals to be punished on their own initiative or that of their superiors. Mayor Goode might, for example, have resigned after receiving the report of the PSIC, thereby accepting the blame and punishing himself. Instead, he ran for reelection in 1987, claiming, in effect, the opportunity to be vindicated or at least forgiven. The police commissioner and the managing director resigned, but they were neither overtly fired nor publicly disgraced.

The electoral process was hardly more conclusive. The publication of the PSIC report triggered a flood of speculation about Mayor Goode's prospects for reelection in 1987. He had been wounded, his friends agreed, but he could rehabilitate himself if he acted to reassert control of his administration, moved ahead with the convention center, solved the trash disposal problem, restored the vitality of city neighborhoods, accepted the commission's recommendations for crisis management, cleaned the streets, or drew from his hat some other small miracle of effective governance. In that ordinary list, MOVE became one among many matters. The deaths and the fire did not transcend the conventional calculus of political goods and bads.

Electoral choices also integrated MOVE into the customary calculus of racial politics—the obscured politics in the commission's report. The choice between black and white candidates removed the sting from the tragedy of a black mayor's having attacked a black organization and burned black homes. At a prayer meeting after the publication of the report, speakers warned of an attack directed not only at Wilson Goode but at all prospective black candidates. Using the same term employed by Ramona Africa, Georgie Woods (one of the best-known black radio hosts in the city) warned: "They know if they can get rid of Wilson Goode—I'm talking about the system. . . . It'll be another 50 years before we have another black mayor in this town. . . . Don't fall for the white man's trick." (*Philadelphia Inquirer,* March 13, 1986)

Twice during 1987, Wilson Goode submitted himself to the voters of the city. In the spring Democratic Party primary he was challenged by Edward Rendell, who had been District Attorney in May of 1985. Defeating Rendell, he ran in the general election against Frank Rizzo, a former mayor who had been in office during the 1978 MOVE siege. Both white candidates attacked the mayor's performance on Osage Avenue, quoting the PSIC's indictment of his failures.

May 13 was, however, submerged in the larger politics of racial identification. Pollsters and analysts attempting to understand the electoral impact of the MOVE episode constructed intriguing images of voters struggling with the demands of judgment: white liberals agonizing over the decision to abandon a black candidate, frustrated blacks wondering whether to vote for a white or stay at home. The electoral process is not, however, designed to couple blame and punishment tightly so that either the defeat or victory of a candidate is unambiguously redemptive. Ballot counts are simple texts. They describe winners and losers rather the souls of voters or the canon of public virtues. Even if the mayor had been defeated, the loss would have been widely interpreted as part of a continuing tragedy rather than a conclusion to a redemptive drama. Goode's victory certainly failed to complete the redemptive sequence even in the eyes of his supporters.

In the end—as at the beginning—the courts appeared as the arena in which redemption would be found. The resignations of the police commissioner and the managing director, the report of the commission, and the two elections of 1987 were treated by many of the participants in the protracted public drama I have described as mere preliminaries setting the stage for a definitive judicial allocation of blame and punishment. When the courts had rendered their judgments, the facts would be known; justice would be done. May 13 would be moved from the present to a remembered past; from a current assault on the moral order to a cautionary memory. The judicial process failed in that role. It became, in some eyes at least, a part of the tragedy that it could not conclude.

The process of judicial blaming was centered on Ramona Africa's criminal trial and on a Philadelphia grand jury's inquiry into the behavior of public officials. The trial provided the lone adult survivor with an opportunity to present her conception of MOVE, the "system," and the events leading up to May 13. Her criminal guilt was, however, decided on very narrow grounds. She was acquitted of charges of attempting to murder police officers and firefighters: she had, it appeared, spent most of May 13 huddled under a blanket protecting the children. She was found guilty of riot because she had confessed to using the threat of violence to coerce public action. Since they could not defend themselves, the MOVE adults who had died on May 13 could not be indicted or tried. They had no day in court, no opportunity to "prove" that they had only defended themselves against illegitimate assaults or to be convicted of attempted murder.

A trial of high public officials and police officers would, of course, have implicitly judged the MOVE adults as well. The decision of the grand jury (and, it was widely assumed, the attorneys who had guided its deliberations) not to indict any officials meant both that the MOVE dead were never tried and that moral outrage was not resolved in a judicial finding of criminal guilt or innocence.

The grand jury, nevertheless, insisted that its report was not only "exhaustive" but "dispositive." It could not, it admitted, "duplicate" the "public outrage" that the disaster evoked—indeed, it would have been a mistake even to cast itself in that expressive role. It had attempted, rather, to "lay out" the "essential facts" in one "cohesive and dispassionate document" and to explain its legal reasoning. "The facts, as we find them to be, can and should speak for themselves." (*Report* 1988, pp. 1–13)

The grand jury (speaking of itself in the third person) provided a summary account of its decision not to bring criminal indictments that it then amplified at great length in a full report (ibid.):

1. The Commission (with the exception of Bruce Kauffman) had been persuaded that police officers had fired on MOVE members attempting to escape from the rear of 6221 Osage and to surrender. The Grand Jury disagreed with this interpretation of the factual record, denying the strongest case for criminal charges against individual police officers presented by the Commission.

2. The jury discovered a strong case that the officers who prepared the bomb dropped on 6221 had lied about the composition of the explosive. It decided, however, that it was essentially inequitable to insist upon this charge when no other public officials were to be indicted.

3. Finally, the Grand Jury came to believe that its intense moral condemnation of the behavior of the city administration could not be expressed in terms that satisfied the criteria set out in the criminal code.

The grand jury distinguished its carefully prescribed legal framework from the informal discourse of the PSIC. "Absent the duty or authority to issue critical charges," the jury insisted with barely disguised annoyance, the commission had "felt free" to label conduct as "grossly negligent" or "reckless" without engaging in the assessment of intentions and prudential behavior that the criminal code (and its community of interpreters) demanded. In contrast, the jury portrayed its conclusions as resting on a close "legal analysis" that distinguished between moral and criminal culpability. (ibid., pp. 11–12)

The jury argued that it could not find the mayor criminally negligent" in approving the bombing, because he could not fairly have been expected to anticipate that the police and fire commissioners would allow the fire to burn out of control. He might have been charged with one or another of a set of even more serious crimes (including murder) if had "intentionally," "knowingly," or "recklessly" disregarded "known," "substantial," and "unjustifiable" risks. The jurors insisted, however, that there was "no evidence" of criminal culpability in the mayor's "state of mind." He was "morally culpable" and "incredibly incompetent." His actions and those of his administration had led to an "urban disaster of scarcely imaginable pro-portion." He could not, however, be charged with a crime. The managing director and the fire and police commissioners were blamed and exculpat-ed in similar terms. For every charge that might be made against them, the jury was inhibited by what it described as evidentiary or legal impediments. The facts never quite spoke for themselves.

The rhetoric was nasty, columnist Chuck Stone wrote, but it sounded of "tinkling brass." "Who cares?" he wondered. "Nobody was indicted." (*Philadelphia Daily News*, May 4, 1988) Several members of the PSIC responded angrily in a similar vein and continued unsuccessfully to press for federal indictments until the statute of limitations expired in 1990. In an epilogue to his account of MOVE's encounter with Philadelphia, Charles Bowser interpreted the failure of the courts to redeem the city within the conventional narrative of racism: "It took three years and four months to sweep the homicides of five innocent children under official rugs." The prejudice that ran through the entire drama, he wrote, "was confirmed by the failure of the grand juries to indict anyone except a black women who was a victim [Ramona Africa, huddling under a blanket] and a black man who misappropriated money [the first contractor building the new houses to replace those that had been destroyed]. . . . The grand juries expanded the tragedy. In addition to the blood of innocent children and the indelible images of the fire, Philadelphia was permanently stained by a gross mis-carriage of justice." (Bowser 1989, p. 175)

Open Stories

There was—and there is—no closure in this account of redemption. Houses were replaced, damages paid, inquiries completed, and lives resumed, but the play was ultimately a "compromise"—the term Mayor Rendell used in 1996 to describe the judgment in Ramona Africa's civil suit. Time, con-ventional wisdom announces, heals all wounds. That is not, of course, pre-cisely right. Those who never knew about May 13, 1985, and are not instructed in its history, can neither forget nor be reconciled. For those who watched events on Osage Avenue unfold on television and who followed the process of redemption closely, the details will fade with time. More signif-icant, large features of the drama will be recast, and the MOVE history will be integrated into deeper views of the social order. I suspect, for example, that the inflected argument about race and class at the end of the commission's report has already faded, dominated by the simpler assertion that the incident would never have happened if either the MOVE members or the neighbors had been white. The MOVE story is refreshed and reinterpreted by attaching it to subsequent events, such as the 1993 assault on the Branch Davidian compound in Waco.

Feelings will also change. Some emotions that began as anger will be transmuted into a sadness that lingers over characters in the plot. (Wilson Goode draws that cloud around himself, asking us to pity him for the ghosts of the dead children and adults who haunt his life.) Others, however, are deepened and elaborated even after the overt signs of rage have passed.

The story remains open and subject to debate both on the street and in the library. The formalization of the plurality of accounts in written texts is an essential part of the process of redemption in a field of open moral communities resistant to an integrative narrative.

I have located seven book-length accounts of the MOVE episode, a novel, a play, and several scholarly articles.[8] Rather than being "dispositive," read as a group these stories enrich and complicate the remembered narrative, making it harder rather than easier to impute a consensual meaning to the "urban disaster."

Virtually everything that has been written about MOVE is explicitly cast within the frame of a personal memory and response. The personalization of history in biography is clearest in John Wideman's 1990 novel *Philadelphia Fire,* in which MOVE appears as a provocation embedded in the perceptions and memories of each of the characters. Within the world of the novel, psychological verisimilitude rather than public veracity defines "truth" even when the imaginary city is called "Philadelphia," and the experiences of one of the characters match those of the author. The incorporation of public experiences into personal identities is barely touched by the rhetoric of fact and the processes of formal inquiry. Charles Bowser's review of the novel captures this intractable pluralism. "Wideman's perspective," he cautions, "is limited by anger, anguish and grief. There is no light beyond the smoke, no redemption in the ashes." There are, Bowser insists, other biographies and other memories that have been shaped by hope as well as anger and by a commitment to repair the damaged world.

Philadelphia, he concludes, is not one story—"not one time or one history" (*Philadelphia Inquirer,* September 23, 1990)—but many.

The accounts of professional social scientists embrace the theme of the intractable plurality of both stories and discursive forms. The MOVE history, Wells (1990, p. 212) argues, resists being "normalized" into a single official or coherent narrative. Like a "surrealistic painting" or a "nightmare," Wagner-Pacifici (1994, pp. 148–149) writes, it remains "inchoate."

That pluralistic image—even in its most mannered conception of an inexplicable tragedy for which everyone is responsible but no one is guilty—dominates every attempt to offer a single compelling account by presenting a viable alternative narrative or to find redemption in a trial by jury. Instead, the redemptive response is to preserve the stories and to enhance the roles of those who mediate between them. Wagner-Pacifici's *Discourse and Destruction* and an earlier study by Hizkias Assefa and Paul Wahrhaftig, *The MOVE Crisis in Philadelphia: Extremist Groups and Conflict Resolution* (1990), both focus on the failure of city officials to appreciate and cultivate the activities of informal mediators who might have discovered a way to reexamine the 1978 killing in return for the end of MOVE's assault on the sensibilities of its neighbors. Nagel (1991), in a complementary argument, observes that the mayor's "unresolved decisional conflicts" led him to shift dramatically from a policy of evasive delay to a "hypervigilance" in which mediation was impossible.

In all these accounts, the MOVE history is integrated into progressive professional cultures that assume that it is possible to enrich the experience of mediators vicariously, to strengthen the psyches of public officials through education, and to build theory—to "chart a path through the discursive forest of rationalities, excesses, silence and incoherence" (Wagner-Pacifici 1994, p. 148). As ecstatic redemption is frustrated by the pluralism of an overlapping field, it is replaced by public orders and by dreams of a procedural grace that may limit the scope of conflict even if they cannot eradicate the "permanent stains" of injustice. Ramona Africa lectures on MOVE at universities in the United States and Europe and serves as guide at an exhibition mounted by the African American Museum in Philadelphia (*Philadelphia Inquirer,* July 26, 1998). So are memories crafted.

12
Ethical Mandates and the Virtue of Prudence

Mind and Marrow Bone

This chapter moves across the Delaware River into New Jersey. The stage for this account of an attempt to realign the social organization of space is charged with emotion and moral fervor, but the script does not originate either metaphorically or literally in an inferno. Here and there, the story is punctuated by stormy zoning meetings, passionate legislative debates, campaign invective, and noisy public rallies. For the most part, however, the arguments with which I am concerned were governed by the stylized norms of legal communication and the restrained rhetoric of professional planning, administration, and policy analysis. In this story, the moral heroes seeking to repair an imperfect world wear judicial robes. They speak of inequality and deprivation but not of death and certainly not of murder. In a style characteristic of the Law, common words and texts bind the protagonists to one another through a debate spanning several decades and crossing conventional institutional boundaries.

The theme that links my account of this highly disciplined drama to the search for redemption after the 1985 MOVE incident is a concern with the virtue of prudence. In the MOVE history, prudence is the missing virtue whose absence permits the construction of a crisis and its transformation into tragedy. The content of the virtue (as it might appear in practice) is defined by the indictment of its flawed versions (appeasement, non-confrontation, avoidance) and its antitheses (gross negligence, excess, administrative disarray, insensitivity, impatience, recklessness).

This chapter treats prudence not as a protection against moral disarray but as a protection against strong ethical mandates that promise or threaten to rearrange communities. Prudence warns us not only to attend to the children but also to be careful of re-creating the world in the name of innocence.

I have chosen a case that is a part of the canon of the community of professional city and regional planners, but the dynamics I describe appear in every profession. Not only planners but also corporate managers, physicians, and rabbis must learn to treat strong mandates prudently if they want to preserve the field of overlapping communities.

Prudence's two faces and its role in balancing conflicting claims often make it difficult to recognize the practice of the virtue. In the community of planners, for example, its votaries admonish one another and anyone who will listen that prudence dictates that we attend to the future, acting now to avoid prospective dangers and to reap the benefits of foresight. We should—prudently—overcome the ubiquitous tendency to calculate our interests so narrowly that we sink our collective ship. At the same time, the virtue directs us to temper our confidence. We should regard with a prudent skepticism estimates of our intelligence that leave no room for uncertainty or perversity and assessments of our good will that leave no room for egoism and privacy. We should understand that ethical principles are bound to conflict with one another and that it is therefore imprudent even to attempt to reconstruct the world or to rewrite our codes as if we could harmonize all interests and all ethical commitments.

The practice of any virtue is necessarily more complex and more contested than the simple statement of an ethical principle. Prudence, however, seems peculiarly slippery. Compared to justice or love, it is all practice and temper, with very little in the way of formal text to guide our shared understanding of its ethical or emotional force.[1] Even Machiavelli, as Garver (1987) remarks, "says very little about prudence at all, instead enacting a conception . . . and giving his audience the means of acquiring it." Experienced planners spend a great deal of time cultivating a prudential disposition in novices, engaging them in the practices of the precious but ambiguous virtue. The recruits must learn when and how it is appropriate to capitalize future goods in the present and when it is not; when it is prudent to avoid risks and when risk aversion is paralyzing; when it is possible to repair the world and when reform is likely to spawn ethical monsters; when formal knowledge enhances intelligence and when it requires that we systematically ignore what we should sensibly regard; when to speak or act and when to wait silently.

Even "compleat" practitioners are unlikely to respond to these judgmental choices in the same way or with an unconflicted grace. They are characteristically torn between rival interpretations of the ambiguous virtue, with very little hope of striking a permanent balance. In an earlier version of this chapter, I captured these judgmental choice with four lines from William Butler Yeats's poem "A Prayer for Old Age":

God guard me from those thoughts men think
In the mind alone:
He that sings a lasting song
Thinks in a marrow-bone

My attention had been called to those lines by J. Anthony Lukas's account of how Judge W. Arthur Garrity, a central figure in Boston's difficult school desegregation struggles of the 1970s, had credited his mentor, Francis Ford, with a "streak of skepticism, even suspicion, lest he embrace a judicial doctrine without an understanding of its practical consequences" (Lukas 1985, pp. 250–251). "In pondering a legal problem," Lukas quotes Garrity as saying of Ford, "he subscribed to the prayer of the poet Yeats."

Ford's use of Yeats may, however, be a revealing misreading, highlighting the ambiguity of the ancient virtue. The poem continues as follows:

From all that makes a wise old man
That can be praise of all;
what am I that should not seem
For the song's sake a fool?

I pray—for fashion's word is out
And prayer comes round again—
That I may seem, though I die old,
A foolish, passionate man

If the marrow bone that protects against a cerebral disposition is skeptical and realistic, it is also poetic, prayerful, foolish, and passionate. In Ford's reading, it is prudent to articulate and refine our tacit knowledge, to imagine and justify our practices ethically, and to construct the world as a series of problems amenable to intelligent solution. Prudence—in our marrow bone—also dictates, however, that we be cautious: danger lurks in the detachment of cosmopolitan professions and in the ways they simplify and abstract social worlds and ethical mandates. We sensibly clutch our wallets tightly when we are told that a plan is "rational," "comprehensive," "systematic," or "in the public interest." (Less defensively, we may smile at the forms of ironic speech. Clearly no one intends those words to be taken at face value.)

Prudence captures us in its complex toil even when abstract principles are grounded in the experiences of a community and rival claims are supported by passionate loyalists rather than outsiders. There are times in the history of every moral community when members insist that prudence requires that an established web of practices and a plurality of moral norms be brought within the discipline of strong ethical mandates. If the community is to survive, the defenders argue, we must (variously) "renew our ancient faith," "return to first principles," "learn again to speak truthfully with one another," or "pursue justice." Such mandates arouse a prudential counter-response: perhaps we should not be so quick to condemn the petty compromises and the corruption of "everyday" life; perhaps there is a practical wisdom in the ways "ordinary" people balance the virtues so that none completely dominates the others.

The forms of this dilemma are particularly complex and subtle when we represent ourselves as living within a field of open and overlapping communities. In such fields, change in one community does not always require a response from all communities. Buffers of inattention and tolerance allow us sometimes to act without reconciling our individual or collective lives to a single coherent moral order.

Some strong ethical mandates, however, spread across a field, threatening the relations between communities and the buffers that divide them. Families, churches, and firms are all challenged when we realign the meaning of privacy in order to reconstruct our conceptions of gender to conform to the demands of justice. Similarly, if we all share a common fate as citizens of Planet Earth, how can we, as members of nations, resist the imperatives of a global environmental ethic or the international redistribution of income? If we are all bound to the self-determination of "peoples" as a first political principle, how can multicultural empires survive the ethical challenge unscathed? Strong ethical mandates may be powerfully resisted, or they may be embraced, but they cannot be ignored. They change the fields into which they are launched.

Prudence may "demand" the redesign of the communal field we imagine in our minds. Simultaneously, however, the hazards engendered when we try to design new boundaries, buffers, and negotiated meanings arouse prudential caution. How will the new field operate? How will it cope with variety, conflict, and change? Might the new ethical imperative be accommodated into the old communal order, or is that order deeply implicated in the immorality we seek to remedy?

Prudent men and women have good reason to be troubled by these questions and to be uncertain in their responses. We enact a concept of prudence that begins with Aristotle's conception of its compelling role in the array of virtues. Prudence, as Aristotle describes it in the *Politics* (1277b), is the distinguishing mark of public leadership. It is "the only virtue peculiar to the ruler" in a polity of roughly equal citizens; a practice of personal reflection and public deliberation. However, that grand vision now often gives way to prudence as caution and moral skepticism if not outright immorality (Nelson 1991). Indeed, we often have trouble distinguishing the two themes in our own speech as caution, skepticism, and political capacity are intertwined.

This chapter explores these troubles and uncertainties as they have been articulated in a series of judicial decisions in the state of New Jersey. The exploration is an appreciation of the ways in which prudence protects an open field from the simplifying imperatives that threaten to transform it into a deep community or to control it with an overarching social contract. Caution in the face of an ethical mandate does not necessarily betray moral sloth, nor need hesitation be justified by an equal and countervailing moral imperative. "Simple prudence"—that is to say, "complex and inflected prudence"—shapes our responses to strong ethical mandates. It should lead us to hesitate before we resolve conflicting values by appealing to overtly higher ethical standards, and it may (it follows necessarily) sometimes make cowards of us.

The New Jersey Problem[2]

In 1940, roughly 30 percent of the population of New Jersey lived in the state's six largest cities. Newark, the largest, had 430,000 residents. The 1990 census indicated that the same six cities included about 10 percent of the state's population. Newark has shrunk to approximately 70 percent of its 1940 size.

In a spatial form that defies conventional images of city and suburb, New Jersey is, nevertheless, highly urbanized. A virtually continuous belt of settlement cuts across the state diagonally, from the Philadelphia suburbs in the southwest through Trenton, the Princeton Corridor, New Brunswick, Elizabeth, Newark, and the suburbs opposite New York. The belt is politically divided into hundreds of jurisdictions.[3] The edges of these local polities are often virtually invisible, designated only by a welcoming sign in an otherwise seamless landscape.

It would be a mistake, however, to imagine that localism is anachronistic or trivial, or that it is soon to be overwhelmed by the interdependencies of a dynamic society. Local governments are responsible for choosing, administering, and financing a substantial portion of their own services. That responsibility creates motive, opportunity, and means for social groups to employ public authority to create and maintain communities; to attract some potential members while effectively excluding others, and to shape residents into citizens by forming their conceptions of rights and obligations. The structure of local government reaches deeply into the design of churches, schools, neighborhood associations, clubs, and Little League teams. Even where the communion does little more than protect the privacy (and the external memberships) of residents, threats to that minimal order are vigorously resisted.

The localities are also instruments of economic development. Stationary units in a field of footloose firms, they variously seek to resist some employers and to retain others, and to replace highly valued out-migrants with comparable newcomers and (at other times) to adapt to great waves of change by encouraging shifts in their local economic base. Like their private counterparts, they sometimes compete vigorously with one another and sometimes enter into coalitions; they are sometimes foolish or venal and sometimes wonderfully imaginative; they are sometimes in control of their own fortunes and sometimes helpless before the winds of economic fortune.

The forms of inter-jurisdictional competition, conflict, and cooperation shape the allocation of authority within the political fabric: who is able to initiate actions and who can block unwelcome intrusions. The communal winners enjoy considerable discretion in balancing taxes and expenditures. They command resources that allow them to insulate themselves from at least some of the shifting winds or to adapt successfully. The losers suffer a quite different fate. Former New Jersey Treasurer Clifford Goldman described their situation to an audience at Princeton University in 1987: "What we have really done is to take a primarily poorer class of people, put them in separate taxing districts, impose on those districts the requirements to support certain services, and essentially in a simplified way, make the poor pay for their own services. We are also taking the property away a little bit each year from property owners in those districts under the burden of 6 to 7 percent tax rates." Goldman concluded: "That's not a system that any moral person would have designed from scratch. It has just evolved over a long period of time." (Council on New Jersey Affairs 1988, p. 43)

Whatever they would have done "from scratch," men and women who represented themselves as moral have vigorously resisted changes in the system Goldman cryptically sketched. Without the props of an explicit ideology other than "local autonomy," they have sought to create and maintain a social order that legitimates inequality in personal income and affirms the value of winning in life's race by allowing advantages and disadvantages to be transmitted across time and generations.

Finally and critically, the order permits municipalities to use their coercive powers to shape and defend local moral orders.

In the last three decades, two streams of criticism and policy making have converged on this pattern of localism. The first—often described as "urban policy"—has engaged the demand that localism be mitigated sufficiently to ensure a minimum level of welfare for the poorest residents of the state and to redevelop the cores of the few large cities within the urban belt. Though this argument was often couched in an intense ethical rhetoric, it did not threaten the dominant pattern. (The threat was particularly muted when it was federal rather than state dollars that financed the reconstruction of Newark, educational programs for poor children in Trenton, or mental health services for poor adults in Camden.) Images of aiding "distressed" cities, working with "urban" schools, and supporting "inner city" neighborhoods shaped discussion without allowing it to undermine the principles that legitimated inequality, stratification, and the political construction of communities.

Though it has no conventional name that allows it to be instantly recognized, the second stream is much more threatening. For roughly thirty years (though precursors are easy enough to find), the attention of political elites in New Jersey has been drawn to a series of overlapping, difficult, and intractably messy questions. How, they wondered, should the infrastructure of the politically fragmented urbanized belt be planned and financed, endangered ecosystems and natural resources spanning jurisdictions protected, the stream of garbage managed, public education financed, and access to dispersed employment arranged? The debate on every one of these issues inevitably centered on the pattern of localism. Whether the debate dealt with garbage, housing, transportation, schools, sewers, water, or labor markets, the boundaries and incentives that divided interdependent localities made it difficult (though not impossible) to write cooperative agreements between jurisdictions, create new regional authorities, or finance an enlarged role for the state government.

The Supreme Court of New Jersey assumed a central role in these political discussions. Virtually every issue that challenged the pattern of profound localism has come before the judges at one time or another. Two protracted conflicts—one dealing with land and the other with education—have forced (or, better, allowed) the judges to assess the ways in which the coercive authority of the state entered into the political construction of inequality and of community. The constitutional imperatives as articulated by the judges threatened not simply the relations between state and local polities but the web of overlapping social circles embedded in the recruitment and exclusion of neighbors and the socialization of children.

The basic moral arguments in the two policy streams were essentially identical. The dramatic forms of the interventions were also similar. In both streams, the judges represented themselves as reluctant heroes. They entered into the redesign of communities and persisted over decades only because of a legislative failure that compelled them to defend constitutional rights that they could not ignore and to respond to morally compelling social needs. If the constitutional texts had been explicit, lower courts would have suppressed the offending behaviors whenever they appeared. However, the imperatives, as the judges read them, were vague though compelling: simple principles dominating a complex field of subordinate practices. That rhetorical form forced decisions: it also evoked prudence in response.

The political dynamics of land use and education were quite different. Often the judges observed that they could strike down exclusionary zoning ordinances and reward builders who had been thwarted by them but they could not practically build and market houses. In contrast, since the state provided education, the judges could (and did) credibly threaten to mandate an income tax to finance the schools, establish revenue-sharing practices, and prescribe curricula.[4]

Prudence took on different faces in these two contexts. In the first, it protected the judges from being pulled by their own commitments into an uncharted policy domain against wily opponents and without substantial political backing; in the second, it cautioned against judicial perfection and organizational imperialism.

I have chosen to deal only with the issue of spatial exclusion and the decisions that have taken their name from Mt. Laurel, the township in which the legal attack on established modes of local autonomy was pressed most decisively. My treatment of these cases is very selective, centered on the mind and marrow bone of the judges in the interplay of ethical mandates and prudence rather than on the substance of housing and land use policy.

Mt. Laurel[5]

The Mt. Laurel litigation began with a complaint by poor residents of the township that local zoning and the allocation of public resources effectively prevented them and their children from replacing their current homes. They claimed, in effect, that they could not be legitimately exiled from Mt. Laurel by public action setting dues they could not meet. They were joined in this limited claim by former residents who argued that they had been displaced by those same public decisions. The scope of the case was subsequently enlarged by a complementary assertion that a class of poor residents in adjacent jurisdictions also had a right to move to Mt. Laurel though they had never lived there. Put more carefully: Public action could not raise the price of entry so that no member of the class could hope to bid successfully for shelter in Mt. Laurel.

In 1975, the Supreme Court agreed that all those claims were valid. It insisted that local zoning ordinances are justified only if they do not deny any citizen either "due process" or "equal protection of the laws" and only if they serve the "general welfare." Mt. Laurel, the Court said, had failed those demanding tests "inherent" in the general wording of Article I, Paragraph 1 of New Jersey's constitution:

All persons are by nature free and independent, and have certain natural and unalienable rights, among which are those of enjoying and defending life and liberty, of acquiring, possessing, and protecting property, and of pursuing and obtaining safety and happiness.

The judges held that it was constitutionally imperative that each town in which there was a possibility of new development ensure places for a "fair share" of its region's low- and moderate-income residents. Because it was grounded in the New Jersey constitution, that finding could not be overturned by a simple legislative majority.

The Court was unanimous in its findings but the judges differed among themselves on subtle but important matters. The majority opinion (written by Justice Frederick Hall) was complemented by two concurrent statements. The first, a brief note by Justice Worrall Mountain, asserted that the result could and should have been grounded in statute rather than in constitutional law. The statutory use of the "general welfare" to justify police powers had the same "amplitude" as the constitutional provisions cited by the majority and were sufficient to "justify, if not compel" the decision.

The second concurrent opinion was written by Justice Morris Pashman. He endorsed the principles of the majority but proposed to "go farther and faster" in implementing them. Pashman was bolder in both his policy recommendations and his description of the enemy embedded in suburban practice. He argued emphatically that there was a "disaster" imminent in the emergent urban pattern. His rhetoric was hotter than Hall's, his indictments more severe, and his ethical commandments more pointed. Nevertheless, I read the Hall and Pashman opinions as tendencies in a single institutional mind; voices in the same body, speaking to the litigants, to larger audiences, and to each other. Writing for his colleagues, Hall on the bench may have been guarded in his diction; however, he shared Pashman's moral passions. In a post-retirement speech he described the exclusion of the poor from suburban jurisdictions and the failure to meet their basic housing "needs" as "social evils that must be corrected if we are to exist as a true democratic society." Having found Mt. Laurel's behavior "immoral," he said, it was not difficult for him to designate it as "unconstitutional" (Hall 1977, p. 112).

In both the Hall opinion and the Pashman opinion, the Court appears as the reluctant leader of an expedition into morally compelling but practically uncharted territories. The broad direction of that expedition was defined by its origins in a critique of the immorality of established exclusionary practice, by its guiding constitutional principles, and by its image of a destination in socially diverse communities that would provide (Hall wrote) the "atmosphere" demanded by "a democracy and free institutions." Despite their sense of working against the grain of practice, both Hall and Pashman presented themselves as speaking for a superordinate communal standard. Pashman was particularly insistent on this prophetic role:

> The people of New Jersey should welcome the result reached by the Court in this case, not merely because it is required by our laws, but, more fundamentally, because the result is right and true to the highest American ideals.

Perhaps all general principles, even when they meet a congenial and accepting response, are altered in the process of institutionalization. The initial "spirit" is inevitably diminished as it is articulated in bureaucratic rules and in detailed legal interpretations. "Fair" distributions lose their glow when they emerge from protracted negotiations rather than leaping from the head of majestic justice. Our faith in good intentions is eroded by the recognition of the perverse (or at least anomalous) consequences of the ways we implement them.

There is, however, something special about the prudential taming of strong ethical mandates that threaten to reorganize a complex field of communities. When the judges in 1975 undertook to discipline their world with the general mandates of Article 1, Paragraph 1, they set out a planning task they could not complete without prudently circumscribing their own interpretation of the commanding ethical code. Their circumscription—at the moment the mandate was articulated—illustrates the difficulty of distinguishing between prudential caution and the crafts of practical judgment and leadership that fascinated Aristotle.

The majority opinion framed this planning task clearly but without aggressively specifying its difficulties. Zoning, Hall simply observed, create amenities and then prevent some citizens from using them. On the face of it, that exclusionary policy offends each individual's right to the "equal protection" of the laws. That denial could never be justified when race was the basis of exclusion. The majority now insisted that exclusion on the basis of income was also interdicted. Pashman's voice captured the profound implications and the difficulties of that assertion. "Justice," he argued, "must be blind to both race and income." The image of blind justice is, of course, a central icon of the legal system. Pashman was not, however, describing the procedures for the assessment of personal guilt or innocence; he was describing a principle guiding the allocation of the benefits of all public action. If justice was properly blind, the government could not benefit one class without providing an identical or equivalent benefit to every class. Public amenities—including the shared environment of "air and water, flowers and green trees"—could not be arranged or regulated in a way that closed them to anyone simply because they could not afford an illegitimately imposed price of admission.

This expansive view of "equal protection" was complemented by a substantive interpretation of the meaning of "the general welfare." Some human wants, Hall argued, were appropriately understood as politically privileged. The New Jersey constitution implicitly required that public actions be arranged so that these "basic human needs"—including housing—be met. A local polity could not legitimately argue that the basic needs of its members had been satisfied and that its land-use or housing regulations were justified if it had failed to promote the "proper provision for adequate housing of all categories of people." Observing a pattern of exclusionary zoning, the Court held out a Kantian remedy: Every locality must act as if its regulations established a general inclusionary principle. In a field of polities designed to fulfill those principles, each locality would assume its "fair share" of the population of low- and moderate-income residents.

The strong ethical mandates to extend the protection of the law equally to each person and to attend to the general welfare threatened the order of a field of communities in which public and private domains were deeply intertwined. The expansive application of "equal protection" would require either a catastrophic disengagement of government from private realms or an enormous expansion of the capacity of the state to proscribe and, if necessary, redress government-supported inequality. The obscure bargain that sustained the image that there was a "private" domain where none existed would be undone.

In a similar way, a patterned, substantive conception of the "general welfare" would require an agency empowered to define politically privileged claims authoritatively, and to oversee and (if necessary) initiate public actions. It would ensure the priority of basic human needs even when they could not be satisfied without reducing the political salience of ordinary wants or violating claims based on rights or deserts. A list of needs that were easily met might be accommodated without difficulty within a pluralistic democratic polity. If, however, the needs challenged deeply embedded practices—if they included, for example, "decent housing," open space, participation in a socially diverse community, equal educational opportunity, and self-respect—then the "general welfare agency" would be a demanding (even a threatening) political master.

Mt. Laurel I, a sympathetic New Jersey lawyer remarked (Mytelka 1977, p. 150), "sparkles with kinetic potential, suggesting revolutionary change" without, however, providing fully developed answers to the questions it raises. Hall particularly spoke in the oblique and ambiguous voice of prudence. Against Pashman's advice, the fair share obligation was confined to "developing" communities, requiring that (in some arena or court) fairness and feasibility be balanced. *Mt. Laurel* was presented not as having revolutionary possibilities but as simply the next step in an unfolding series of cases in which the Court had required a "general" rather than a "parochial" referent for the "welfare" clause. The constitutional principles the Court evoked were described as limited in their scope, whatever their theoretical reach. As a "matter of policy," they were to be applied only to "major questions of fundamental import."

Hall did not, however, simply play Prudence to Pashman. Both judges wrote within a common fabric woven from three distinctive threads. The first thread was the concept that the ethical mandate could be satisfied if jurisdictions assumed their "fair shares" within a "region." Hall and Pashman represented each jurisdiction as embedded within a socially diverse territory that was a microcosm of the larger society and a moral object: Mt. Laurel was censured for harming the general welfare of "its" region. If regions were correctly designated and if (as newly enabled polities) they attended to the fair allocations that their own good health required, then a constitutional and moral wall would protect the resulting housing pattern against legal challenge.

In an open social system in which capital, labor, energy, goods, and information all move easily across space, there is no uniquely compelling—let alone "true"—protocol for the designation of regional boundaries or fair shares. That, of course, did not prevent the judges from trying to ground regions and shares in the forms and formalities of social science and professional planning. They commissioned studies (Burchell et al. 1983) and listened to expert witnesses. In one particularly dramatic episode, they put 21 planners from both sides of a case in a room sans lawyers with instructions to settle on a formula for the allocation of regional fair shares. One commentator praises (Haar 1996, p. 71 and passim) the work of the three Superior Court judges assigned to Mt. Laurel cases in revealing terms:

> . . . the three judges prevented the doctrine from remaining an incorporeal dream that historians of a later generation would criticize as the product of an overzealous supreme court insufficiently versed in the realities of real estate and local government or as an instance where the trial system had been burdened with an essentially legislative-administrative task that it could not discharge.

The judicial facts, constituting a public order, were crafted over many years as the judges shaped obligations that disciplined the practices of courts, municipal governments, developers, and state agencies. "Region," "fair share," "need," "development," and "sound planning principles" entered the lexicon of a professional Mt. Laurel community that included judges, special masters, lawyers, planners, and state officials. The process of forming that community and its distinctive discourse has worked through *Mt. Laurel I* and its successors, through legislative debates, through the internal deliberations of the Council on Affordable Housing created in 1985, through the attempts of the Office of State Planning to create regional polities and to insert them into the process of development planning, and through bargaining among jurisdictions and between developers and municipal authorities. "Mistaken words" that challenge the Mt. Laurel discourse now appear as attacks on a web of obligations that can no longer be readily disentangled.

The second thread in the prudential fabric is nearly transparent. The ethical mandate announced in *Mt. Laurel I* stems from the constitutional obligations of the citizens of New Jersey: the state polity, whatever its conventional practices (or its moral theories in practice), was dedicated by its constitution and its "highest ideals" to the meanings the Court ascribed to Article I, Paragraph 1.

Though cast in this central role, the state of New Jersey is almost wholly invisible in *Mt. Laurel I. In Mt. Laurel II* its salience is reaffirmed in striking sentences that adopt Justice Pashman's earlier characterization of the land as a public resource:

The basis for the constitutional obligation is simple: the State controls the use of land, all of the land. In exercising that control it cannot favor rich over poor. It cannot legislatively set aside dilapidated housing in urban ghettos for the poor and decent housing elsewhere for everyone else. The government that controls this land represents everyone. While the State may not have the ability to eliminate poverty, it cannot use that condition as the basis for imposing further disadvantages.

The paragraph concludes, however, without specifying the state's obligations to meet basic human needs or to redress the inequalities in which it was implicated. The state, the Supreme Court announced, had delegated control over land to municipalities. All municipalities that had acted in the exclusionary modes practiced by Mt. Laurel were bound to accept their obligations, remedy their behavior, and, in effect, reform their character.

In *Mt. Laurel I,* Justices Hall and Pashman both inveighed against the selfishness and parochialism of exclusionary municipalities. The Court's opinion in *Mt. Laurel II,* written by Chief Justice Robert N. Wilentz, was even more biting:

. . . Mt. Laurel remains afflicted with a blatantly exclusionary ordinance. Papered over with studies, rationalized by hired experts, the ordinance at its core is true to nothing but Mount Laurel's determination to exclude the poor. . . . We have learned from experience . . . that unless a strong judicial hand is used, Mount Laurel will not result in housing, but in paper, process, witnesses, trials and appeals.

However, the anger directed at "widespread non-compliance" only emphasized how strongly the decisions affirmed the political framework whose failings they sought to rectify. The Court repeatedly announced that it would welcome legislative intervention. In Wilentz's words: "Powerful reasons suggest and we agree, that the matter is best left to the Legislature" in order to "protect" the "interests" created by the Constitution and by "underlying conceptions of fairness in the exercise of governmental power." The Court did not, however, attempt to wrestle with the legislature so as to control its decisions directly. Instead, it ratified the salience of municipalities, asking them to stretch but not exceed their modest capacity to promote low- and moderate-income housing. The play was scripted so that municipalities—persuaded that the Court was in earnest—would require legislative action in order to create a stable and defensible cartel. The cartel's rules—as realized in the Fair Housing Act of 1985 and accepted by the Court—required that each jurisdiction permit (though not necessarily create) its fair share of what came to be described as "affordable housing." The rules also ensured that the major community-forming features of localism and its role in a system of stratification would be protected.

The third thread in the prudential fabric was a pervasive confidence in professional planning. Hall's and Pashman's initial characterization of the sprawling, low-density urban pattern in New Jersey was written in the terms of the conventional professional critique of ill-planned suburbia. Their remedies are also cast in those professional terms. There is no reason, Hall assured Mt. Laurel and other developing communities, why compliance with the Court's decision would prevent them from becoming and remaining "attractive, viable communities." The fundamental principles of zoning would particularly be undisturbed:

They can have industrial sections, commercial sections and sections for every kind of housing from low cost and multi-family to lots of more than an acre with very expensive homes. Proper planning and governmental cooperation can prevent over-intensive and too sudden development, insure against future suburban sprawl and slums and assure the preservation of open space and local beauty. We do not intend that developing municipalities shall be overwhelmed by voracious land speculators and developers if they use the powers which they have intelligently and in the broad public interest.

The use of "sound planning criteria," Wilentz insisted, would now allow the Court to enrich and vary its conception of fairness:

. . . there is no reason . . . in our Constitution to make every municipality a microcosm of the entire state in its housing pattern, and there are persuasive reasons based on sound planning not to do so. The Constitution of the State of New Jersey does not require bad planning. It does not require suburban spread. It does not require rural municipalities to encourage large scale housing developments. It does not require wasteful extension of roads and needless construction of sewer and water facilities for the out-migration of people from the cities and the suburbs. There is nothing in our Constitution that says that we cannot satisfy our constitutional obligation to provide lower income housing and, at the same time, plan the future of the state intelligently.

The commitment to planning, by enriching the conception of fairness, tamed the ethical commitment by grounding it in images of physical design, environmental quality, competitive claims, and budgetary constraints.

Planning transformed a fundamental insistence on blind justice into a set of goals for "communities of place," "affordable" housing, and the efficient provision of an urban infrastructure. In order to encourage the construction of houses, wealthy jurisdictions were allowed to satisfy their Mt. Laurel obligations by financing low- and moderate-income housing outside their boundaries. The process of taming strong mandates began in the decisions of the robed judges and continued in the work of those (less dramatically garbed) engaged in the implementation of the Fair Housing Act and in the preparation, assessment, hesitant implementation, and adjustment of a state-wide development plan approved in 1992. Because planners and politicians value ordinary people and the satisfactions of everyday life, policy imperatives have been grounded in banal measures of public preferences and opinions rather than in ethical mandates.

The rhetorical forms of professional planning are sometimes presented by critics (inside the house and out) as ways of dominating the citizens of the modern state—as expressions of mind over marrow, system over life-world. And so they may be! However, the talk of planners—the data, the models, the contingent forecasts, the economic calculations, the policy analyses—also pays tribute to the virtue of prudence. The constitutional mandates, the moral demands of shared New Jersey citizenship, the radical implications of "equal protection," and even the credibility of regions as anything but an artifice crafted through negotiation are difficult to discern in the counting and the calculating.

Planning, a moral aristocrat and warrior might observe with disdain, is a cautious, petit-bourgeois craft. The professional processes of intelligence and scheming resist the reduction of ethical practices to strong mandates. They legitimize the variety of communities despite the taint of coercion, they compromise heroic virtues that devalue "thick" representations of what is good in our lives, and (perhaps most significant) they elevate ethical mandates so that they can be worshipped without walking among us.

13

Liberal Republics and the Open Field

Constructing the Field

The stylized myths of community organize our moral landscapes so that we can navigate within them. The contractual myth encourages us to distinguish between voluntary and involuntary associations; to assess and mitigate contractual flaws. The image of a community integrated by a deep moral order sets our eyes on the creation and maintenance of shared practices and common ties.

The notion that communities are overlapping and open makes sense, I hope, of the pluralism that is our everyday experience as we seek to resolve our moral uncertainties. We sustain openness when we cultivate public orders and conventions for reconciling differences but do not exaggerate their ability to resolve dilemmas, ambiguities, and essential conflicts—when we do not confuse our orders, however precious, with a single, consensual social truth.

The open fields of the third myth are both varied and protean. Some fields make it easy to create but difficult to sustain communities. Even relations cast in the forms of deep religious commitments are represented as temporary and partial. Other fields, in contrast, invest substantial authority in at least some communities in a way that limits entry, external inspection, and the challenge of ephemeral associations. In some fields, communities fail faster than they can be created. Other fields appear in our minds as stable ecosystems that maintain and restore their balance through overtly tumultuous processes. Gales of destruction produce waves of communal innovation.

Most of the fields that shape communal relations have no distinctive names. We ascribe to "society" or "culture" the tasks of monitoring relations between communities. With greater specificity, we recognize professions that claim to mediate between communities. For example, as we struggle with the dyad of firm and family we are variously supported by therapists, employment counselors, friends, novelists, and lawyers. Though they may address different concerns and act at cross-purposes, these intermediaries encourage us to believe that an imperfect and shifting accommodation of work and family is within our grasp. With all its flaws, that accommodation appears as preferable to either withdrawal from one of the communities or the complete integration of the two worlds.

The intermediaries as guardians of the field organize themselves into communities that socialize and discipline members, claim rights, affirm obligations, and create and protect domains of competence. (The community built around the Mt. Laurel decisions and practice illustrates that dynamic.) The guardians may sometimes project a transcendent image, as if they were outside the relations they protect. They are, however, inevitably cast as players within the field: one community among many. They are subject to all the ordinary sins of the flesh, including the prideful belief that they can go beyond openness to a full moral integration that flows through them and is crafted in their image

The protective tasks and the temptation to go beyond them are exaggerated when the guardian of the open field is a liberal republic. Those polities shape the field and are moral communities; at the same time, they are moral communities in their in their own right, using their authority and power to act collectively, to socialize and discipline members, and to endow them with rights and obligations.

The two roles—that of guardians of the field and that of members of discrete moral communities—are both complementary and contingently in conflict. The ambivalent relationship of the two roles is articulated in familiar debates over the appropriate range and depth of the "substantive" values pursued by liberal republics as communities and as guardians (Galston 1991; Walzer 1997). Does a liberal republic endanger its role as a guardian of openness if (as a moral community) it promotes one type of family over another, if it privileges some groups, or if it adopts the forms of a civic religion? Does it cripple its own communal capacities if it insists on a pluralism so deep that it strips both memory and history of a unifying content (Schlesinger 1998)?

I enter those debates and those illustrative questions indirectly. Returning to the themes of chapter 4, I am interested in the ways in which the relations between the roles of liberal republics as guardians of the field and as communities are grounded in the conception of members as citizens and as stakeholders. What is required of individuals cast in those parts? How may they manage to act intelligently in the face of the difficult cognitive and affective demands of the third myth? The end of the tale complements the argument made in chapters 11 and 12. The myth of open moral communities tames strong ethical mandates and deep redemptive claims. In the same way, it requires a thin conception of the virtues of citizens.

Liberal Republican Polities

In republican polities, formal institutions and tacit practices hold governors accountable to the "people." Since the great revolutions of the eighteenth century, republicanism (and latterly "democracy") have gained a unique political legitimacy. It is difficult to find a label for an undemocratic regime that is not a term of opprobrium—to imagine such a regime (whether led by colonels, by mullahs, or by the vanguards of a revolution) as anything but temporary.

Republics serve, shape, and coerce both their members and other communities with which they are entangled. They limit the sting of their awful power, however, by creating and sustaining "private" domains that are beyond their authority, though not beyond their power. Privacy operates to limit the gaze of officials and of citizens. When talk and deed respect the form, liberal republics do not interfere in private domains and should not be held accountable for private acts.

However, "privacy" is a complex and contested notion. It does not signal a consensual boundary that everyone understands even at the moment that it is violated. It is, instead, an attribute of activities—"my" speech, sexual practices, ways of addressing God, or factory—that may also simultaneously be designated as "public." Abortion and homosexuality are intensely private matters to some, public matters to others. The politics of liberal republics are dominated by the constant collective creation and defense of privacy. It follows necessarily that they are equally dominated by the collective creation and defense of the public domain—by *public* and *private* (as in current debates over regulation of the Internet) repeatedly entangled and disentangled.

The liberal construction of privacy is complicated when republics endow other communities with authority and coercive capabilities. "Incorporation" allows associations of all kinds (from firms and labor unions to churches, ethnic groups, residential settlements, families, and welfare organizations) to act as what the British call *quangos*—quasi-autonomous non-governmental organizations. Paradoxically, the extension of authority is accompanied by an insistence on openness that extends the gaze of officials and citizens into otherwise private affairs.

Openness is an asymmetric policy. Formed in the struggle against serfdom, slavery, and caste, liberal polities are attentive to restrictions on the ability of individuals to leave communions—whether they are labor unions, firms, cities, confessions, or marriages. Even personal contracts are regulated to prevent the overtly voluntary acceptance of conditions so onerous that they are tantamount to slavery (Rosenblum 1998).

Freedom to enter is a more complex and conflicted value. Without a broad array of opportunities to join communions, the freedom to exit is negated. If employees who refuse a contract offered by their employer are blackballed across the entire labor market, then exit is an empty or perilous option. If refugees escape one jurisdiction but are prohibited from settling in any other locale, then the freedom of movement is vacuous. Much the same is true if spouses are allowed to divorce but not to remarry. On the other side, however, if the polity insists on removing all selective barriers on entry (no immigration restrictions, no novitiates prior to membership, no rejection), the "private" discipline of communities is destroyed.

The conflict between open entry and selectivity pervades the relations between liberal polities and the field of communities with which they are engaged. Openness (as a policy and as a deep value commitment) is characteristically grounded in the conception of citizenship: no communion should discriminate among persons in terms that are inconsistent with equal membership in the liberal polity itself. The deeply integrative thrust of that moral principle is, however, tamed by competing interpretations of its demands, and of the appropriate reach of the regulatory practices of the polity. The interpreters—ordinary citizens and guardians of the moral order—struggle with difficult questions and with protean resolves: What are the requirements of equal membership in the polity? Must they dominate the entry requirements of every community, or are some immune from their application? Are the assignments of stigmas to race, ethnicity, poverty, gender, sexual preference, family origins, and caste equally onerous? Must they all be wholly expunged before the conditions of entry are legitimated by the polity? How far, in effect, does the Mt. Laurel principle extend? Does unequal "economic citizenship" in the United States now threaten a "deep sense of national community" (Ackerman and Alstott 1999, p. 6)?

Beyond exit and entry, the internal processes of communities as municipalities endowed with coercive public authority are also subjected to the regulatory practices of liberal polities. In various ways, they are tested against a standard of "reasonability." An incorporated business firm, for example, makes a contribution to a university. Before granting a tax deduction, government officials may sensibly ask "Is that contribution reasonably related to business purposes or is it a fraudulent diversion of the stockholders' resources?" After collective bargaining, a labor union signs a contract: "Were the members adequately consulted?" When the members of a community are children, liberal polities characteristically insist that they have the authority to oversee a fiduciary relationship. If adults fail as trustees within the terms of the polity or if they prevent their children from assuming the role of citizens, polities intervene, at least temporarily substituting their moral orders and practices for those of the failed or flawed community.

The external boundaries of liberal republics are often open and contested. With or without the sanction of the Law, capital, labor, information, and materials move across their porous borders. In a similar way, their internal boundaries are shaped and reshaped as they incorporate communities and place them in a changing open field.

This rather jumbled and protean representation of the liberal polity is quite different from the familiar images we associate with nationalist ideologies and the stories and rituals of the nation-state. In those images, the external boundary and the terms of membership are authoritatively defined; the internal structure—even in its complex federalist versions—is highly specified in detailed legal tracts. For the purposes of moral guidance, and for many more mundane tasks, the polity may appropriately be represented—in the words of Rawls (1993, p. 40)—as a "complete and closed social system."

That familiar image is cast within the myth of deeply integrative moral orders. Liberal polities express (again to borrow phrases from Rawls) the "overlapping consensus" of their societies. Their essential normative commitments touch the "main purposes of human life." The liberalism of the polity is defined by the ways it relates to other "comprehensive" traditions and ideologies within its own "society." Within this mythic form, the theorists debate the requirements of coexistence: How "thin" or "thick" is the appropriate conception of rights and goods in the moral order of "political liberalism"?[1]

In contrast, my representation of liberal polities is set within the open myth. Some of the communities that crowd the field are comprehensive in their world views, but most (including specialized governmental agencies) are narrow in scope and normatively "flat." Even when they essentially sustain and complement one another, the communities are different, Participants shift loyalties, temporal rhythms, and discursive forms while maintaining command of their communal repertoire. When they compete or conflict, the shifts are inflected moral accommodations rather than deep imperatives or rewritten contracts.

The members of liberal republics confront these moral complexities in distinctive symbolic roles as stakeholders and as citizens. In the first case, intelligent individual behavior is defined by the tasks of protecting and enhancing privileged interests. In the other case, members enjoy extensive rights but modest obligations. The competence of citizens is measured against the task of choosing and sustaining intelligent governors who will struggle with the relationship between the two roles of the liberal republic.

Stakeholders

'Stakeholder' and 'citizen' are sometimes used as simple synonyms. Will Hutton, a British political analyst and editor, has coined the notion of a "stakeholder economy and society" to describe a program that involves enhancing the capacity of the British state and the public obligations of individual citizens (Hutton 1995, 1997). In the United States, the lexical table is turned in the other direction. Critical of the performance of government and skeptical of its transformative potential, advocates of "civic renewal" associate the virtues of citizenship with engagement in the "third sector," and with "civil society" (the traditional territory of voluntary associations).[2]

I have come too far in this essay to hold out much hope of authoritatively disentangling the terms. Indeed, I hope that by now readers will anticipate my argument that the ambiguous elements complement one another.

The term 'stakeholders' evokes initially a tradition of political exclusion: only those who have a stake in public affairs (usually through the ownership of property) are sensibly entitled to vote. Absent that conservative stake, "levelers" would use the franchise to appropriate the wealth of others to the grief of the commonweal. The debates among Cromwell's officers at Putney in 1647 were echoed in the American state legislatures early in the history of the republic, and in the British Parliament considering the Great Reform Bill of 1832. In somewhat altered form, the exclusionary argument continues in efforts to limit voting on bond issues to property owners and to limit voting on school matters to the parents of students. The rapid spread of contractual communities in which only homeowners vote illustrates the contemporary vitality of the notion that stakes privilege some citizens and (it follows) that their absence diminishes the political entitlements of others.

The notion that only those with stakes are entitled to vote glides subtly into an inclusionary standard. In one application, this standard leads to the redistribution of private property so that political citizens are economic stakeholders.[3] In another canny political version, stakeholders are those who are capable of disrupting public negotiations. Rather than wait for disaster to strike, skilled planners engage all the potentially disruptive players. Treating every person or group who is either necessary for success or capable of disruption as a stakeholder, commands attention to the task of engaging (or entangling) them in a process to which they will be obligated at the end of the day.

The final image of stakes and stakeholders challenges established political boundaries and entitlements. Stakeholders leap over great distances and conventional borders at a single bound, threatening to sweep away the ordinary dynamics of representative democracy in favor of committees who are empowered to challenge every established value. In this image, individuals, groups, and communities look out at the world and ascribe goods and bads to long-established practices and to prospective schemes: I am entitled to participate in every matter in which I am at risk of losing a prospective benefit or suffering a direct harm. I am intelligent if I cultivate a cogent conception of my stakes and the ways of protecting them.

The influences that play on this ascription of stakes to phenomena near and far are themselves objects of design. Social investments in environmental monitoring alter the threshold at which hazards become apparent; market innovations allow small and widely distributed costs or benefits to be aggregated so that they are worth reckoning. I create a stake when I persuade friends in Philadelphia who had never thought about such matters that their welfare is threatened by a road-building project in the Amazon rain forest. I transform a stake when I persuade someone that an anticipated benefit is a probable hazard, or when I create an organization that cultivates claims and give them a compelling voice.

Some stakes may, of course, be secrets of the heart that are never voiced in public. For the most part, however, stakes must be publicly articulated if hazards are to be avoided and investments protected. Even in liberal regimes with very broad tolerance, some claims and some rhetorical styles are so suspect or so stigmatized that stakeholders may complain that their right to a voice has been inhibited. Differences within and between political regimes repeatedly engender conflict in the regulation of widely distributed computer networks, of offshore radio transmitters, and of satellites. Even where there are no legal barriers to communication, differences in practical access may be sensibly interpreted as limiting the right to a voice.

Even when all these difficulties in articulating stakes are acknowledged, in liberal regimes very little is added to the general conception of free speech by elaborating the special rights of stakeholders to voice their claims. For the most part, in such regimes assertive stakeholders' claims are not limited by law or by conventional practice. I am free to endorse the ways in which the exemplary practices of your family sustain my stake in the moral order, or to criticize the ways in which trade practices of a distant nation endanger my firm or human rights as I understand them.

None of us, of course, can attend equally to every feature of the current and the emergent political landscape. We ascribe no stakes to features that are invisible or that defy alteration—to features that, for good or for ill, touch us so lightly that we cannot afford to shift our attention to protect prospective benefits or to mitigate hazards. Most of our stakes may, therefore, be planted close to home, in our "places." Jurisdictional boundaries, however, have very little moral weight against the claim of a stake (Yackle 1994; Sunstein 1990; Yeazell 1994). Indeed, the rights of stakeholders are sometimes treated as so compelling that representative institutions are esteemed only when they achieve agreements that might be expected of a fully specified and collaborative field of stakeholders. If some stakeholders are missing or if competitive politics inhibit collaboration, republicanism is a sham that should give way to a genuinely democratic practice.

In liberal regimes, the major limits on the influence of stakeholders have less to do with the right to voice than with the moral or legal obligations to listen and with the practical incentives to attend to the views of others. Candidates for elected office, for example, may or may not be morally obligated to hear the voices of their constituents, but they certainly have powerful incentives to keep their ears cocked if there is serious competition for the posts they seek. Quite ordinary citizens (and some not so ordinary) who seek to mobilize resources, build coalitions, or collaborate must similarly master the craft of listening. In both autocratic and liberal regimes, the practices of legislators and administrators are shaped by incentives to monitor the settings they seek to govern. Autocrats, fearful that thwarted stakeholders will subvert their control, must devise ways of listening that do not encourage strategic deception but, at the same time, do not elicit participatory fantasies. In liberal regimes, the governors face even more difficult dilemmatic choices. They often listen in settings (such as public hearings) that reward strategic manipulation and encourage the belief that grievants (cast as "the people") will or should triumph over the deliberations of legislatures and agencies.

Judges and juries in liberal regimes are, of course, not only practically but also legally bound to listen in settings governed by highly stylized communication practices. The special (and hence contested) right of stakeholders to "voice" is largely centered in the right to be heard in those settings: to have legal standing (even in the courts of distant jurisdictions), to sue in one's personal name, or to be represented as a member of a class.

Legal obligations to listen fade subtly into moral responsibilities, but I find it difficult to treat listening—or, indeed, any other practice—as a virtue without limits. Listening may be part of the respect that I owe to other human beings; however, I am not morally bound to listen for as long as you are willing to talk, nor am I bound to ignore claims of affection, respect, and trust in order to allocate my attention equally between competing stakeholders.

Theories of social justice imply an ethical practice in which "we" are bound to listen to claims of violated rights, unmet fundamental needs, or unacknowledged deserts (Miller 1976). The putative authority of such theories, however, establishes the conditions for a division of labor. If we are, as Goodin argues, bound to nurture both those who are particularly "vulnerable" to our behavior and those whose vulnerability is general or structural, it doesn't follow that our communicative obligations are identical (Goodin 1985). I am morally obligated to hear my own children's voices, but a chain of delegates necessarily mediate between me and all the innocent children who are harmed by my profligate use of resources, my selfishness, and my weakness of will. The delegates may indict me for my moral failures, but they cannot—or better, they should not—cultivate a moral order in which I am bound to watch a television program that gives voice to the innocents.

Citizens

Individuals often surprise us with the claims they fail to assert. Don't they understand, we wonder, that they will be harmed by this intervention or benefited by that proposed facility? Symmetrically, we are often surprised by stakes that are claimed, and we wonder whether they are strategic rent seeking. In contrast, "citizen" seems like such a simple notion: Citizens are members of "polities." The status is documented and publicly acknowledged. Citizens enjoy the rights of members and carry the burdens of the associated obligations. Others may share in some of these rights and obligations, but the notion of membership implies a difference in the package held by citizens and by aliens.

It would, however, be a mistake to be deceived by that simplicity. Women and children have been citizens of countries in which they could not vote. Some citizens are entitled to rights as members of communities that others do not enjoy (Smith 1997, pp. 10–12). Even the rights of aliens have been variously graded: resident aliens often command rights that distinguish them from refugees, hostile belligerents, and allies. Individuals may simultaneously be members of several different polities with ambiguous or contested domains. The field of polities is complicated by a very large overlapping set of "private" communities—such as families and business firms—shaped by the disciplines of public institutions and reciprocally influencing the capacity of those institutions to act collectively, to recruit and socialize new recruits, and to encourage "good citizenship." The current fascination with the influence of civil society on the possibility of democratic governance only emphasizes the difficulty of marking the boundaries of polities once we begin to probe the meaning of conventional distinctions.

An instrumental craft and a set of normative virtues are attached to the role of stakeholder. We praise stakeholders who are analytically insightful and sufficiently skilled in reframing issues to articulate potential agreements; we rue the instrumental dullards who seed the world with stumbling blocks. Eager to master the arts of negotiation, we look to a small publishing industry and army of consultants to counsel us on "getting to yes." We recognize that some stakeholders are indeed rent seekers, scattering claim markers in the hope of striking a lode. Others, however, are heroic in their identification with causes that offer collective rewards but little prospect of personal gain.

The instrumental and moral scope of citizens is much more constrained than that of stakeholders. There are no citizens without polities, no polities without practices, no practices without institutions and moral communities to sustain them. When I claim the rights of a citizen or do my "civic duty," I carry the weighty baggage of those complex engagements into political arguments. Committees of stakeholders bound together by protracted litigation or by stable environmental conditions may last a long time. There is, however, something essentially temporary about their role, even when disputes drag on forever. Stakes are creations of issues, not of communities; of interests, not of membership. The abiding claims of citizenship are threatened by the instrumental flexibility of stakeholders who free themselves from rules, practices, and boundaries.

I don't mean to suggest that "citizens"—even as ideal types—are saints. In liberal republican regimes, we praise and sometimes even vote for leaders who rise above their own personal interests to speak for the commonweal. In some regimes, we ask them to put their investments in blind trusts, to avoid even the appearance of a conflict of interest, to publish their tax returns, and to identify campaign contributors. Citizens at large are not similarly constrained. We assume that their political speech will and should promote their interests—that they act, in effect, as stakeholders. Indeed, we rightly assume that governors attempting to understand the distributional implications of policy options would be crippled if ordinary citizens were to suppress their own preferences in favor of the prudential voice of the wise legislator. We don't ask ordinary citizens to excuse themselves from participation in conflicts in which they have a personal interest, nor do we insist (in a version of term limits) that they be quiet after a period of advocacy.

The normative claims of the polity should, however, subtly shape the speech and the political intelligence of members as citizens. We praise the "virtues" of a "good" citizen and rue the failings of those who evade their civic duties. Periodic movements of communal renewal encourage visions of what Shklar (1991, pp. 10–12) described as the "ideal citizen," wholly devoted to public activity, who "live(s) in and for the forum," cultivating the arts of direct democracy rather than representative democracy. Those movements are, however, characteristically short-lived. The call for "perfect republican virtue," Shklar wryly observed, has few takers in the United States. It conjures a "republic unlike the United States as it now is, ever has been, or is ever likely to be in any imaginable future." In the terms I have used, (merely) "good" citizens who observe the law, exercise their right to vote, and speak with a civil tongue (Kingwell 1995) meet their obligations as members of a liberal republic protecting an open field of communities.

Good citizens may also, of course, be loyal colleagues, devoted parents, moral partners, and generous neighbors. However, one can interpret those virtues as marks of citizenship only by expanding the domain of the polity and integrating civil society into a single moral order. The myth of open moral communities, in contrast, is served by a thin conception of political membership.

What may we sensibly expect of the "intelligence of citizens" in liberal republics? Citizens need not confidently know the "public interest" in order to speak, nor need they be intimidated by claims that their concerns are parochial or selfish. The beginning of intelligence is the recognition that the roles of citizens and governors are entangled and protean but nevertheless worth distinguishing. If we fail to distinguish them, we are seduced by an impossible and even dangerous image of a world in which every citizen is bound by the political and intellectual obligations of a governor and nothing more is required of a governor than of the citizen on the street.

The alternative to that image begins with the observation that the governors are not a homogeneous class, nor, even in the most centralized regimes, are they members of a single organization. The governors of a modern state are embedded in inter-organizational fields with an intense though rarely neat or coherent division of labor and with multiple and contested integrative links, fuzzy boundaries, and opaque or at least only translucent windows: many created out of one! The work of the governors requires a great deal of specialized knowledge. The sensible operation of shelters for the homeless cannot depend on the housing ministry's understanding of foreign affairs or forest management. A local councilor should be able to manage land-use disputes without grasping the distributional impact of international trade policy.

The intelligence of that inter-organizational field, in contrast, depends on at least three critical elements: the existence and capacity of monitors signaling when issue domains should be sensibly attached or uncoupled, a principled regard for the procedural rules that sustain the predictability and legitimacy of political relations, and a process of collective choice that is grounded in public deliberation and justification (Gutmann and Thompson 1996). These three elements of intelligence take many institutional forms. The technical support for legislative deliberation varies widely both across and within nations. In some polities, rule-regarding behavior is maintained by privately initiated litigation in the courts; in others, that path is rarely used. In all liberal republics, the roles of integration and deliberation are supported by an independent press and by networks and career paths that link government agencies to epistemic and professional practice communities. The degree of independence and the character of the inter-communal relations are, however, quite different from one polity to another.

The most distinctive element in this triad is the notion that collective choice is grounded in the deliberation of the governors. The moral authority of a liberal republic rests on the ways in which the governors deliberate with one another at the same time as they address their public constituencies.

That moral authority is constantly vulnerable because the norms of intelligent deliberation among the governors and the address to citizens are contingently—maybe congenitally—in conflict. The success of internal deliberations depends on the ability to limit the political agenda and to resist the intrusion of ephemeral issues; the success of address to citizens depends on an expansive and timely openness to their aspirations and fears. Internal deliberations depend on willingness to be persuaded and to invest in the act of persuading one's peers; on a civil tongue, prudence, and stable public standards of logic and evidence; and on a discursive practice that allows familiar or passionate issues to be reframed or reorganized. Although those qualities may appear in the public address, they often yield in that open arena to the discursive tasks of mobilization and to the affirmation of shared values.

There are good if not always honored reasons to discipline public discourse in a way that enhances the intelligence of both governors and citizens. A polity in which large numbers of potential voters do not understand major policy choices and the political process narrows the electoral advantage of intelligent governors and imposes a burden of unintelligent claims on post-electoral (or, better, inter-electoral) governance. The modest proposal that citizens as voters should be intelligent enough not to frustrate intelligent governance doesn't have the grand resonance of the populist sensibility: it doesn't rest the intelligence of the polity on the wisdom of the people, nor does it eradicate the ideologically troubling distinction between citizens and governors. It certainly lacks the majesty of collaboration and consensus. In compensation, however, it has the advantage of its rhetorical poverty. It doesn't require that voters allocate enormous resources to making gross distinctions between candidates and parties, or that they imagine themselves grandiosely as legislators attending to the entire political agenda.

Liberal republics are robust as moral communities and moderate in their role as guardians of open fields if they ask a great deal of governors and relatively little of citizens. The institutional implications of that modest but important role were understood in roughly similar terms by republican theorists from Machiavelli to Madison. They characteristically argued that the intelligence of ordinary citizens was limited by their inability to overcome the blinders of passion and faction. Popular intelligence was, of course, also limited by simple ignorance, but that was so intractable a feature of the social system that it barely merited serious attention. In real places, it was possible to imagine ways of arranging the "springs of government" to enable republican institutions to survive and prosper despite the popular blinders.

In contrast, in the nineteenth and twentieth centuries we cultivated the definition of the intelligence of both governors and citizens in terms of the capacity to use formal information and knowledge in shaping political action. Around the world, states depend on that cognitive intelligence for both day-to-day management and strategic policy making: calibrating weapons, setting tax rates, mapping land uses. (And, it follows, states are vulnerable to the pathologies of those epistemic forms.) Passion and faction—the old enemies of intelligence—have been transmuted into preference and interest where they serve as compelling though not uncontested foundations for ethical choice. The new enemy, ignorance, is dangerous but tractable—a practical flaw that can be remedied, rather than a moral failing built into human nature.

The shift in the understanding of intelligence makes it difficult to specify the principle of adequacy: How much popular knowledge is enough to empower intelligent governors? There is no reason, however, to be intimidated by that difficulty. The modest principle frees us from overburdening citizens by confusing their political role. It provides a symbolic orientation in the face of moral uncertainty—the circumstance with which this essay began—that allows us to attend to our identities as citizens in a political community rather than as abstractly equal and thickly obligated persons.

Conclusion

My acknowledgments and a few scattered allusions in the text signal that the chapters in this essay were written over an extended period of time. For the most part, however, I have adopted a common literary conceit: the text was written in a single instant so that no time elapsed between beginning and end, and all the ideas fit together in a seamless fabric. In the spirit of the text's interpretive style, I have tried to make that conceit credible; however, I propose at the end to undo it. I have woven together responses to distinct intellectual problems. One problem (even better, one tentative resolution) led to another. My efforts to integrate the responses do not, however, create a seamless argumentative fabric. The responses bear the marks of the problems from which they sprung and of a wary apprehension of difficulties yet to be addressed.

I abandon the conceit of a timeless and entirely coherent author without making any claim to a heroic integrity. Confession is a self-serving tactic intended to increase the text's persuasive power by providing ("in conclusion") more alternative readings than might appear in a seamless fabric. I have multiplied the number of places at which, I hope, readers will recognize themselves, encouraging them both to affirm and to challenge the text.

As I indicated in the preface, by the mid 1970s I had turned my attention from telecommunications to planning theory. Repeatedly, however, I looked back over my shoulder, trying to link old concerns and new. Chapter 4 and the account of the intelligence of citizens and governors in chapter 13 testify to my strained neck and to the abiding influence of early fascinations. Some readers will, I hope, see this essay as a prologue to a telecommunication planning effort grounded in a communitarian sensibility.

My approach to planning theory was deeply informed by my abiding interest in communication. I repeatedly wondered how we managed to understand one another at all when so many ordinary terms were contested. How could we construct and use general theories when they seemed inevitably partial and ambiguous? Those were the issues I explored in essays transformed here into the fable in chapter 5 and the account of "now" in chapter 7.

There was no sign of the three mythic communities in those early essays. Misunderstanding, in those accounts, was grounded in the complexity and diversity of individuals and communities, not in the abstractions of stylized myths. I described what I was doing as a social rather than a philosophic epistemology. I was concerned with the intellectual bias of organizational forms; with what could be practically known rather than what could be known in principle.

There is a visible seam along that line. I suspect that some readers will be content to accept my account of the implications of the initial pluralism without attaching to it the community myths and the political arguments they evoke. Indeed, the myths are not necessary to explain or validate contested political lexicons and normative conflict. They are stitched to the initial pluralism in order to extend the possibilities of resolving nagging ethical uncertainties and negotiating public orders. The myths are evoked to sustain agreements, not to trumpet diversity.

The major elements of the agreement argument are presented in chapters 1–3 and then elaborated in the accounts of prudence and redemption in chapters 11 and 12. There are, however, seams within this fabric that are only thinly disguised by the literary conceit. I first used the concept of a "deep community" in the early 1980s to explain why cities in the United States had not developed a synthetic conception and practice of communication planning. That curiously negative formulation (a synthetic conception of communication would have mistakenly implied that cities were or should be imagined as deep communities) suggested that some communities were indeed deeply integrated moral entities. What were the poetics of policy and planning arguments within such communities? How, in particular, did they compare with the literary forms of arguments when we conceived of individuals creating social worlds through a series of contracts, or when we shifted from the attributes of individual communities to those of a field of diverse, overlapping, open entities?

Those questions about poetics and my responses to them are important elements in the final text of this essay. They appear particularly in my repeated appreciation of irony and ambiguity in policy and planning discourse. I don't, however, run the analysis of literary strategies fully to ground. Instead, I have subordinated that analysis to a series of ideas that I describe as a "communitarian sensibility." Some readers will, I expect, see the seams in the fabric and regret the gaps left by my redirection.

"Communitarian sensibilities" first appeared in the plural in a paper I wrote in 1993. In the current text it appears in the singular as the title of part I and, in my mind, as the principal concern of the essay. Whatever their role in validating moral orders, communities are critically important in maintaining and adapting them. In order to play those instrumental roles, they must recruit, socialize, and discipline members, distinguish between members and strangers, collect resources, and cultivate a domain of competence that makes the game worth the candle.

The central notion in this conception of community is the construction of individuals and organizations as members with rights and obligations. If there are no members, and if there is no process to create and maintain rights and obligations, there is no community.

Many associations meet those criteria. Some are formal and some informal; some temporary and some long-lived, some large and some small, some democratic and some authoritarian, some deserving of profound respect and others frightening. The communitarian sensibility is a disposition to assess the impact of innovative opportunities or compelling moral claims on communities rather than simply on groups with shared volitions or interests. The sensibility informs the design, the repair, and the dissolution of communities and communal fields with a wary skepticism about strategies that are grounded in improbable structures.

I particularly distinguish three such improbable structures as parents of flawed strategies. In the first, individuals are imagined or permitted to be members of one and only one community and to be subject to its exclusive discipline. In the second, the array of communities is endowed with a political permanence that makes it enormously difficult for communions to be born or to die, to take on new roles, or to allow old roles to expire. In the last, the field of communities is so arranged that everything is in its appropriate social and physical space. In that world, where neatness is a cardinal virtue, local polities are immune from distant vetoes when they deal only with local matters; a consensual distinction between private and public domains is carefully maintained.

I don't believe that I have borrowed the term from anyone else, but the idea of a "communitarian sensibility" is not new. By any of its names, the sensibility has its enemies and its critics. They will discern in my version the fragments cobbled together and the arguments only partially addressed—mind still arguing with itself. Some of the enemies and critics are partisans of one of the three improbable structures. Others, more subtly, resist a capacious definition of community or my emphasis on exclusion and discipline: Is a highway convoy really a community? Isn't a stable small town or urban neighborhood a precious example of a real community? Must love, friendship, nurturance, and sociability be limited? Though I have not made much of a point of it, I certainly recognize that the communitarian sensibility limits the claims of social justice and muddies the rhetoric of reason with instrumental calculations. The critics will surely wonder whether the gain is worth the cost.

Having come this far, I will be content if readers find those critical questions engaging.

Notes

Chapter 1

1. On the struggle to reinvent a republican tradition that will satisfy this lament, see Sandel 1996.

2. Rosenblum (1998, pp. 319–348) distinguishes in a similar way between "associations" and "identity groups." Our essential agreement may, however, be obscured by our lexical differences: she ascribes the moral implications of membership to associations, and she describes identity groups stripped of those implications as "communities." In contrast, the communities that engage me in this essay all shape moral orders. Many of those communities are formal associations, but some are not.

3. On the maintenance of communal boundaries see Walzer 1983. For critical treatments of the preference for local responsibilities see Care 1987 and Goodin 1985.

4. Crawford and Ostrom (1995) provide a guide to the terms of such a reflective inquiry.

5. See, in particular, "We live through institutions" in Bellah et al. 1991. See also Bellah et al. 1985.

6. An "intelligent highway" that electronically controlled the speed and spacing of vehicles would, presumably, destroy those ubiquitous but ephemeral communities and their customs.

7. Walzer (1983, pp. 38–39) argues in the same vein: "Neighborhoods can be open only if countries are at least potentially closed. Only if the state makes a selection among would-be members and guarantees the loyalty, security, and welfare of the individuals it selects, can local communities take shape as 'indifferent' associations, determined solely by personal preference and market capacity."

8. For an example of that distress, see Barber 1988.

9. Mintzberg (1979, 1983) elaborates on these images of practices in the dynamics of firms.

Chapter 2

1. This argument is similar to Barber's (1988, pp. 152–176) critique of Oakeshott's historicism.

2. This issue of organizational design is central to Williamson 1975, Chandler 1962, and Mintzberg 1979.

3. The concept of transparency carries with it considerable emotional baggage. See Hunt 1984 on its use in the Reign of Terror to justify a window on private behavior and thought. In the current discussions of "digital government," the same term is used to describe information systems that allow both citizens and public managers to see into the workings of governments.

Chapter 3

1. In the film *The Truman Show* (Paramount Pictures, 1998), the circle of actors around the hero exposes him completely to the television audience.

2. See Okin 1989 and Peterson 1981.

3. See Horkheimer 1984, McIntyre 1988, and (particularly) Nozick 1993.

Chapter 4

1. For contrasting approaches to these substitutions, see Mitchell 1996 and Talbott 1995.

Chapter 5

1. For a sympathetic but incisive critique of these efforts, see Frohock 1987.

2. John Dewey is probably the most important figure associated with the notion that science and liberal democracy are uniquely coupled. See, for example, *Democracy and Education* (1916).

3. For a compelling illustration of the uses of this simple dimension, see Lindblom 1977.

Chapter 7

1. See Adam 1995; Bender and Wellbery 1989; Hassard 1990.

2. See Leviticus 25: 8–17.

Chapter 8

1. See Beck's (1992) critical assessment of that professional faith.

2. See also Alborn 1994.

3. According to Krimsky and Golding (1992, p. xi), "the field of risk studies grew out of the practical needs of industrialized societies to regulate technology and to protect their citizenry from natural and technological hazards."

Chapter 9

1. The original version of this account was written in the summer of 1982 as one of several attempts to integrate the work of twelve task forces, a long list of consultants, several ensemble groups, and a seemingly endless series of meetings. The integrative device I adopted was to map the various ways in which participants in what I will call P:PPF defined "Philadelphia." This revised version, mellowed by time and a different purpose, is less prescriptive than the original and more appreciative of the ability of the participants to offer one another the gift of ambiguity. Some of the P:PPF talk and the great stack of written reports are dated, shaped by the pained local response to the decline in federal grants to cities. I have, however, provided an interpretation of general themes in the conversation that remain (in 1999) abiding qualities of the talk of the town. For my purposes, the project concluded yesterday. I subsequently published a revised version of the internal report as "What is Philadelphia? The city as polity" (Mandelbaum 1984).

2. For a telling account of those conflicting strains, see Bissinger 1997.

Chapter 10

1. The original publication was titled "Reading Plans" (Mandelbaum 1990). It was followed by "Reading Old Plans (Mandelbaum 1993) and a review of three current but remote plans that I have informally called "Reading Plans III" (Mandelbaum 1997).

Chapter 11

1. The discipline of writing controls the presentation of Voices from the Community (American Friends Service Committee 1986), which consists of extracts from 45 long interviews with "everyday thinking people" organized by the AFSC. Ordinary conversations are not neatly organized by topic, nor are they introduced and summarized in reflective essays.

2. For an important exception, see Shklar 1984, particularly pp. 7–44.

3. A tenth MOVE member was tried separately, convicted, and sentenced in 1982. An eleventh member, who renounced her membership in court, was acquitted.

4. Long excerpts from the transcript of the criminal trial can be found in Anderson and Hevenor 1987.

5. For an incisive critique of that management style, see Kelling and Coles 1996.

6. See the statement by Carl Dix (Harry 1987, pp. 193–196).

7. See next chapter.

8. See the bibliography in Wagner-Pacifici 1994.

Chapter 12

1. The classic texts are Aristotle's *Nicomachean Ethics* and *Politics*. My attention was drawn to prudence by Nussbaum (1990), by Pincoffs (1986), and by Dunn (1990). Kronman (1985) reminded me how much my early sense of the concept was shaped by Alexander Bickel.

2. For a useful background to the issues and relationships explored in this chapter, see Pomper 1986.

3. If Newark had followed Manhattan's example and annexed the adjacent New Jersey counties in the nineteenth century, it would today be among the largest and richest cities in the United States.

4. The history of the school issue since 1970 is summarized in the latest (and probably last) decision in the case of *Abbott v. Burke*, decided in May of 1998.

5. The two major decisions discussed here are Southern Burlington County NAACP v. Township of Mount Laurel 67 N.J. 151, 336 A.2d 713 (1975)—"*Mt. Laurel I*"—and 92 N.J. 158, 456 A.2d 390 (1983)—"*Mt. Laurel II.*" In 1986 the New Jersey Supreme Court validated the newly passed Fair Housing Act in *Hills Development Co. v. Township of Barnards* 103 N.J. 1, 510 A.2d 621, a decision sometimes described as "*Mt. Laurel III.*" For a detailed account of these cases, see Haar 1996.

Chapter 13

1. The quoted phrases are explicated in the first lecture in Rawls 1993.

2. See Eberly 1994, Ackerman and Alstott 1999, and the web sites of the Pew Partnership for Civic Change (http://www.pew-partnership.org/index.html), the Civic Practices Network (www.cpn.org), and the National Commission on Civic Renewal.

3. On these themes, see Healey 1997 and Innes 1990.

Bibliography

Abbott v. Burke, 153 N. J. 480; 710 A. 2d 450; 1998 N. J. LEXIS 451.

Ackerman, Bruce, and Anne Alstott. 1999. *The Stakeholder Society*. Yale University Press.

Adam, Barbara. 1995. *Timewatch: The Social Analysis of Time*. Polity Press.

Alborn, T. L. 1994. A calculating profession: Victorian actuaries among the statisticians. *Science in Context* 7: 433–468.

American Friends Service Committee. 1986. *Voices from the Community*. AFSC National Community Relations Committee.

Anderson, John, and Hilary Hevenor. 1987. *Burning Down the House: MOVE and the Tragedy of Philadelphia*. Norton.

Aristotle. 1985. *Nicomachean Ethics*. Hackett.

Aristotle. 1984. *The Politics*. University of Chicago Press.

Assefa, Hizkias, and Paul Wahrhaftig. 1990. *The MOVE Crisis in Philadelphia: Extremist Groups and Conflict Resolution*. University of Pittsburgh Press.

Attiyah, Phillip. 1981. *Promises, Morals and Law*. Oxford University Press.

Barber, Benjamin. 1988. *The Conquest of Politics: Liberal Philosophy in Democratic Times*. Princeton University Press.

Barry, Brian. 1965. *Political Argument*. Routledge.

Beck, Ulrich. 1992. *Risk Society: Towards a New Modernity*. Sage.

Bellah, Robert, Richard Madsen, William M. Sullivan, Ann Swibler, and Steven M. Tipton. 1991. *The Good Society*. Knopf.

Bellah, Robert, Richard Madsen, William M. Sullivan, Ann Swidler, and Steven M. Tipton. 1985. *Habits of the Heart: Individualism and Commitment in American Life*. University of California Press.

Bender, John, and David E. Wellbery, eds. 1989. *Chronotypes: The Construction of Time*. Stanford University Press.

Billig, Michael, Susan Condor, Derek Edwards, Mike Gane, David Middleton, and Alan Radley. 1988. *Ideological Dilemmas: A Social Psychology of Everyday Thinking*. Sage.

Bissinger, Buzz. 1997. *A Prayer for the City*. Random House.

Bohman, J. 1992. *New Philosophy of Social Science: Problems of Indeterminacy*. MIT Press.

Borges, Jorge Luis. 1964. The Library of Babel. In *Labyrinths*. New Directions.

Bowser, Charles. 1989. *Let the Bunker Burn: The Final Battle with MOVE*. Camino Books.

Breyer, Stephen. 1993. *Breaking the Vicious Circle: Toward Effective Risk Regulation*. Harvard University Press.

Bryson, John M., and Barbara C. Crosby. 1992. *Leadership for the Common Good: Tackling Public Problems in a Shared Power World*. Jossey-Bass.

Burchell, Robert, W. Patrick Beaton, and David Listokin. 1983. *Mount Laurel II: Challenge and Delivery of Low-Cost Housing*. Center for Urban Policy Research.

Burt, R. A. 1984. Constitutional law and the teaching of the parables. *Yale Law Journal* 93: 455–505.

Care, Norman S. 1987. *On Sharing Fate*. Temple University Press.

Chandler, Albert. 1962. *Strategy and Structure: Chapters in the History of American Industrial Enterprise*. MIT Press.

Chatman, Seymour. 1978. *Story and Discourse: Narrative Structure in Fiction and Film*. Cornell University Press.

Cohen, Sande. 1986. *Historical Culture: On the Recoding of an Academic Discipline*. University of California Press.

Connolly, William E. 1987. *Politics and Ambiguity*. University of Wisconsin Press.

Cottle, Thomas. 1976. *Perceiving Time: A Psychological Investigation with Men and Women*. Wiley.

Council on New Jersey Affairs. 1988. *New Jersey Issues: Papers from the Council on New Jersey Affairs*. Princeton University.

Cox, L., Jr., and P. F. Ricci, eds. 1990. *New Risks: Issues and Management Advances in Risk Analysis, volume 6*. Plenum.

Crawford, Sue E. S., and Elinor Ostrom. 1995. A grammar of institutions. *American Political Science Review* 89: 582–560.

Dewey, John. 1916. *Democracy and Education*. Macmillan, 1953.

Dunn, John. 1990. *Interpreting Political Responsibility: Essays, 1981–1989*. Princeton University Press.

Dunn, William N. 1981. *Public Policy Analysis: An Introduction*. Prentice-Hall.

Eberly, Don E., ed. 1994. *Building a Community of Citizens: Civil Society in the 21st Century*. University Press of America.

Edelman, Murray. 1988. *Constructing the Political Spectacle*. University of Chicago Press.

Ellickson, Robert C. 1982. Cities and homeowners associations. *University of Pennsylvania Law Review* 130: 1519–1608.

Feinberg, Joel. 1980. *Rights, Justice and the Bounds of Liberty*. Princeton University Press.

Finkel, A. M., and D. Golding, eds. 1994. *Worst Things First: The Debate over Risk-Based National Environmental Priorities*. Resources for the Future.

Fish, Stanley E. 1980. *Is There a Text in This Class? The Authority of Interpretive Communities*. Harvard University Press.

Frohock, Fred. 1987. *Rational Association*. Syracuse University Press.

Gale, R. M. 1968. *The Language of Time*. Humanities Press.

Galston, William A. 1991. *Liberal Purposes: Goods, Virtues and Diversity in the Liberal State*. Cambridge University Press.

Garver, Eugene. 1987. *Machiavelli and the History of Prudence*. University of Wisconsin Press.

Gauthier, D. P. 1990. *Moral Dealing: Contract, Ethics and Reason*. Cornell University Press.

Goode, W. Wilson, and Joann Stevens. 1992. *In Goode Faith*. Judson.

Goodin, Robert E. 1985. *Protecting the Vulnerable: A Reanalysis of Our Social Responsibilities*. University of Chicago Press.

Gouldner, Alvin W. 1979. *The Future of Intellectuals and the Rise of the New Class*. Seabury.

Grant, George Parkin. 1985. *English Speaking Justice*. Notre Dame University Press.

Greenhouse, Carol. 1986. *Praying for Justice: Faith, Order and Community in an American Town*. Cornell University Press.

Gundersen, A. G. 1995. *The Environmental Promise of Democratic Deliberation*. University of Wisconsin Press.

Gutmann, Amy, and Dennis Thompson. 1996. *Democracy and Disagreement*. Harvard University Press.

Haar, Charles M. 1996. *Suburbs under Siege: Race, Space, and Audacious Judges*. Princeton University Press.

Hacking, Ian. 1990. *The Taming of Chance*. Cambridge University Press.

Hall, Frederick W. 1977. An Orientation to Mount Laurel. In *After Mount Laurel*, ed. J. Rose and R. Rothman. 1977. Center for Urban Policy Research.

Hardin, Russell. 1988. *Morality Within the Limits of Freedom*. University of Chicago Press.

Harry, Margo. 1987. *Attention, MOVE! This Is America*. Banner.

Hassard, John, ed. 1990. *The Sociology of Time*. St. Martin's Press.

Healey, Patsy. 1997. *Collaborative Planning: Shaping Places in Fragmented Societies*. Macmillan.

Higham, John. 1994. The future of American history. *Journal of American History* 80: 1289–1309.

Hills Development Co. v. Township of Barnards 103 N. J. 1, 510 A. 2d 621 (1986).

Hirschhorn, Lawrence. 1980. Scenario writing: A developmental approach. *Journal of the American Planning Association* 46: 172–183.

Hochschild, Arlie Russell. 1997. *The Time Bind: When Work Becomes Home and Home Becomes Work*. Henry Holt.

Horkheimer, Max. 1984. *Eclipse of Reason*. Continuum.

Hornstein, D. 1992. Reclaiming environmental law: A normative critique of comparative risk analysis. *Columbia Law Review* 92: 501–571.

Hornstein, D. 1994. Paradigms, process, and politics: Risk and regulatory design. In *Worst Things First*, ed. A. Finkel and D. Golding. Resources for the Future.

Hunt, Lynn. 1984. *Politics, Culture, and Class in the French Revolution*. University of California Press.

Hutton, Will. 1995. *The State We're In*. Jonathan Cape.

Hutton, Will. 1997. *The State to Come*. Vintage.

Innes, Judith Eleanor. 1990. *Knowledge and Public Policy: The Search for Meaningful Indicators*, second expanded edition. Transaction.

Innes, Judith Eleanor. 1998. Information in communicative planning. *Journal of the American Planning Association* 64: 52–64.

Kadushin, Charles. 1969. *Why People Go to Psychiatrists*. Atherton.

Kaplan, Thomas J. 1986. The narrative structure of policy analysis. *Journal of Policy Analysis and Management* 5: 761–778.

Kelling, George L., and Catherine M. Coles. 1996. *Fixing Broken Windows*. Free Press.

Kingwell, Mark. 1995. *A Civil Tongue: Justice, Dialogue, and the Politics of Pluralism*. Pennsylvania State University Press.

Kronman, Anthony T. 1985. Alexander Bickel's philosophy of prudence. *Yale Law Journal* 94: 1567–1616.

Kymlicka, Will. 1989. *Liberalism, Community and Culture*. Clarendon.

Lash, J. 1994. Integrating science, values, and democracy through comparative risk assessment. In *Worst Things First*, ed. A. Finkel and D. Golding. Resources for the Future.

Lincoln, Bruce. 1989. *Discourse and the Construction of Society: Comparative Studies of Myth, Ritual, and Classification*. Oxford University Press.

Lindblom, Charles E. 1977. *Politics and Markets: The World's Political-Economic Systems*. Basic Books.

Lindblom, Charles E. 1990. *Inquiry and Change: The Troubled Attempt to Understand and Shape Society*. Yale University Press.

Lindblom, Charles E., and David K. Cohen. 1979. *Usable Knowledge: Social Science and Social Problem Solving*. Yale University Press.

Lukas, J. Anthony. 1985. *Common Ground: A Turbulent Decade in the Lives of Three American Families*. Knopf.

MacIntyre, Alasdair. 1984. *After Virtue: A Study in Moral Theory*, second edition. Notre Dame University Press.

MacIntyre, Alasdair. 1988. *Whose Justice? Which Rationality?* Notre Dame University Press.

Mandelbaum, Seymour J. 1972. *Community and Communications*. Norton.

Mandelbaum, Seymour J. 1984. What is Philadelphia? The city as polity. *Cities* 1: 274–285.

Mandelbaum, Seymour J. 1985. Historians and planners: The construction of pasts and futures. *Journal of the American Planning Association* 51: 185–188.

Mandelbaum, Seymour J. 1990. Reading plans. *Journal of the American Planning Association* 56: 350–356.

Mandelbaum, Seymour J. 1993. Reading old plans. *Journal of Policy History* 5: 189–198. Reprinted in *Urban Public Policy*, ed. M. Melosi. Pennsylvania State University Press.

Mandelbaum, Seymour J. 1997. Reading plans III. *Journal of Planning Education and Research* 16: 230–232.

Mandelbaum, Seymour J. 1998. Ironists under the skin. *Journal of Planning Education and Research* 18: 78–81.

Marris, Peter. 1986. *Loss and Change*, revised edition. Routledge.

Marris, Peter. 1996 *The Politics of Uncertainty: Attachment in Private and Public Life*. Routledge.

McCloskey, D. 1985. *The Rhetoric of Economics.*. University of Wisconsin Press.

Mill, John Stuart. 1989. *On Liberty*. Cambridge University Press.

Miller, David. 1976. *Social Justice*. Clarendon.

Mintzberg, Henry. 1979. *The Structuring of Organizations: A Synthesis of Research*. Prentice-Hall.

Mintzberg, Henry. 1983. *Power In and Around Organizations*. Prentice-Hall.

Mitchell, William J. 1996. *City of Bits: Space, Place, and the Infobahn*. MIT Press.

Mitchell, William T., ed. 1981. *On Narrative*. University of Chicago Press.

Moran, Emerson. 1987. "Should the mayor resign?" *Philadelphia* 78, no. 5: 120–124, 166–178.

Myrdal, Gunnar. 1944. *An American Dilemma: The Negro Problem and Modern Democracy*. Harper.

Mytelka, Arnold K. 1977. Judicial remedies. In *After Mount Laurel*, ed. J. Rose and R. Rothman. 1977. Center for Urban Policy Research.

Nagel, Jack H. 1991. Psychological obstacles to administrative responsibility: Lessons of the MOVE disaster. *Journal of Policy Analysis and Management* 10: 1–23.

National Science Foundation. 1995. Interagency announcement of opportunity: NSF/EPA partnership for environmental research. Report NSF 95-48.

Nelson, D. M. 1991. *The Priority of Prudence: Virtue and Natural Law in Thomas Aquinas and the Implications for Modern Ethics*. Pennsylvania State University Press.

Nozick, Robert. 1993. *The Nature of Rationality*. Princeton University Press.

Nussbaum, Martha C. 1990. *Love's Knowledge: Essays on Philosophy and Literature*. Oxford University Press.

Oakeshott, Michael. 1933. *Experience and Its Modes*. Cambridge University Press.

Oakeshott, Michael. 1962. *Rationalism in Politics and Other Essays*. Basic Books.

Oakeshott, Michael. 1975. *On Human Conduct*. Clarendon.

O'Brien, M. 1989. A proposal to address, rather than rank, environmental problems. In *Worst Things First*, ed. A. Finkel and D. Golding. Resources for the Future.

Okin, Susan Moller. 1989. *Justice, Gender, and the Family*. Basic Books.

Peterson, Paul. 1981. *City Limits*. University of Chicago Press.

Phelan, J. 1989. *Reading People, Reading Plots: Character, Progression and the Interpretation of Narrative*. University of Chicago Press.

Philadelphia Special Investigation Commission. 1986. The Findings, Conclusions and Recommendations of the Philadelphia Special Investigation Commission (Philadelphia, March 6).

Pincoffs, Edmund L. 1986. *Quandaries and Virtues: Against Reductivism in Ethics*. University of Kansas Press.

Pollak, Robert. 1995. Regulating risks. *Journal of Economic Literature* 33: 179–189.

Pomper, Gerald, ed. 1986. *The Political State of New Jersey*. Rutgers University Press.

Rawls, John. 1971. *A Theory of Justice*. Harvard University Press.

Rawls, John. 1993. *Political Liberalism*. Columbia University Press.

Report of the County Investigating Grand Jury of May 16, 1986. Court of Common Pleas of Philadelphia County Trial Division—Criminal Section, 86-007363 (April 20, 1988).

Ricoeur, Paul. 1984. *Time and Narrative*. University of Chicago Press.

Roe, Emery. 1994. *Narrative Policy Analysis: Theory and Practice*. Duke University Press.

Rose, Jerome G., and Robert E. Rothman. 1977. *After Mount Laurel: The New Suburban Zoning*. Center for Urban Policy Research.

Rosenblum, Nancy L. 1987. *Another Liberalism: Romanticism and the Reconstruction of Liberal Thought*. Harvard University Press.

Rosenblum, Nancy L. 1998. *Membership and Morals: The Personal Uses of Pluralism in America*. Princeton University Press.

Sacks, Oliver. 1987. *The Man Who Mistook His Wife for a Hat and Other Clinical Tales*. Harper and Row.

Sandel, Michael J. 1996. *Democracy's Discontent: America in Search of a Public Philosophy*. Harvard University Press.

Schlesinger, Arthur M., Jr. 1998. *The Disuniting of America*, revised and enlarged edition. Norton.

Sher, George. 1987. *Desert*. Princeton University Press.

Shklar, Judith N. 1984. *Ordinary Vices*. Harvard University Press.

Shklar, Judith N. 1991. *American Citizenship: The Quest for Inclusion*. Harvard University Press.

Slovic, Paul. 1992. Perception of risk: Reflections on the psychometric paradigm. In *Social Theories of Risk*, ed. S. Krimsky and D. Golding. Praeger.

Smith, K. R. 1990. The risk transition. *International Environmental Affairs* 2: 227–251.

Smith, Rogers M. 1997. *Civic Ideals: Conflicting Visions of Citizenship in U. S. History*. Yale University Press.

Southern, David W. 1987. *Gunnar Myrdal and Black-White Relations: The Use and Abuse of an American Dilemma, 1944–1969*. Louisiana State University Press.

Stokey, Edith, and Richard Zeckhauser. 1978. *A Primer for Policy Analysis*. Norton.

Southern Burlington County NAACP v. Township of Mount Laurel, 67 N. J. 151, 336 A. 2d 713 (1975).

Southern Burlington County NAACP v. Township of Mount Laurel, 92 N. J. 158, 456 A. 2d 390 (1983).

Sunstein, Cass R. 1990. *After the Rights Revolution: Reconceiving the Regulatory State*. Harvard University Press.

Suttles, Gerald. 1972. *The Social Construction of Communities*. University of Chicago Press.

Suttles, Gerald. 1990. *The Man-Made City: The Land-Use Confidence Game in Chicago*. University of Chicago Press.

Talbott, Stephen L. 1995. *The Future Does Not Compute: Transcending the Machines in Our Midst*. O'Reilly & Associates.

Taylor, Charles. 1989. *Sources of the Self: The Making of the Modern Identity*. Harvard University Press.

Turner, Stephen. 1994. *The Social Theory of Practices: Tradition, Tacit Knowledge, and Presuppositions*. University of Chicago Press.

U.S. Environmental Protection Agency. 1987. Unfinished Business: A Comparative Assessment of Environmental Problems.

U.S. Environmental Protection Agency. 1990. Reducing Risk: Settings Priorities and Strategies for Environmental Protection.

Wagner-Pacifici, Robin. 1994. *Discourse and Destruction: The City of Philadelphia versus MOVE*. University of Chicago Press.

Walzer, Michael. 1983. *Spheres of Justice: A Defense of Pluralism and Equality*. Basic Books.

Walzer, Michael. 1985. *Exodus and Revolution*. Basic Books.

Walzer, Michael. 1997. *On Toleration*. Yale University Press.

Wells, Susan. 1990. Narrative figures and subtle persuasions: The rhetoric of the MOVE Report. In *The Rhetorical Turn*, ed. H. Simons. University of Chicago Press.

White, Hayden. 1987. *The Content of the Form: Narrative Discourse and Historical Representation*. Johns Hopkins University Press.

Wideman, John Edgar. 1990. *Philadelphia Fire*. Henry Holt.

Wildavsky, Aaron. 1988. *Searching for Safety*. Transaction Books.

Williamson, Oliver E. 1975. *Markets and Hierarchies: Analysis and Antitrust Implications: A Study in the Economics of Internal Organization*. Free Press.

Wolfe, Alan. 1998. *One Nation, After All*. Penguin.

Yackle, Larry W. 1994. *Reclaiming the Federal Courts*. Harvard University Press.

Yeazell, Stephen C. 1994. *From Medieval Group Litigation to the Modern Class Action*. Yale University Press.

Zelizer, Vivian. 1979. *Morals and Markets: The Development of Life Insurance in the United States*. Columbia University Press.

Index